HONOUR KILLING

Ayse Onal

HONOUR KILLING

Stories of Men Who Killed

SAQI

London San Francisco Beirut

ISBN: 978-0-86356-617-2

Copyright © 2008 by Ayse Onal

Chapters 1, 2, 3, 4 and 9 translated by Ümit Hussein, Chapters 5, 6, 8 and 10 translated by Mehmet Onal and Chapter 7 translated by Deniz Perin.

A full CIP record for this book is available from the British Library.
A full CIP record for this book is available from the Library of Congress.

Manufactured in Lebanon

SAQI

26 Westbourne Grove, London W2 5RH
825 Page Street, Suite 203, Berkeley, California 94710
Tabet Building, Mneimneh Street, Hamra, Beirut
www.saqibooks.com

To Mai

Contents

INTRODUCTION

by Joan Smith

In June 2007, three men were convicted of the murder of a twenty-year-old woman from South London. Only one of them had actually taken part in the killing, which was particularly savage, but the others had ordered it: the murderers were hit-men who strangled the victim, stuffed her body in a suitcase and buried it in a garden in Birmingham. They boasted that they had stripped and raped the young woman before her dreadful death, and all but one of them disappeared from the UK shortly afterwards. What made the case peculiarly horrible was the fact that the two men convicted and sentenced to life imprisonment for ordering the murder were the girl's father and uncle.

The murder of Banaz Mahmod caused an outcry when the facts began to emerge during the trial. She had been forced to marry a Kurdish cousin when she was sixteen, but left him and fell in love with an Iranian man from a different Kurdish clan. She was photographed kissing him on a Brixton street by men who had been ordered to follow her by her father and uncle, and their rage on seeing the picture precipitated her death. Her sister Bekhal told a *Sunday Times* journalist what happened: 'It was a kiss on the lips. No, not a snog. But they took a picture and gave it to my uncle and that was it. It was all over for Banaz just because she really loved that man.' Bekhal herself now lives in hiding, fearing reprisals from her family. In 2002, when she was seventeen, she ran away from home after being beaten for refusing to marry a cousin who was twice her age. She said:

> I wanted to have a life, holidays, travel the world, have a good job, have kids, have a family, get married. But families like mine are very strong and go back generations and generations. The family is all mixed blood of cousins to cousins and nephews, and becomes so deep and so intimate and incestuous that the members of it lose themselves.

Like some of the young women whose stories are told in *Honour Killing*, Bekhal Mahmod comes from a large Kurdish family. Her relatives fled to London to escape Saddam Hussein's tyrannical regime in Iraq, but her description of the stifling atmosphere in which she and her sister grew up would be instantly recognisable to Ayse Onal from her work in Turkey. According to a report from a London-based think tank, The Centre for Social Cohesion, the Kurdish regions of Turkey and Iraq have some of the highest rates of 'honour' killings in the world: 'In Turkey, Kurds, who make up no more than a quarter of the population, carry out a disproportionate number of honour killings. A 1999 survey of women in predominantly Kurdish south-eastern Turkey found that 74 per cent of rural women believed that their husband would kill them if they had an affair.' When such families move to other parts of Turkey – or to countries such as Germany and the UK – they bring their traditional codes of behaviour with them and exact terrible punishment if their daughters, sisters and wives do not display total obedience. Remziye Öztürk, the spirited young woman whose tragic story opens Ayse Onal's book, came from a Kurdish family which moved to a sophisticated modern city, Istanbul, but – like Banaz Mahmod's father and uncle in Mitcham

– flatly refused to relax the strict rules of conduct imposed on girls and women.

Murders of Kurdish women are rare in Britain. Four are known to have been victims of 'honour' killings, two of whom were taken abroad before they were murdered; in May 2007, nineteen-year-old Shawbo Ali Rauf was taken to Iraqi Kurdistan from her home in Birmingham and stoned to death after her family found unfamiliar numbers on her mobile phone. In all four cases, the murders were carried out either by older male relatives or by hit-men paid to commit the crime. Until very recently, official figures suggested there were around a dozen 'honour' killings in the UK each year, predominantly in families of South Asian origin, but many people working in the field believed that this was an underestimate. As in Turkey, the practice has had its apologists; in a poll of 500 British Hindus, Sikhs, Christians and Muslims carried out for the BBC's Asian network in 2006, 10 per cent of the respondents said they would condone the murder of someone who offended their family's honour. In February 2008, however, a senior British police officer radically changed the terms of the debate. Giving evidence to the Home Affairs Committee of the House of Commons, Commander Steve Allen, who speaks for the Association of Chief Police Officers, said that around 500 cases of forced marriage and 'honour' killings – the two practices are inextricably linked – are reported to the police and the Foreign Office forced marriage unit each year:

> Is it under-reported? Massively. What we will never know, or cannot know at the moment, is the extent to which it is under-reported. If you were to ask me to hazard a guess, if the generally accepted statistic is that a victim will suffer thirty-five experiences of domestic violence before they report, then I suspect if you multiplied our reporting by thirty-five times you may be somewhere near where people's experience is at, but we simply do not know.

What Allen is suggesting is that as many as 17,500 young people are victims of forced marriage and honour-based crimes in Britain each year. In one British city alone, Bradford, more than 200 teenage girls disappear from secondary schools each year and fail to return from trips to the Indian sub-continent; it is feared that some are being forced to marry relatives and are at risk of violence, including murder, if they resist. According to Nazir Afzal, a Crown Prosecution Service lawyer who is an expert in the field, a child's withdrawal from school should ring alarm bells: 'Often, if a girl or boy is taken out of school early, it's a trigger that a forced marriage may be on the cards.'

Family members who know the truth about an 'honour' killing are often too scared to cooperate with the authorities, or actually collude in the crime. Nazir Afzal again:

> These cases resonate beyond the immediate family as we often deal with cases where significant members took part in the act; in the murder. And in the case of Banaz [Mahmod], for instance, in addition substantial numbers of the community did not assist and support prosecutors; instead they supported the family members who were responsible for the killing. They really didn't care and it showed ... We don't see this as domestic violence – it's beyond that. The murder of Banaz was so brutal that it was a clear warning to others; it was a way of saying 'don't step out of line or this could be you'.

In the same year that Banaz Mahmod's father and uncle were convicted of her murder, British police also managed to get a conviction for the murder of Surjit Athwal, a twenty-seven-year-old Sikh woman who was taken to India and killed because she wanted a divorce. Surjit's body was never found, and her husband and elderly mother-in-law were brought to justice years later when a relative finally decided to give new evidence to the police. Sometimes the violence extends beyond women to their children as well: in July 2006, thirty-two-year-old Uzma Rahan and her three young children were murdered at their home in Cheadle Hulme, Greater Manchester, by her husband Rahan Arshad, who suspected she was having an affair. At his trial, Arshad told the court he was angered by the fact that his wife had begun wearing Western clothes. 'It wasn't right for a mother and someone who came from Pakistan to change the way she dressed all of a sudden,' he said. On the day of the murder Arshad attacked his wife with a rounders bat, hitting her twenty-three times before turning it on his children. Not long before her death, Uzma had told friends she feared becoming the victim of an honour killing: 'Count the days before he kills me,' she said. Like Banaz Mahmod, who appealed to the police for help several times – on one occasion a policewoman dismissed her as 'dramatic and calculating' – no one took Uzma Rahan's fears seriously enough to save her life. While most victims of 'honour' killings are women, men have been murdered too. In November 2004, a nineteen-year-old student at Oxford Brookes University, Arash Ghorbani-Zarin, who was of Iranian descent, was murdered by the Bangladeshi family of his girlfriend, Manna Begum, after she refused to break off her relationship with him. The girl's father, Chomir Ali, told his sons, aged sixteen and nineteen, to kill Arash after discovering that Manna was pregnant and the couple intended to marry.

In the UK, such crimes have become visible only recently. The police are used to dealing with domestic violence, even if their response is not always as swift as victims and their advocates would like. Two women are killed each week by partners or ex-partners, according to Home Office figures; several British men have murdered their children to take revenge on former partners, sometimes killing themselves as well, and it is clear that no ethnic group has a monopoly on gender-based violence. But 'honour' crimes differ from domestic violence in several significant ways, and pose special problems for the criminal justice system. They are usually planned in advance and often involve fathers, uncles and brothers acting together to enforce strict codes of conduct, with varying degrees of approval from other family members. Few perpetrators believe they have done anything wrong, and they may be supported in this view by relatives who were not actively involved in the crime. Like some of the men interviewed by Ayse Onal in this book, they believe that their family's 'honour' was at stake and they had no choice, expressing little or no remorse when they are tried and convicted. One of Banaz Mahmod's hired killers, thirty-year-old Muhamad Hama, boasted that he stamped on her neck to 'get her soul out' during the two hours of rape and torture which preceded her murder. Rahan Arshad expressed no remorse for killing his wife, whom he described as 'that fucking bitch', but said he was sorry about the murders of his children.

Indeed, many people dispute the use of the term 'honour' killing, arguing that the real issue at the heart of such crimes is control. In the UK, as in Turkey, there is a conflict between young people from traditional families who aspire to the freedom enjoyed by the rest of society and their families' insistence that they have the right to control every aspect of their behaviour. Shafilea Ahmed, a seventeen-year-old girl from Cheshire, described that conflict in a series of poems and song lyrics, including one ironically titled 'Happy Families':

> I don't pretend like we're the perfect
> family no more.
> Desire to live is burning.
> My stomach is turning
> But all they think about is honour.
> I was like a normal teenage kid
> Didn't ask 2 much I just wanted to fit in
> But my culture was different
> But my family ignored.

Shafilea wanted to be a lawyer. Her body was found in a flooded river in Cumbria in February 2004, five months after she disappeared from her family's home in Warrington. She had recently returned from a trip to Pakistan, where she had been introduced to a potential husband and drank bleach in an attempt to avoid a forced marriage. Four years later, in January 2008, a coroner ruled that Shafilea had been unlawfully killed in what he called a 'very vile murder'. 'Her ambition was to live her own life in her own way: to study, to follow a career in the law and to do what she wanted to do. These are just basic fundamental rights and they were denied to her,' said the South and East Cumbria coroner, Ian Smith. At the time of writing, no-one has been charged with Shafilea Ahmed's murder.

It is not just the silence of relatives which makes such crimes difficult to investigate and prosecute. In the UK, as in Turkey, 'honour' crimes are most often associated with the country's Muslim population, although girls from other religious backgrounds have also become victims; Karma Nirvana, the Derby-based organisation which helps South Asian victims of forced marriage and 'honour' crimes, was founded by Jasvinder Sanghera, a woman from a Sikh family whose parents ostracised her after she fled a forced marriage. The police, schools and other organisations have been reluctant to become involved in what they tend to see as family disputes, allowing girls to be returned to situations in which they have already been threatened or experienced violence. Melissa Power, a friend of Shafilea Ahmed, said that Shafilea was found looking cold and frightened in a park near her college in October 2002 after she had been absent for more than a week. 'She was brought to college and said she had escaped from the house in the early hours of the morning,' Melissa said. 'She had faded bruises and scratches to the left of her neck. She said she had been locked in the house and hadn't been allowed out.'

In France, which has a larger Muslim population than the UK, a feminist organisation called Ni Putes Ni Soumises – 'Neither Whores Nor Doormats' – was set up in 2002 by Fadela Amara and a group of young women of mainly North African descent in the banlieues where many immigrant families live. In 2003, they marched through French cities and into the centre of Paris, denouncing French racism and the abuse of Muslim women by fathers, uncles and brothers. In 2005, they published a booklet which provides advice to young Muslims about their rights, including this uncompromising denunciation of forced marriage:

> You could be a victim of forced marriage. That is to say, someone may select a partner for your life, without consulting you. Forced marriage is still practised today in families which reproduce this archaic custom. But this practice sacrifices your future and your happiness. It is forbidden in France. The law protects you ... Don't forget that marriage is a mutual arrangement.

Forced marriage is not illegal in Britain, although a growing recognition that it is a serious form of abuse of young people – around 15 per cent of victims are male – has led to the law being changed to give victims the right to sue in civil courts for the first time. But the publicity surrounding high-profile cases and a new candour on the part of the authorities are changing public opinion, and there is a growing realisation that what lies behind honour-based crime is a resurgence of patriarchal attitudes. These are tribal as well as religious, and they always prioritise the needs and aspirations of the clan – as interpreted by its senior males – over the will of individuals. It is an early form of social organisation, incompatible with modern notions of individual freedom and universal human rights, which causes incalculable damage to men as well as women; sons, cousins and nephews find themselves trapped into dynastic marriages, although the sexual double standard allows them latitude to find sexual outlets elsewhere. One of the reasons for such marriages is to keep property within the family, and it is clear that girls and women are regarded as a form of capital which the senior males are able to dispose of at will. But the special burden imposed on women is not just obedience but having to embody the family's honour, so that their sexual continence or otherwise is regarded as reflecting on the status of the entire clan. And what emerges so powerfully from Ayse Onal's interviews with Turkish men who have murdered sisters, daughters and wives is the fragility of a masculine identity which depends on other people's behaviour: what should enhance their status in the world also has the capacity to destroy it.

Men who live in honour-based cultures are perpetually fearful, suspicious and angry, fuelling the violence with which they react when they believe their anxieties have been confirmed. Ayse Onal has done an immense service by revealing what it is like to live in such families and the terrible cost, not just to the women who are beaten and eventually killed, but to the perpetrators and other relatives. Families are torn apart, racked by guilt and opposing loyalties, but that is just the end product of a process which militates against full participation in modern democratic societies and the economic prosperity they generate. In Turkey and the UK, there is a striking correlation between honour-based codes and a reluctance to educate girls and young women, which results in girls failing to finish their education and being married at an early age. This is a tragedy for the girls themselves, many of whom aspire to careers, but it also perpetuates poverty within their families. In that sense, 'honour' crimes are not just individual horror stories but a disaster for entire families, preventing them from playing a full role in civil society. It is for this realisation, as well as giving the victims a voice, that we have to thank brave journalists such as Ayse Onal.

February 2008

1

REMZIYE

I had only just returned home when the phone rang. I was tired from days of travelling, and fed up because the convict I'd requested to interview had refused to see me. The young man, who had killed his fourteen-year-old sister five years before, had refused to utter a single word on the subject, and had gone so far as to complain about me to the prison authorities. I was still smarting as I picked up the receiver.

'They're dead.'

It was my cameraman.

'Who's dead?' I said.

'Your protégés, they died in a car accident in Austria.'

A lump formed in my throat. 'You mean Remziye?' I asked.

I was greeted by silence at the other end of the line. Then, 'No one knows whether or not there was any criminal intent. It's been over two weeks since the accident. We've only just found out.'

'What about the child?' I asked.

'No one knows.'

The line went dead.

And they say bad news travels fast. My tiredness had lifted; the searing pain in my chest revived me. I went outside and jumped into the car. I drove without any idea of where I was going; I did not see Istanbul as I passed it.

The lives of the people who occupy the crammed buildings of this city, which are piled on top of each other from the outskirts to the centre, are worlds apart, separated by insurmountable obstacles. Children scavenge for food in rubbish bins while their rich counterparts pass by in flashy chauffeur-driven cars on their way to school. There are no thick black lines dividing the social classes in Istanbul. Just as the most destitute can be found in the choicest districts, there are mansions belonging to the filthy rich in the poorest areas.

While some girls are being killed for honour, others walk freely through the same streets with their latest lover. The poor do not hide their poverty from the rich, nor the rich their riches from the poor. Without the merest glance in the other's direction, without ever touching, lives that have hit rock bottom and lives that have soared sky high make love, fight, carouse and die in the same streets. For this reason alone Istanbul is unique. For this reason it is possible for those who live in Istanbul to suffer the same hardships without ever knowing they have done so.

I didn't meet Remziye Öztürk until she was a teenager but, when I met her, she told me the story of her life and so I have written this chapter according to what happened to her, from childhood onwards, even though I didn't know these things until the end of her life.

The Öztürks are a large, religious Kurdish family from Bitlis who took refuge in Istanbul. Being Sunnis, they settled in a conservative district of Sultanbeyli, backing onto Ümraniye. They live in a large *gecekondu** district on the Asian side of the city, populated by Kurdish immigrants. Sunni and Alevi Kurds have traversed the same path of

---

* A shanty house, erected quickly without permission.

migration, but mysteriously their religious beliefs are so divided that it is as though there are ruled lines separating the neighbourhoods that they have built. Local services – such as refuse collection and electricity supply covering the Sunni district – end on the outskirts of the Alevi district as abruptly as if they'd been severed with a knife. Those who live in the Alevi district have to either create their own local services, or renounce their beliefs. The Sunni Kurds consider the Alevi Kurds degenerates who have betrayed the faith, while the Alevi Kurds fear the Sunni Kurds who demand that everyone be like them.

A few houses further north live the Öztürks' older uncles; a few houses further south, their older aunts. They have expanded from the first Öztürk house the way moths cluster around a light bulb: a huge neighbourhood made up of only one family.

It hasn't even been a quarter of a century since they migrated from Mutki, one of the most conservative administrative districts of Bitlis, to Istanbul. The family's father had been made very anxious by the Kurdish revolt, which, clearly, from the first raid in which scores of children were killed, was going to be very bloody. He had bundled up his belongings and moved to Istanbul. While the women in the tribe were scurrying back and forth packing up for their new home, the men had bought an illegal plot of land for the Öztürks to build a roof over their heads and on it they had constructed a *gecekondu* worthy of their family dignity.

In Istanbul *gecekondus* are built so that they can eventually be transformed into apartments. Although the political parties are mainly dependent on the middle classes for the majority of their votes, they have always played on the *gecekondu* vote. Approximately one in four *gecekondu*-dwellers actually use their vote, and party voting figures are invariably unreliable. After every election there is a *gecekondu* pardon, whereby the houses in violation of town planning rules are legalised. So every dweller eagerly anticipates the opportunity to turn their temporary house into a permanent apartment building. Storeys are added to the houses as sons get married, so the family that built the original *gecekondu* becomes a rich property owner a quarter of a century later, when the building is five storeys high.

The Öztürks conformed to this tradition to the letter; although they had not quite managed five storeys, since first immigrating they had become the proprietors of three storeys, with two apartments per floor.

Remziye was a stranger to the Bitlis chapter of the family history. She was born when the second storey of the *gecekondu* in Sultanbeyli had been completed. Her father, who planted a tree in the garden after the birth of each son, chopped a tree down when she was born. Among tribes, being the father of daughters is partly shameful and partly problematic. Because girls often run away with men they want to marry, they are the most common cause of blood feuds, second only to land disputes. For this reason it is an established tradition to marry off daughters as soon as they are born. This also ensures that the sons of the family stay out of trouble. And so, to protect her family from any potential problems that might arise in Istanbul where the lifestyle was so full of temptation, the moment Remziye was born a 'cot betrothal' to her uncle's youngest son was performed. Unbeknown to the newborn baby she was now shielded against the devil's incitements. The two babies' families made an agreement upon their honour that the babies would be married. And to seal the match the baby boy's swaddling clothes and the baby girl's hair were threaded with the same blue beads to ward off the evil eye.

Remziye grew up dominated by four older brothers, two of whom were married. At the age of eight, according to her mother's wish, her head was covered. All the girls' heads in their neighbourhood were covered, but Remziye was the youngest.

At her mother's insistence she was sent to primary school several years later than her contemporaries. Remziye wore a uniform inside school and kept her head covered outside, and she finished with top grades. She flew home waving the certificate she believed would make her family truly proud, with one request: to be taken to the seaside. But her wings were clipped before she'd even entered the house.

Her mother, considering such notions inappropriate for a girl, and a poor girl at that, flew into a rage. Not only had she herself never seen the sea, but she wasn't even aware that there was any sea in Istanbul. Her daughter was getting ideas above her station. None of her sons had gone on to higher education; they had found it difficult enough finishing primary school. Remziye's success highlighted her sons' failure. Before the men in the house had even seen them, Remziye's mother burned her daughter's glowing reports on the stove. But when, in that same year, Remziye was the first to recite the *Qur'an* by heart in the girls' course at the mosque, her mother's anger abated.

The family put a barbed wire fence all the way around their *gecekondu*. They planted trees in the gaps in the fencing and reserved the rest of the plot for planting vegetables. They had a coop in which they raised over fifty chickens, and directly beside it a small barn where they kept a few sheep and a cow.

When the last born after Remziye was also a girl her father refused to look at his wife ever again. He had forgotten that she had given him eight sons. Instead of resenting her husband, her mother blamed Remziye. Her daughter was so quick-witted and intelligent that she frightened men. In the mornings, bright and early, she would feed the chickens, milk the sheep and cow, then run to school. In the afternoons, after school, she would take the sheep out to pasture, and then go to the *Qur'anic* course at the mosque.

As soon as the two-hour class was over she'd run home holding that day's section of the *Qur'an*, then prepare the evening meal. At weekends she would prepare wafer-thin *yufka* bread – dampened with water, wrapped in a cloth and stored in the pantry – with such skill it put her mother in the shade.

In summer they would go to Bitlis and, over the course of three months, prepare tomato paste, honey, pepper, preserves, dried fruit and vegetables, dried pasta, sheets of dried fruit pulp, walnuts, braised meat preserved in oil, butter and curd cheese for the whole tribe. Towards the middle of autumn they would bundle up the provisions they had made and the entire tribe would return to Istanbul, like a modern caravan convoy.

Remziye deeply resented having to do this. The men in the family did practically no work, while the women tilled the fields, prepared provisions for winter and did all the household chores. Yet it was the men who were served the thighs of the fried chicken, the freshest of the fruit compote, the crunchy edges of the pastry *böreks*.

Her mother was tired of Remziye's irreverent protests. The girl, who didn't dare open her mouth in front of her father, seized every opportunity to question her mother whenever the men weren't around. Why didn't her father ever work? Why hadn't her brothers continued with their education? Why were the girls forbidden to watch television when the men were around? Why was it always the girls who worked? On one occasion her mother had had enough of Remziye's endless bombardment.

'If the women didn't do these jobs why would the men ever listen to them? A woman either does the devil's work and brings trouble on her husband's head, or she works and lets him take it easy. Do you want to know what happens when a girl doesn't work?' And with that Remziye's mother brought the rolling pin down on her daughter's head.

As her brothers got married and settled into the apartments on the upper storeys, Remziye's workload got heavier. As if the care of her own younger sister was not enough, the care of the new brides' babies was also left to her. Still she did not utter a single word of complaint. As her mother said, the harder she worked the easier it would be for her to obtain permission to go on to secondary school. That summer in Bitlis she used every imaginable ploy to persuade her father to let her go. Her father would not give her a definite answer but just said, 'Let's get safely back to Istanbul first.'

But going back to Istanbul did nothing to help her cause. Besides, school had started at the beginning of September and the family didn't return until the beginning of October. Remziye seized an opportunity to go and find her primary school teacher. She begged him to persuade her father to let her have an education.

When the teacher came to Remziye's house one evening he was given a warmer welcome than he might have expected. Not only did the family serve him freshly made, buttered, *yufka* bread with honey but they also prepared a separate package for him to take home. It looked as though the teacher had persuaded the family because Remziye's father had said, in reply to his request that Remziye should have an education, 'We'll see, we'll do whatever bodes best.'

But no sooner had their guest left the house than each of her elder brothers set upon Remziye in turn and beat her. Remziye was stunned. The sociable, tolerant, hospitable family of a moment before had vanished. In its place was a savage pack, foaming at the mouth. She was familiar with her father's temper, but her mother was transformed beyond recognition. With a hatred that put her father's hatred in the shade she removed Remziye's hijab and yanked her hair. How could she have made a stranger party to their private business?

Remziye cried all night. In the morning her mother made her stand before her and ordered her to tell the teacher that her father had given her permission, but that she herself had changed her mind about going to secondary school. Escorted by her older brother, she went to school. Remziye did as she had been told. Noting her swollen eyes and the purple bruise on her temple that was just visible beneath her hijab, the teacher did not believe her. But because her older brother was standing behind her he pretended that he did. He decided to report the case to his superiors and make sure that the girl continued with her education. But it was all in vain. The family was very obliging to the people who came to persuade them, insisting it was Remziye herself who no longer wished to study. Before long the matter of school was shelved forever.

Although what followed was pure anguish for Remziye, it also signalled total defeat for the family. Remziye refused to wear the voluminous outer garment known as the *çarşaf* and the family grew tired of beating her. They were perturbed by her stubbornness and, in the end, they decided to marry her off and pass the responsibility for her on to her husband. Remziye's mother prepared a large pot of *perde* (curtain) *pilav* and invited all their relations for dinner. A sumptuous feast was laid before the men. The women crowded into the kitchen. They would have whatever was left over once the men had eaten their fill and left the table.

Remziye knew that *perde pilav* was fed to someone who was about to join the family through marriage. An oval pot is lined with a thick 'curtain' of flat *yufka* bread and, after the *pilav* has been prepared with almonds and shredded chicken, it is turned upside down and the first mouthful fed to the prospective bride. The *pilav* symbolises abundance, the almonds the bride bearing sons and the *yufka* curtain the keeping of the family's secrets by those who are about to join it. But Remziye couldn't see a bride anywhere.

As her father respectfully passed the first mouthful of *pilav* to her elder brother he explained that in the past they used to put partridge in the *pilav* instead of chicken, and grumbled, 'Where can you hunt partridge in this desert called Istanbul?' Then he said, 'Putting game in the *pilav* is a sign of a family's strength.'

Her uncle's youngest son ate the second mouthful of *pilav*. Remziye watched the men performing the ceremony among themselves and it didn't come as much of a surprise to her to learn that the ceremony was in honour of her cot betrothal to her cousin Nizamettin, which had been arranged sixteen years before, on the day she had been born. Remziye knew that all the baby girls in the family were betrothed at birth.

Nizamettin was a sullen, reserved young man, with a striking resemblance to Remziye's elder brothers. Remziye had never seen him laugh, and when he spoke his tone was loud, aggressive and argumentative. She couldn't even begin to contemplate him as her husband. Or rather she could, but she shuddered at the contemplation. Moreover, Nizamettin didn't treat her like a fiancée, he kept her at arm's length. Remziye knew the men in the tribe had an obligation to tradition, but she had still hoped for a shift in their attitude.

She didn't want to be like her mother, a lost woman married off to a relation, whose sole purpose was to serve her man among multitudes of children. Like the girls she saw on television, she wanted to uncover her head, go to school, go out and about and have a career. She wanted to come home from work and prepare dinner with her husband; she wanted to live in an apartment block where, as she'd seen on television, the people didn't know each other; she wanted to do as she pleased without anyone making a song and dance about it. She was aware that study was the only path to achieve all this, but as a betrothed young woman going to school was out of the question. Once she married Nizamettin she would go to a house two streets down the road as a bride and live her life doing the same chores she did in her father's house. She would drag out her days having never breathed freely in the world. And she didn't want too many children either. In fact, she didn't want any, but she knew she had to have a few, otherwise her relations and neighbours would assume she was barren and spread malicious gossip about her.

Because Remziye was now engaged she didn't protest when her mother changed her headscarf. Seeing the black *çarşaf* her mother wore, which concealed everything but her face, she knew she was privileged to get away with just wearing a scarf. She no longer had to wear the thin transparent muslin *yazma* that covered her head and reached her shoulders. She would pile her long hair on top of her head and secure it with a hairpin, gather it in a fine mesh known as a *bere*, made of black calico, then cover it with a flowered silk kerchief as wide as a tablecloth that came down to her shoulders, one end of which was secured with a pin.

Her rebellious soul had gradually been whipped into sorrowful surrender; the intensity of her desires had dulled. All that remained of her fiery spirit was a few embers on the verge of extinction. Remziye passively embroidered and crocheted in preparation for the marriage that was to take place at the end of the summer.

It was then that Ismail arrived. He was building a *gecekondu* for a family that had just moved to the plot next to their garden. As was customary, her mother sent lunch and hot tea to the workmen building the neighbours' house. When Remziye handed Ismail the lunch tray through the trees she sensed the young man's excitement. Once she even felt him surreptitiously caress her hand and was embarrassed and excited. It was the first time in her life that a stranger had touched her skin. The young couple plunged headlong into what began as hushed, secret conversations but which quickly became ever bolder, ever longer caresses, progressing from fingers to wrists.

Her mother grew disgruntled about the unnecessary length of time it took Remziye to serve lunch, but she could never have suspected that romance had bloomed between her daughter and Ismail. As soon as Remziye got into bed at night she would fantasise about going to the seaside she had never seen, as the wife of this swarthy, handsome builder; she would imagine them drinking tea, holding hands and kissing, and her heart would race. She would try to prevent her elder brothers, whose mattresses were lined up beside hers, from noticing her beating heart. The world had suddenly turned into a beautiful place. The smell of the chickens' cage didn't bother her any more, nor did she care about making her hands rough from picking vegetables.

When the neighbours' *gecekondu* was almost completed, Remziye could not think how she and Ismail would meet once the building was finished. When she asked him, the young man said he was taking as long as he could but told her that she mustn't worry, even when it was finished. He was going to send his family to ask for her hand in marriage. He slipped a telephone number into her hand. Remziye couldn't bring herself to tell him she was already engaged. She was afraid he would leave her if she did.

That night Remziye realised something was up after Ismail's shift was over and he returned home. Although the sun had not even set the whole family was gathered together and were sitting in silence with their heads bowed forward. Her eldest brother's wife stood up and slapped Remziye hard. From her apartment on the upper floor she had seen her laughing and talking with the *gecekondu* workman. Her sister-in-law's slap did not hurt, but Remziye was terrified of the possibility of her family finding out about Ismail. She knelt before her father, placed her forehead on the ground as though in the act of *namaz*, and started to plead with him.

'How could you think I would ever laugh and talk with a stranger, father? My sister-in-law is trying to blacken my name; I was only taking back the trays my mother sent. Please will you, at least, believe me?'

Her elder brother took her from under her father's feet and began beating her. He said, 'I'm going to beat you till you tell the truth.'

Her mother encouraged him, saying, 'If she won't tell the truth, kill her, my child.'

After watching for a little longer Remziye's father asked for a *Qur'an*. He wanted his daughter to place her hand on it and swear she was telling the truth. Had any male's hand ever touched hers?

Remziye placed her hand on the *Qur'an* and swore. Inside, she begged God to forgive her.

Her father was persuaded. Nevertheless he still sent for Nizamettin quickly, in order to eradicate any suspicion. He told him to prepare for the wedding now, in Istanbul, rather than in the summer in Bitlis. Nizamettin obeyed his uncle's wishes with his habitual icy coldness. He would begin the marriage preparations straight away.

Remziye despised her prospective husband. He hadn't even looked at her swollen face or asked her why she'd been crying. While the whole family was sleeping Remziye stared at the ceiling, trying to think how she could escape. Violence could not whip Remziye into submission and the rebellious spirit that she had assumed was broken, had risen once again, with all its might.

The following morning, taking care not to be seen by her sisters-in-law on the upper floors, she made as if she were going to the chicken coop. Ismail had started work. She told him in whispers that they needed to run away urgently. The young man was taken aback; he hadn't been expecting this. He had no wish to find himself on the wrong side of this very extensive tribe from Bitlis. But the girl's face was covered in bruises and her face swollen. Something was clearly very wrong. He didn't answer straight away; he didn't want to dash her hopes. He decided he would tell her when he finished work that evening that he couldn't run away with her, but that he would send his family to ask for her hand.

But he wasn't able to put his decision into practice. That evening Remziye was nowhere to be seen. When the sun was about to set Ismail gathered together his tools, changed out of his work overalls and started walking towards the street to catch the bus. And there, he couldn't believe his eyes: Remziye was at the bus stop. Under the disapproving glare of onlookers the two lovers did the unacceptable at the Sultanbeyli bus stop: they embraced. With growing danger came greater courage.

Ismail took Remziye to his house. His family, who lived in another *gecekondu* at the upper end of Sultanbeyli, received their daughter-in-law, whom Ismail had never mentioned, reluctantly. Not only were they afraid that this girl they knew nothing about might bring trouble on their heads, but they disapproved of her boldness in suddenly uprooting herself and coming to a strange house out of wedlock. But they were not hostile towards her. After they had eaten a silent meal they decided she would sleep in the same room as Ismail's sisters, and that Ismail would stay at a relation's house until they were married.

For the first time Remziye realised that life in all *gecekondus* was pretty much the same. Ismail had sisters too. Remziye found the girls' behaviour very familiar. They performed their tasks in silence with their heads bowed, walking as if on eggshells as though fearing rebuke at any moment. Remziye ate a few mouthfuls, trying not to catch Ismail's eye. After seeing Ismail off to a relation's house, she curled up on the mattress spread out on the floor in the girls' room and tried to get to sleep. Despite having acted of her own free will she felt very weary.

In the middle of the night there was a pounding at the door, like the drums during Ramadan. Half asleep and reciting the *zikir*,* Ismail's father opened it. Remziye's elder brothers, her cousins and Nizamettin were at the door, their faces like thunder. Remziye was devastated that they had found her, but there was nothing she could do. She bowed her head, and before she could even take leave of Ismail's family, was marched ahead of her captors. She departed just like that, in the silence of the night. She gave thanks internally that they hadn't found Ismail at home. Had they done so they would both have been killed.

She was taken home in a three-car convoy: she had no idea who had

---

* A devotional act that often includes the repetition of the names of Allah, supplications and aphorisms from *hadith* literature, and sections of the *Qur'an*.

lent her brothers the cars. Her mother, father and her other relations were all up and in a rage. In reply to her mother's insistent questioning her brothers assured her that Remziye was still untouched, but they had to decide whether or not she was to be killed. They bound her hands and shoved her into one of the rooms, and once the door had been locked they all went off to sleep. The family decided to keep Remziye prisoner until she had been brought to heel.

In the days that followed she was unable to get any news of Ismail. No one ever mentioned the matter; it was as though she had never run away. She wasn't allowed out, not even into the garden; she only did the chores inside the house. Nizamettin informed Remziye's father that he was calling off the wedding. The family began to look for an elderly widower who would be able to pay substantial *başlik parasi*.* They sent word to Bitlis and the surrounding villages where their relations lived.

Remziye longed to object to the future they were planning for her, but it was impossible. And then an unexpected opportunity presented itself and she became convinced that God was on her side. A respected member of the tribe died. The men of the house went to the *sala namaz*, a prayer recited before the muezzin recites the *ezan*, and the women went to lament for the deceased. And they forgot all about Remziye. Unsure whether she was being put to the test, Remziye waited for a while. She was afraid that if she took one step outside, one of her elder brothers would spring out from a secret hiding place and kill her.

When she heard the sound of the *sala* she found the courage to go out into the garden and climb over the wall. She ran all the way to the main road without stopping. When she thought she had left the house sufficiently far behind, she pleaded with someone in a shop to

---

*   A sum of money payable to the bride's father upon her marriage, after which she would be regarded as her husband's property.

let her make a telephone call, and she rang Ismail. She had memorised the number he had given her weeks before, as if it was a holy secret.

The young man came for her, but Remziye sensed his unwillingness. She could see that he was frightened, because there was no turning back now. This time Remziye's family would kill her if they found her. Reluctantly Ismail suggested that they should go to the house of one of his lesser-known relations.

Remziye had more courage than Ismail. She also knew what she had to do to make him a party to her resistance. She had to create an opportunity for them to be alone. Loving Ismail meant freedom. With a passion that Ismail was incapable of resisting, Remziye propositioned Ismail and they made love over and over again. From then on they regarded themselves as man and wife in the eyes of God. And, as a married woman, there was no need for Remziye to bow her head any more. She and Ismail would get themselves a *gecekondu* somewhere far away, as soon as possible, and set up home.

Remziye insisted they have an *imam nikah*, a religious marriage ceremony. The family they were staying with brought the imam to the house who granted the girl's wish, but because a religious marriage, although respectable in the eyes of society, is not recognised by Turkish law, they also needed to have a civil ceremony, for which documents of identification were necessary. They applied to the *mukhtar** and placing their trust in this man, who was curious about what had happened to Remziye's own documents, they told him the story of their forbidden love from beginning to end. The *mukhtar* behaved like a father towards them and started the proceedings for obtaining new documents straight away. Kissing his hands, they left his office in deep gratitude.

They sat down to their evening meal feeling more cheerful than they had in weeks. But before they had even taken their first mouthful the door of the *gecekondu* was broken down. The Öztürk tribe, headed

---

*   A village administrator similar to a councillor.

by the *mukhtar*, charged in. Suddenly the house was packed, as if for a mass meeting. Panic stricken, Remziye looked around for Ismail. She saw him jumping through the open window. With a heavy heart, she wrapped her headscarf around her head, knowing that this time fate had taken her well and truly captive.

Her brothers, mistaking someone else for Ismail, knocked him to the floor and, paying no heed to Remziye's screams, proceeded to beat him almost to death. Remziye managed to stammer, 'That isn't Ismail.' Ignoring Remziye, her brother looked at the *mukhtar*. It was only after he had confirmed that the girl was telling the truth that they let the poor man go. Kicking, punching and hurling insults at Remziye, they dragged her from the house. As the blood poured from her mouth, Remziye wondered at the *mukhtar*'s cruelty. She would never trust anyone again.

Remziye was thrown into the room where she had been held prisoner two weeks before, this time with her feet tied. As she lay bound and trussed on the mattress she could hear the family discussing her fate in the other room. Her mother insisted that if they didn't kill her they would never again be able to look anyone in the eye, either in Bitlis or in Sultanbeyli. But Remziye was amazed at her father. That hard man who never smiled was the only one who objected to having her killed. The oldest paternal uncle was to make the final decision.

Out of a perverse politeness her brothers and cousins didn't open their mouths before their elders, but her sisters-in-law shouted a string of vehement curses about Remziye's behaviour. From their high-pitched discussions Remziye learned something else of which she had been totally ignorant until now. Her youngest uncle's daughter, Fidan, had also run away with a stranger. She too had been caught and, just like Remziye, was awaiting the verdict on her fate. They thought it would be best to take them both to Bitlis and kill them in the village. But Remziye's father, who had argued against the girls being killed and in favour of their being married off to elderly widowers in the village, had a sudden change of heart.

'Let's kill the girls here,' he said. 'Azmi can do it. He's sixteen, but on his birth certificate he's younger. He'll get a light sentence.'

They decided Remziye's younger cousin would be killed first. As the death squad was departing her mother counselled the young boys with a detachment that made Remziye's hair stand on end.

'Whatever you do, don't kill them in the house. There'll be the bother of getting rid of the bodies. Shoot them among the trees and then dump the bodies somewhere.'

Silently the boys went to the house where Fidan was imprisoned. Remziye felt the gunshot that killed her little cousin in her own heart. Then the footsteps of the returning youths approached, to take her to her own death. Over and over again, she repeated, 'I don't want to die.'

Her eldest aunt switched on the light in her room, helped Remziye up and untied her feet. In contrast to her ruthless words in the other room, she was strangely kind to Remziye now. She carefully retied Remziye's slipped headscarf, straightened out the creases in her long wrinkled skirt and took her before the assembled family. Then she withdrew.

'Did you hear?' Remziye's father asked her. 'My sons killed Fidan. Now it's your turn. Take the *shahada*.'*

Remziye raised her head and looked at her father. 'I want to read the *Qur'an* and perform *namaz*,' she said. 'I don't want to die a sinner.'

Without looking at his daughter the man said, 'Go ahead, it will be the last chance you'll get. You can tell God you repent.'

In a half whisper Remziye said, 'I have to perform my ablutions.'

---

*   Islamic confession of faith, repeated before death, declaring that there is only one God and accepting Muhammad as the final prophet.

To his sons, who were on their feet ready to act, Remziye's father said, 'Let her be.'

He asked for a *Qur'an*, which he began to read out loud. After a while he closed it with great reverence and, after kissing it and touching it to his forehead, placed it on the highest shelf. 'Everyone go to bed now,' he said. 'Let Azmi finish this job, God speed, in the way he sees fit.'

When her father had finished speaking Remziye went out into the garden, with Azmi behind her. She went into the shed between the trees that served as a toilet, bathroom and storage space for tools. She began to perform her ablutions, making sure her head was visible through the broken window.

Azmi, who could not smoke in his father's presence, began to roll a cigarette, while keeping one eye on the movements of Remziye's headscarf.

Remziye made her ablutions, stepped outside and told Azmi she was going to perform her *namaz* under the tree. The young boy, traumatised by all the stress he was under, was already rolling his second cigarette. He didn't even respond; he was waiting for his father's signal to shoot.

Remziye walked behind the shed. She removed her shoes and placed them beside the prayer mat she had spread out on the ground. Her heart was pounding, because she was about to carry out a desperate escape plan. She stuffed the old clothes she had smuggled out with her into her headscarf and tied them to the lowest branch of the tree. In the darkness they cast a shadow on the prayer mat which, she hoped, would fool Azmi into thinking she was still there, at least for long enough to give her time to escape.

Quiet as a mouse, she lifted the barbed-wire fence and, heedless of the spikes tearing into her flesh, wriggled through. Barefoot, her head uncovered and with blood pouring from where the barbed wire had cut into her, she began to run. She didn't know where she was running and as she ran the weather suddenly turned, and it started pouring with rain.

Remziye didn't know how far she had run. She was soaked, spattered with mud, hungry, thirsty, cold and exhausted, but alive. She didn't have a single penny, or any idea of the time, or where she might be. With all her strength spent, she sat on the covered steps of a building and God sent the miracle she needed. The steps she was sitting on belonged to a Cem house. She knew a Cem house was the temple of the Alevi Muslims and she remembered that her family had always been very disparaging about them. Three youths, who had appeared from a side street and were going into the building, caught sight of the desperate girl sheltering on the steps. They carried her into the building and cleaned up her bleeding, swollen feet. From somewhere they produced a pair of slippers. They placed them on Remziye's feet, hooked their arms through hers and took her to a house.

Although it was past midnight, the large Alevi family gave Remziye a kind, cheerful welcome that was beyond what she could possibly have hoped for at that ungodly hour. They didn't ask who she was, or why she had run away, or from whom. The mother of the house, whose red hennaed hair was peppered with white, wrapped her up in blankets, gave her mint tea and fussed over her. The young boys who had carried her to their home had disappeared.

As Remziye was drifting into a dazed sleep she vaguely heard the woman's last sentence, 'Don't worry, my child, there won't be any men in this house tonight. I'm sending them all to stay with relations. You make yourself at home and go to sleep. Think of me as your Muslim sister and you'll feel better.'

The following morning, for the first time in years, Remziye woke up very late. The delicious fragrance of boiling tea and freshly prepared *börek* wafted in the air. It was the first time Remziye had woken feeling lighthearted and thankful. The girls in the family were gathered around the table squabbling over the *böreks*. Remziye washed her face and hands, folded up her mattress and sat down at the table. Her cousin Fidan, who had committed the same crime, was dead, but she had survived.

She told her story to her Muslim sister, and the woman stroked Remziye's hair, which she had uncovered for the first time in years. Confidently Remziye's Muslim sister declared, 'No one can come and take you away from this house; they'll have to carry our corpses out before they can take you.'

She summoned one of her sons and instructed him to find Remziye's Ismail. Towards evening Ismail came to the house with one of the youths who had found Remziye at the Cem house. The lovers embraced for a long time and the whole family was overcome with emotion. The couple had nowhere to go. Remziye was very fearful. She knew that if they caught her again she stood no chance of escaping alive.

Remziye's Muslim sister solved all her worries for her. She and Ismail would be her guests until they found somewhere to take refuge. But no one, not a single person, should know where they were staying. Remziye and Ismail fell on the woman's hands and kissed them with gratitude. In recompense to God for granting her the miracle of staying alive Remziye prepared *pilav* from green lentils, put on a jet-black *çarşaf* to stop anyone from recognising her, and went to the Cem house to distribute the food to all the visitors.

Because Alevi women do not cover their bodies, her distributing *pilav* dressed in a *çarşaf* attracted a lot of attention. But no one recognised her. The head of the Cem house, the Alevi *dede*, extended his hand to this wronged, desperate couple and had the necessary identification documents for their civil marriage prepared in secret. The marriage ceremony was also performed in secret. But as Remziye embarked on her new life as the legal wife of Ismail, she knew that fresh troubles couldn't be far away.

The neighbours in this poor Alevi district organised a collection among themselves, and with their help the couple acquired a one-room house and several items of furniture. But they could not resolve their biggest problem: Ismail couldn't work. Because the tribe was searching for them everywhere he had to go to great pains not to be seen. The family that had helped them was very generous, but because they were so poor themselves, the most they could do was share their poverty.

Remziye began to sense that Ismail was depressed by the fugitive life they were leading, and that the constant threat of being killed was wearing him down. She was certain that had she not left him any other option, Ismail would not have taken the risks they'd taken. But there was no turning back if they were to stay alive. In addition, Remziye was pregnant. Nothing could have made her happier, and if she had a child there would be no danger of Ismail abandoning her. She nursed hopes that now that she was a married woman with a family, her tribe would spare her. Once she had her baby she planned to send word to her father that she would like to kiss his hand, but things did not go as she had hoped.

Remziye gave birth in a *gecekondu* in the heart of Istanbul, with the help of her experienced Muslim sister. The baby was a girl. This not only dashed all hopes of going to kiss her father's hand, but meant Remziye had to live in deadly secrecy. It was only once she herself became a mother that she finally learned why women hate daughters and want sons. Having sons meant having strength. Nevertheless, thinking it might help to heal the blood feud, they named the child Emine, after Remziye's mother.

But each day brought increasingly unnerving news. Thinking they would eventually succeed in wearing down the fugitives and making them surrender, the tribe was raiding every house indiscriminately and assaulting Ismail's family who had been forced to abandon the neighbourhood where they had spent their whole lives to move to a secret location. But Ismail's father couldn't change the location of the humble shop where he sold kitchenware and cleaning products. It would have amounted to self-inflicted bankruptcy. Remziye was held responsible for all their hardship. Where, at first, they had rejected her with subtle hints, they now did so with blatant insults. There was neither peace nor reconciliation on the horizon. Remziye envisaged a future of relentless attacks, poverty and abandonment.

At the slightest flicker of the curtain, or ring of the doorbell, or sound of a raised voice, her heart leapt into her mouth. She could no longer sleep at night. Whereas in the past she had had the courage to look out into the street, now she couldn't even go near the window. When she did manage to sleep, dropping off towards dawn, she would awake in fear, thinking Ismail was going to kill her. During the day she felt she was imprisoned in a cage and that, if she came out of her dark prison, she would attack everyone in her path, like a rabid dog.

For Ismail, the nightmare Remziye lived at home continued outside. He would find a temporary job, but within days the tribe would discover his whereabouts and often he would leave without even collecting his wages. Ismail couldn't understand how this extensive tribe had the time to devote to hunting them down.

Ismail and Remziye went to the district attorney, but he hadn't recognised how serious the situation was, and put their fear down to a simple family misunderstanding.

'If anything happens to you I'll sort it out,' he had said, and dispatched the disheartened couple back to their home.

The news reaching Remziye's ears from all directions gradually wore down her resistant, rebellious soul. She knew they were heading for disaster and that only her own efforts could save her, but she was at a loss as to what to do. One day, as she was gazing vacantly at the television, her heart started to race. The presenter was inviting viewers to contact them by telephone if they had a problem they wanted the programme to resolve.

She clasped her baby to her and ran to the house of her only friend, her Muslim sister, to use her phone. But the lines were permanently engaged and it was impossible to get through.

Remziye spent every lunchtime the following week sitting in front of the television, trying to get through to the programme. And once again it was her worldly-wise sister who provided the solution. An acquaintance of hers worked at the post office; with his help they managed to get through to the programme. Knowing the entire nation was listening, Remziye told the story of her flight from death, concealing her name and other details of her identity.

The presenter wanted to meet Remziye after the programme to give her the money donated by viewers during the broadcast. In fact, the presenter of that lunchtime women's programme did something else too: she contacted the director of the weekly news analysis programme that I presented and, aware that I was doing some work on this subject, asked if I would like to meet Remziye.

Naturally I jumped at the chance. I was there before Remziye had even arrived at the television studio. I waited for her, tingling with excitement.

At that time I had no way of knowing that her adoptive family, including the sister and the young boys who first found her were all together, celebrating. I learned of the first day's excitement from her, when I met her.

It was as though they had won the lottery. In *gecekondu* neighbourhoods news spreads with incredible speed, in a mysterious way that no one can quite understand. The entire neighbourhood crowded into her adoptive sister's house. As was the custom, they made *lokma*, balls of fried dough filled with syrup, and distributed them to the neighbours. They prepared a banquet of grilled meat for themselves. Remziye realised with astonishment that everyone in that neighbourhood, where she had gone to such pains to keep herself hidden, actually knew her very well. But she didn't let it dampen her spirits. For the first time she had conquered her fate and triumphed and she didn't want to cast a shadow over this victory with a new fear.

But, because she didn't trust anyone after the *muhktar*'s betrayal she refused the programme's offer to send a car to pick her up. She didn't want to give her address to anyone, especially not complete strangers. She dressed and smartened up her husband who, because he couldn't work, slept late during the day and stayed in the coffee shop till all hours of the night. She swaddled her baby and went to the studio in her sister's friends' car.

Remziye, who had thought Istanbul consisted of Sultanbeyli, was overwhelmed by the size of the building she entered and the freedom of the girls who worked there. She saw that the world she'd seen only on television really did exist. And she thought how much she'd give to be one of those busy, bustling reporters. But she had become a mother before she was nineteen. She cursed her fate. But, for the moment, everything happened as magically as if a fairy had waved her wand over their lives. Someone calling from Austria wanted to help them. Lots of people had sent in baby clothes and small sums of money.

When we brought Remziye back to her neighbourhood with her contented baby sleeping in her arms, many people were waiting for them. The neighbourhood was ringing with the tale of the fugitives, and in the days that followed all of us in the news team threw ourselves into the Remziye case. The Austrian consulate general had been deeply moved by the fugitives' tale and granted them visas immediately. Someone in Austria, a Turk whom they'd never met, was going to pay all their expenses. Another nerve-wracking six months ensued. And despite all our efforts to change her name and the details of her story, Remziye's tribe still found out that her story had made the news. Not content with running away with a man, Remziye had shamed the family in front of the whole nation and they thought her conceited and presumptuous; they were determined to exact their revenge.

They called the programme over and over again, threatening to kill Remziye and Ismail. They discovered the location of Remziye's *gecekondu* from some small children playing in the street, but thanks to Remziye's adoptive sister's quick thinking Remziye escaped certain death. Her sister dreamed up a ploy to delay her pursuers, giving Remziye the chance to abandon everything and flee. Remziye believed that God was protecting them, through her sister leading her brothers up the wrong path. Thankfully Ismail wasn't at home when Remziye's pursuers attacked. Had he been in, escaping from Remziye's brothers might not have been so simple; it might well have turned into a bloodbath.

As Remziye's elder brothers entered her house, she was already in a taxi sent by her sister, clutching her baby. She had money now, and it protected her from death. By the time Remziye, Ismail and the baby got onto the plane bound for Vienna they had had to change houses four more times. But the spontaneous collection organised by the television workers and those who had heard of her plight had brought about a miracle in their lives. Remziye no longer had to try and stretch every penny. When changing houses, she could afford the rent that she had to pay in advance. For the first time in her life she was tasting the freedom that money can buy.

The first time I met Remziye she requested something very simple of me. Her large black eyes shone from the *çarşaf* that covered her from head to toe when she said she wanted to see the Bosphorus. She said that she had spent all her short life in Istanbul but, she told me, 'My father said there is no sea in Istanbul. How can there be no sea here?'

Together with her baby, who was now one year old, and her husband looking on in wonder, we sat in a restaurant with tables overlooking the sea. It was a fish restaurant, shimmering in magical light. Remziye was too excited to eat a single mouthful, but she stuffed the baby full.

When I asked how she felt she said, 'I've climbed up to heaven from the bottom of a dark pit.'

We talked for many days and I noted every detail of her story. My cameraman filmed the sections she consented to, and we discussed how they could escape death. We pushed envelopes containing donations that people had sent her into her hand. For the first time in her life she had her own money and she had earned it all by herself. Her husband, who was overshadowed by her strong personality, watched her in admiration. He was bewitched by these talents he hadn't known his wife possessed.

I went to see them off despite all their protests. She didn't once remove her black *çarşaf* until she had boarded the plane. Her three-year-long flight from death had made her so suspicious that she hadn't even told me which flight she was leaving on, or her last address. I had had to find out her flight details myself, but because they were flying for the first time, I wanted to be there to help them.

I bought them coffee in the airport. Remziye was heavy-hearted, but her husband, who was more at ease than Remziye, was happy. To him, leaving Istanbul meant leaving behind all their financial difficulties; it meant that they would be able to walk in the street without worrying; it meant that Remziye could discard her *çarşaf* and when her child was hungry she would be able to do something she had never yet been able to do, she could go to the shop swinging her arms by her side.

'Tell me, Remziye,' I said. 'What gives you girls the courage to take your lives into your own hands and run away, knowing you risk death? What is it that makes you so brave?'

With deep sincerity Remziye held my hands in her own small white ones. Her eyes were filled with unshed tears.

'I want to answer you as someone who has turned herself into a prisoner in the name of freedom. Of course there's the freedom of being able to go to the shop to buy bread, but true freedom is not being dependent on anyone, not even on your husband after you're married. True freedom is not being beaten and knowing, when you walk past your elder brother, that he won't beat you; knowing when you walk past your sister-in-law that she won't beat you, that your father won't beat you. Being treated like a human being, in other words. That's the only thing we run away for. Girls don't take their lives into their hands and run away for the sake of their husbands. They do it for the sake of freedom. They can only be free with the help of a man, that's why there's always a man in their baggage when they set out on their journeys. But many of them lead the same life they have run away from in their husband's home. It's tragic. They risk death to run away to freedom, but even if they escape death they're often sentenced to the same slavery they have fled from.'

She was silent for a while and heaved a troubled sigh. She closed her eyes and continued, her voice even more quiet.

'Even if you do take your life into your own hands, the rest is determined by fate. We're prepared to risk death to be free and many of us do die, as you know. Like my cousin Fidan. I feel as though I've cheated her by staying alive.' She went on, 'It's very important to be loved, to be able to throw your arms around your older brother and feel not fear, but his warmth! To be able to say, "My big brother is behind me, no one can touch me." But girls like me are always afraid. If my big brother sees me laughing, or if he sees my hair, these things have always made me afraid that he will beat me.

'We spend our childhoods with our mothers, but when we reach the age of fourteen or fifteen we're married off. It doesn't matter if he's widowed, it doesn't matter if he's old, as long as he's got money! When there's money all our customs are forgotten. When there's money no one wants to kill the girl. They don't want a poor husband.

But we move in poor circles, where are we supposed to find the rich husbands they won't kill?'

There was deep regret in her voice, and then she was silent for a moment. She seemed to be searching for the right words. Then she lifted her beautiful face and looked into mine. 'You might not want to kill someone who carries your own blood, who's a part of your life, but because you're pressurised by the elders and our customs ... there's actually a lot of guilt in all this ... there's the question of being behind bars for years. Your life is ruined. Once you get out you're not treated like a human being, you have a criminal record, you have all kinds of things.'

She fell silent again, and tears started to pour down her face. Startled by her crying, Emine, who was sucking her thumb on her mother's lap, started crying too.

Ismail and I said nothing, but I realised that this young woman was all alone with her fear, and I knew it would be very difficult to find a way to comfort her.

I turned to Ismail and asked, as sensitively as I could, 'Why do you think they usually kill the girls, whereas they hardly ever lay a finger on the men they run away with?'

'Because,' said Ismail, 'if they kill me it will start a new blood feud. Someone in my family will kill one of their family. And so it will go on. They don't want new blood feuds. If they only kill the girl it won't start any new problems between the two families.'

'Why did they decide to kill you, in that case?'

'Because we held out. Because I accepted Remziye after they had taken her back so I deserved to die as well.'

'If your sister ran away would you shoot her, after everything you've been through?'

Ismail replied without hesitation. 'There's running away and there's running away. If the person running away gets married like I did, that's fine, but if their intentions are bad it goes without saying I'd kill them both.'

While I was searching for something suitable to say to him in reply, Remziye, who had wiped away her tears, handed their tickets to the attendant. It was time for them to leave. We walked together as far as passport control.

'Do you know why the stranger in Austria is helping you, Remziye?' I asked.

She put her head on my shoulder and replied, 'Because twenty-five years ago the girl he loved was murdered by her family and dumped in the river. He only managed to escape by running away to Austria.' Sadly, she added, 'In other words, he's getting his own back on fate.'

The immigration officer stamped their passports and handed them back. Remziye turned to say goodbye. I hugged her tightly.

She whispered in my ear, 'The closer I get to escaping, the more afraid I am of being captured.'

The family of three fugitives went through passport control. Remziye turned and looked at me one last time. I got the impression she was apprehensive about her journey into the unknown. As I was trying to smile at them encouragingly they disappeared from view.

I never saw them again.

2

HANIM

Slightly built, he was wearing a baggy grey Urfa *shalwar** tapering abruptly at his ankles, with a faded green polo-neck sweater. Over the sweater he had on a short embroidered jacket the same colour as his trousers. He had rather a large forehead, with the odd wisp of cropped hair. He was taciturn, but his silence lent his face the same mysterious appeal as that of a religious leader. His eyebrows were knit in a permanent frown. His name was Murat. According to his file he was twenty-five, but he looked as if he was well past his thirties.

'Have you read my file?' he asked.

I had, but I didn't want him to know. 'No, I haven't,' I said. 'I prefer to hear it from you.'

'Seven years ago I killed my mother and then gave myself up,' he said in a barely audible whisper.

I knew Murat's crime, but hearing it recounted firsthand made my blood run cold. Killing someone was extraordinary in itself, but matricide was just unthinkable.

I was obviously unable to hide my feelings very well, for he soon

---

*   Traditional dress worn by both women and men in eastern Turkey.

said, 'If you can't bring yourself to talk to a man who murders his mother we can stop filming now.'

'No, no, please! You must realise it's not every morning I meet someone who has killed his mother. Please forgive me,' I said.

With the first hint of a smile since we'd met he nodded to the cameraman to signal that it was okay to start filming again.

He didn't want us to use his name or show his face. But he did give us permission to use his story without altering a single detail. When I said, 'Thank you for trusting us,' he said, 'People who have spent a long time in prison are like dogs; they have the same instinct for telling friends and enemies apart,' which I took as a compliment. The air cleared a little, and although the expression on his face was still distant we began to speak in a more relaxed manner.

'I once heard someone say, in a film, that every murderer is actually the victim of the person he has murdered. We are murderers with our bodies but victims with our souls. That's why, while it is justice that punishes our bodies, it is our crime that punishes our souls. Which do you think is worse?' he asked.

I didn't reply. I was afraid of breaking the spell, afraid that I wouldn't hear the whole extraordinary confession.

'This is the first time in years I've referred to that woman as "Mother". I don't know why, but that's the way it's coming out of my mouth. Maybe it's only by saying "Mother" that I can purge myself of my crime, maybe it's an overdue beginning,' he said softly.

We smoked endless cigarettes and we met on many mornings after that, and I knew, when I left that prison after the last interview, that the man I had left behind was an extremely lonely, guilty, repentant man.

Murat's mother, Hanim, hadn't even turned sixteen when she married Ibrahim the night watchman. At least, as far as she knew she hadn't turned sixteen. Being unable to read or write, she had no idea what her official age was. It had even been rumoured in her poor neighbourhood on the outskirts of Urfa that she was beyond marriageable age.

Her father had been planning to marry her to a merchant from Birecik, who had promised to give her a necklace of five gold lira coins and a thick bangle of twisted Trabzon gold. Hanim, who hadn't been consulted, was ready to accept whatever fate had in store for her. She only dreaded the thought of leaving Urfa. To her, the world beyond Urfa seemed like a dark, bottomless well. She knew the world to be a big place, but still her heart told her it consisted only of Urfa. She had been to few places even in Urfa. She had only visited the holy lake with the magic fish two years before, when her father's last wife had taken her there to pray.

Her father had been married by an imam to two wives. Her mother had died many years before and Hanim's recollection of her was hazy. She had no idea how old her mother was when she died, or indeed how old she herself was when it happened. She loved her two stepmothers very much; they formed a protective wall between her father and herself.

Hanim had no expectations beyond living like everyone else, mothering many sons and surviving squabbles with her husband's other wives. But the future was to deny her such hopes. Stepdaughters, customarily, were made to perform all the heaviest household chores, in return for food and a roof over their heads. Hanim was in charge of the household cleaning, and the washing and cleaning out of the chickens' cages, while her father's two wives cooked and baked bread once a week. Hanim never complained. Being the youngest of nine sisters from the two stepmothers, and older than her six brothers, her half-woman, half-child existence didn't strike her as at all burdensome.

A young local man called Ibrahim set his sights on Hanim, flaunting the night watchman post he had inherited from his father as an attraction. For a long time Hanim didn't know who Ibrahim was, she'd never seen him in her life. And anyway, half the men in Urfa were called Ibrahim, after the Prophet in the legend in which the Assyrian King Nemrut has a dream that his reign will come to an end at the hand of a boy child to be born that year. Nemrut orders all baby boys born that year be put to death but the Prophet Ibrahim's mother gives birth to him secretly in a cave, and when Ibrahim grows up he returns to his family's home and begins to speak out against Nemrut and paganism. Ibrahim is captured and cast into a fire from the top of the hill, where Urfa Castle stands. But God transforms the fire into water and the logs into fish, and the Prophet Ibrahim falls into the newly formed lake in a garden of roses. Ever since this miracle, the lake that resulted from the fire being turned into water, and the fish it contains, have been considered sacred.

Hanim's two stepmothers insisted that instead of the suitor from Birecik who was forty years her senior, she should be married to Ibrahim the night watchman, who was only ten years older. Both women agreed that Birecik would lack the strength to father children, and only wanted a wife to care for him in his old age. Ibrahim was not handsome, but he was young and strong. Hanim was to have been the third wife of the merchant from Birecik, whereas she would be Ibrahim's first wife. Hanim ventured no opinion on this match either. She wasn't convinced that a first wife is always the most cherished. The fact that her father doted on his last wife, who was young enough to be his daughter, belied this theory, but she didn't make a fuss. She was certain that her stepmothers had her best interests at heart.

The stepmothers persuaded her father that the young Ibrahim was the better choice. He wouldn't be able to provide her with gold jewellery – indeed, it was doubtful whether he could provide the mandatory *mihir** – yet there could be no better husband than a respected man with a gun, who was employed by the state.

---

*   A dowry of money or gold given to the bride as security in the event of divorce or death.

In Urfa the weddings of orphaned girls were quiet, sombre affairs. A red sash was tied around the bride's waist and an old piece of muslin served as a veil. A ceremony was performed by the imam, followed by prayers, after which she was dispatched to her husband's home and the marriage was deemed complete. On the eve of the wedding the women partook in the ceremonial bridal bath and celebrated the henna night; the day after they sampled the banquet, which was to be served to the men.

Ibrahim had insisted on a civil wedding, but Hanim, only sixteen, wasn't old enough to be officially wed so, in the end, he agreed to a religious marriage until she came of age.* The red sash was tied, the white muslin placed over her face, and the ceremony was performed at her father's home, with the male witnesses testifying, while Hanim, her older sisters and her two stepmothers waited in another room. Afterwards they drank sherbet.

When Ibrahim's father was killed in a terrorist attack, the state took Ibrahim on as a replacement, and his mother moved in with them. She despised Hanim. She had no problems with her four other sons' wives, because they lived in their own homes, but she saw Hanim as a rival, and she lost no time in making Hanim's life a living hell. Ibrahim, whose love for his wife was so intense its equal could not be found in any other man in Urfa, was partly to blame for this. But before the second year of his marriage was up he sent his fractious mother to live with his older brother in Viranşehir. He couldn't bear to see her mistreat his beloved wife.

And yet it was his mother who had chosen Hanim, with whom he'd fallen in love before he even set eyes on her. In Urfa girls were traditionally paired off, from a young age, with male cousins; girls who didn't conform to this tradition and ran away with someone else were murdered, along with the man they'd eloped with. Ibrahim's mother had chosen girls from the family for her older sons, but

---

* The mimum age for a civil marriage in Turkey is eighteen.

for her youngest son she had looked for an orphaned girl with no family, thinking she would be easier to manage. Hanim was the ideal candidate, not least because of her extraordinary beauty.

No one, until her husband, had ever told Hanim that she was beautiful. Her only sexual experience had been with her stepcousin Halil, who followed her into the chicken coup when she was cleaning it and aroused her body and her soul among that sickening stench. He would grope the girl's waist from behind and usually fumble under her clothing to squeeze her firm breasts or curved hips. Hanim didn't utter a sound and continued cleaning the cage as though nothing had happened, but she took such a long time over the cleaning that the boy understood her to be a willing party, and, despite saying that he was like a brother to her, her cousin, when he returned from military service, looked for any opportunity to renew these henhouse sessions, right up until Hanim's marriage.

Once she was married, Hanim gave birth to four daughters in quick succession, but these births occurred before her civil marriage ceremony. By the time she had Murat, she was twenty-one and she and Ibrahim were legally married in the eyes of the state, but this meant that only Murat was registered as the legitimate child of legally married parents. From the day he was born Hanim gave her son preferential treatment over her daughters. He was her little king.

The arrival of so many robust children in such quick succession gave the impression that Hanim had a very active sex life, but this was far from true. Her husband worked at night and slept during the day. If, when he awoke, he told his wife to heat water it meant that he intended to take a bath when he returned from work, which indicated that he was going to have sex with her. The sex would last no more than a few minutes, and it grew more and more infrequent.

Hanim began to feel increasingly nostalgic for her cousin Halil's advances. Her husband had never been able to arouse her in the same way. As time passed she began to believe that the husband of whom her stepmothers spoke so highly was, in fact, weak. Ibrahim was permanently tired, because of his night shifts, and he was unattractive, ill kempt and haggard looking. There had also been a considerable increase of violence in the town: attacks and local skirmishes between the newly established army and Kurdish militants had added to Ibrahim's workload.

Hanim had grown very tired of the husband who doted on her and granted her every wish. She pitied him but she did not love him. Every month without fail Ibrahim handed over his pay packet to his wife, telling her to do whatever she liked with it. But, like the logs thrown into a gaping oven, the salary she had at her disposal was never enough and poverty remained a chronic problem in their household. Nevertheless, Hanim managed to perform some miracles: all the children finished primary school, and all the girls were sent to workshops to learn how to make rugs. The girls would be married off, one after the other, at a tender age.

One summer, Murat was sent to his grandmother's in Viranşehir, and it was there that he heard strange rumours about his mother and the man she allowed into the house at night, after his father had gone to work. Murat's grandmother had never forgiven Hanim for having her banished from her home. She was very old by then, but her heart hadn't softened. Her son might have turned a deaf ear, but she could still make her grandson hear what she had to say.

At first Murat didn't mind his grandmother's hints and questions about his mother. He knew Uncle Halil who came to the house late at night. Not only was Uncle Halil like a brother to his mother, but every time he came he gave all the children money and brought them presents of fruit and groceries. Murat was the one to whom he paid most attention, sitting him on his knee for hours and stroking his hair. These lavish shows of affection, which he didn't even get from his own father, were surely due to his being the only son.

One night, towards morning, when Murat hadn't yet turned nine, he woke up feeling strangely uneasy. He went to the toilet – he had to go outside into the courtyard to do so – and, on returning, he heard whispers coming from his mother's room. He raised the curtain door of the room and peered inside. In the pitch black, all he could make out was the outline of the mattress on the floor. He understood from his mother's happy peals of laughter, which he'd never heard before, that she was not alone. He understood that the giggling and groaning were indicative of forbidden pleasures, but he couldn't understand who she was sharing these pleasures with. He lay down on his thin mattress in the room he shared with his older sisters and kept his eyes fixed on his mother's room.

He saw his mother walk out on tiptoe. He saw her seeing Uncle Halil off, in the dark. Murat heard her murmuring the words she normally reserved only for him, 'My lion, my hero, my ram,' she said, as she held Halil close. Murat closed his eyes tightly, terrified of seeing anything else. But he could sense his mother silently surveying the room where her children slept. Once she had made sure they were all asleep, she went back to bed, humming a folk song under her breath.

Murat had no idea how long he lay there with his eyes shut. He only remembered that his father had returned home well after daybreak, that his mother had welcomed him joyfully and prepared him something to eat, that his father had told her to heat water, that she had done so but that his father had nodded off before the water was even heated, and that his mother had gone out into the courtyard, where she poured the water and began to clean.

Murat never saw Halil and his mother in the same bed again; But Halil was at their house almost every night and although Murat no longer wanted to accept the presents Halil brought, or the money he gave him, he never found a way to refuse. He began to go to bed first every night, he was the last to wake up and he stopped speaking. Sometimes weeks would go by without him seeing his father, and his mother, worried about the changes in him, first took him to the local fortune teller, then to the Holy Lake so that the imam there could recite prayers for him. Although there wasn't the slightest difference in Murat's behaviour, his mother bragged to the neighbours about the miracle of the Holy Lake that changed her son's altered sleep patterns and restored his desire to speak.

That summer when the schools broke up for the holidays and he once again went to stay with his uncles and his bad-tempered grandmother, Murat had become a silent, serious child. There was not a trace of gaiety left in his mother's little king. Perhaps, if his grandmother had renewed her cruel insinuations about his mother, Murat would have betrayed her and confessed everything. But the vindictive grandmother didn't live long enough to provoke Murat again, that year she died quietly in her sleep.

Murat soon discovered what kind of a relationship his mother had with Halil. But he swore to himself to keep it a secret, until the day he died. He struggled constantly with his love for his mother and his hatred of her betrayal, and his hatred won every time. Since the day he'd seen Halil and his mother together he hadn't hugged his mother, not even once. Whenever she tried to say the words, 'My lion, my hero, my ram,' he covered her mouth with his hand without looking at her face. Hanim couldn't understand her son's silent rejection.

Murat's father had no idea that he had grown up, or that he carried such a heavy burden. He was planning an early retirement and talked of moving to the village and devoting himself to cultivating land. But whenever he mentioned moving, Murat's mother opened her eyes wide and swore, 'They'll carry my dead body out of here before I go to the village.'

And then there came a time when Uncle Halil wasn't around for a while and Murat's mother was no longer her usual cheerful self, she became an irritable woman who hardly ever smiled. Ibrahim was incapable of entertaining her, Murat realised; in fact she was even more irascible when he was around. But Murat saw that his father adored his mother, although, years later, when there were women in his own life, when he weighed things up in his own mind, Murat understood that his father's devotion was in fact pitiful submission, the thing that is often most despicable to a woman. He also understood that women are often attracted to strong, cold men, and that his mother was in love with the first man who had come into her life and had never betrayed him. But at the time Murat was much too young to understand all this.

Murat became a fervent devotee of the sermons at the bazaar mosque. He didn't know why he attended these sermons so diligently, but he wanted God to shed His divine light on an unidentified question he carried deep inside, without crushing or shaming him. By attending sermons, never missing the communal Friday prayers, praying at home on a regular basis and fasting, he took refuge in the safe harbour of religion. Although he spoke little, whenever the subject of his religious devotion was raised he was quick to criticise those whose worship was based on hearsay, advocating the need to read directly from the source or to learn from the *hodjas*.* At every gathering he stressed that the most sacred religious commandment was, 'Thou shalt respect and honour thy mother and father.' His mother proudly showed off her son's conviction to the neighbours. The other boys of Murat's age were loutish, violent hoodlums who caused trouble at home and were beyond anyone's control. Murat was held up as an example of model behaviour. The neighbours repeatedly told Hanim, with envy bordering on resentment, how fortunate she was to have such a son.

Before he knew it Murat had reached adulthood. He was now a handsome young man whom all the local girls watched from behind curtains. But he was unemployed. After leaving primary school he'd gone to work as a labourer on his uncles' land, but he'd grown tired

*   *Hodja* is the local word for imam.

of the village and returned home where he started loitering around the stallholders at the bazaar. His eldest uncle had four large stalls in the centre of the market place and Murat thought he might be able to run one of them, so went to talk to him. The uncle reacted with unexpected generosity. Of course he could have the stall, he deserved it, he could even have the most profitable stall. And so began Murat's work as a retailer. And true to his word, his uncle really had given him the most profitable stall.

The bazaar was nothing like the poor neighbourhoods on the outskirts of town. It was bustling and colourful, and there was never a dull moment. The poverty that had plagued them since his childhood was at last a thing of the past. Not only did the stall bring in very good money, but the mainly female customers fell under Murat's spell. He had not yet had any romantic experiences, but he was aware that women were interested in him. Women were more daring than he could have imagined and they thrived on danger. He was amazed that women could flirt with him when the stall was at its busiest, with their husbands right beside them.

He realised that, for reasons he didn't understand, he only looked at married women and this made him very uncomfortable. He felt like a kleptomaniac, caught red-handed stealing someone else's property. Once again he felt a storm brewing in the depths of his soul. When God didn't provide the answer to the question he couldn't ask, it dawned on him that he was hoping to learn the answer from married women. But still he lacked the courage to initiate an affair with one.

In the end the courage came from another. An attractive woman started coming to shop at the stall every day at around the same time. Unlike the other women she neither haggled nor criticised the quality of the goods. When Murat realised that he, and not the items on the stall, was the object of her interest, he started puzzling over how to engineer a meeting, but she was quick off the mark.

One day a note she pressed into his hand told him where she would be waiting for him. He left one of his cousins in charge of the stall, and went to meet the woman who became the first love of his life. She was a married woman who claimed that her husband beat her, and that her infidelity was her way of getting her own back on him. Every time Murat made love to her, his mother would appear before his eyes. He was consumed with guilt, but somehow that made the affair more appealing.

It was around this time that he met Sevda. She was the prettiest of the few girls who went to the only secondary school in the bazaar. It was clear from her clothes and the way she carried herself that she came from a well-to-do family. Murat started to wait for her after school. The girl was swept off her feet by this serious young man who waited for her tirelessly under the street lamp. They started to meet in secluded spots, away from prying eyes. Murat fell passionately in love with her.

It didn't take his married lover long to gather that Murat was in love with someone else, and she soon found out who the other woman was. She began to put pressure on Murat to stop seeing Sevda, but Murat told her he preferred to end his risky affair with her. He had no idea that these words would change his life, though he did have a sense of terrible foreboding when the young woman fixed her gaze on Murat's face, spat and said, 'But yet you never thought your mother's affair risky,' which was like a punch in the face to Murat.

So that was the way it worked, he thought. Women guilty of the same crime could use it as blackmail against others. Inflamed by passion, she made several other cutting remarks that Murat either couldn't remember, or didn't wish to remember, when he talked to me.

Forcing down the lump of shame in his throat, Murat said, 'You'll see, in a few days, how much someone will have to pay for what you've just said.'

The woman was alarmed by the wrath and the shame glinting in Murat's eyes. 'What did I say?' she said, trying to soften the situation.

'I know exactly what you meant. The glass was already full; now it's overflowed. But you will be one of the causes!'

From that day on Murat was possessed by an obsessive suspicion. He strove constantly to work out how many people were aware of the affair he had thought no one knew about. He set the customers, his friends and his relations, small tests that wouldn't arouse their suspicion. Each time he imagined they knew, he sank deeper in torment and, once again in his life, he distanced himself from the people around him. He recoiled from large gatherings; he was so ashamed. When walking along the street, if someone coming towards him looked at him for five seconds he'd torture himself with the illusion that they knew. He wouldn't join in with the conversations and discussions about honour that were held in certain circles. Whenever these topics came up he'd either hang his head in silence or get up and leave. He believed that for the rest of his life he'd be unworthy of the dignity of discussing such issues. Unfortunately honour was the most common topic of daily conversation in the bazaar in Urfa.

While Murat was torn between his new suspicion and his new love, his uncle summoned him. For some time he had been keeping his distance from his uncles too, doing everything he could to avoid coming into contact with them, but when Murat met this uncle, he said, straight away, 'There's something you need to do.' Murat didn't need to ask what it was. They both knew what he was referring to.

Murat said respectfully, 'I'll do whatever is required of me, uncle.'

'You should,' said his uncle. 'It's up to you to clean this stain on our honour and our dignity. You're young. In a few years' time you'll be out like a lion and then you can marry the girl you love, and the other stall girls as well.'

Murat didn't know how his uncle had found out the deadly secret of his childhood but, without uttering another word, he signalled to his uncle for permission to leave and left the market.

A few days later his uncle summoned him again. He said, 'My lion, my hero, my manly nephew. If you don't do this, I won't be able to show my face in the market. Your father doesn't know what's happening, what could he know anyway, working nights and sleeping during the day? You'd think the reason he's hiding in the dark is because he can't look anyone in the face. He hasn't got the dignity to be ashamed of what's going on, or the courage to cleanse his dignity. It's up to you. If you were to run away where would you run to? When it comes down to it, this bazaar is where you'll come back to. You will always walk with your head down, your shoulders stooped. Murat, my son, until you've done what you must do no one will give you their daughter. If *you* won't do it we'll have blood on our hands, and we have children and responsibilities. Our homes would go to wrack and ruin. You haven't built your nest yet; you wouldn't be leaving anyone behind to go destitute. We'd look after you like a prince in prison. You'll get out in a few years. There hasn't been a pardon for ages, so there'll be one soon. If you clean up this business now it will coincide with a pardon and you'll be out before you've even served five years. You'll be able to walk around the bazaar with your head held high and your dignity intact. The rest is up to you. But if you don't act quickly we're finished with you. We can't bear to live like this anymore.'

Hanging his head, Murat waited for his uncle to finish speaking. When he was leaving he stuffed a wad of bank notes into Murat's pocket, which he meant to refuse, but didn't. His back was soaked in sweat.

He began to walk without knowing where he was going. He had accepted it now, there was nothing he could do about it. If he did what his uncle said, wouldn't everyone ask why now, after so much time, and why not before? They lived in a conservative neighbourhood:

one person's knowledge was enough for everyone to know. Just as his uncle, who had never really accepted his mother, knew, so others must know too.

People provoked him with innuendos, comments, looks or anecdotes that hinted at what they knew, but Murat feigned ignorance, and tried not to rise to the bait. But the water slowly began to fill the glass. All the thoughts he poured into it began to rise with a manic energy that he could no longer control – until he could think of nothing else from the moment he woke up until the moment he went to bed.

His choice was this: either *he* died or his mother died. He thought long and hard about committing suicide. If he were to die it wouldn't change anything. In fact it would make things even worse. He imagined holding the barrel of the gun to his head, but couldn't imagine finding the courage to pull the trigger. If he died no one would know why he had killed himself. And he could hardly leave a note. What motive could he give? If he killed his mother, those twenty people who knew about her 'error' would turn into hundreds, thousands, the whole town. He resolved not to do it. He would kill Halil instead. This was not only an easier option than killing himself, but also required less courage than killing his mother. But then something incredible happened. Just at that moment the muezzin recited the ritual *sala* prayer. The imam of the bazaar mosque was announcing a death. It was Halil. He had had a heart attack.

Murat looked up to the heavens, interpreting it as a divine message. God was telling him not to interfere, that He would take care of what needed to be done, that it wasn't his responsibility and suddenly it struck him that the only way out of this nightmare was to get married. Then he wouldn't have to kill his mother, or at the very least he could abandon the town where he lived. He could go to large but distant cities like Istanbul, Ankara or Izmir, where it would be easy to disappear.

He ran back to his neighbourhood to catch Sevda as she came out of school. Everyone had gone home but she was waiting for him in their usual place. She told Murat that her brother had started to suspect, and that he had told her he would kill her if he found out that she was flirting with anyone. And just to show her he meant business he had beaten her the previous night. The girl was trembling with fear as she told Murat this but, despite the risks, she squeezed Murat's hand tightly.

'Take me away,' she said. 'Take me away tonight.'

'I can't,' said Murat. 'I came today to say we should get married. Let's go to your house and ask for your hand first. If they refuse then we can think about running away.'

But Sevda insisted, 'They won't let me marry you. You haven't got a proper job. Take me away now so we can be at peace.'

'We can't be at peace,' said Murat, 'They'd come after us and kill us both.'

In the evening he mentioned the matter to his mother. It was the first time in years that they'd spoken like mother and son. He wanted to get married and he had found the girl he wanted to spend the rest of his life with.

His mother said 'Don't worry, my son, I'll send word to Sevda's mother that we're going to go and see her daughter.'

Then she got up and opened the door of the large cupboard that was piled high with mattresses and quilts. She pulled out the mattress right at the bottom and rolled it out. She tore off the patch in its centre and inserted her hand into the hole, withdrawing a small bundle. Inside was a necklace of five gold lira coins, and a wad of notes. She held them out to Murat.

'I saved this for you my son. You can pay for the wedding with it.'

Murat felt the sweat pouring off his back and his forehead. The wad of notes his uncle had given him that morning was also sitting untouched in his pocket. He wanted to say to his mother that he wouldn't take her gifts, but no sound would come from of his mouth. Tears streamed down his face. He saw that his mother too was beating herself and crying, and he realised for the first time how beautiful she was. Murat was struck by how much younger she looked than her thirty-seven years, her cheeks pink like those of a girl in early adolescence, her eyes languorous, as though they'd been blackened with kohl. In eight years he hadn't once embraced her. There was a great fire smouldering inside him. He felt an unbearable urge to hold her and to weep out loud, unashamedly. The stronger his desire became, the more he steeled himself. The tears flowing down his face reached the end of his nose and dripped onto his trousers, where the wet patch expanded like a spreading ink stain.

Murat fell asleep in that position. Much later he heard, from the clatter of pots and pans, that his mother had put food on. He thought it might be the last meal she ever cooked. In his sleep he'd heard his father say, 'May it be for the best, as he wants to get married you do what's necessary.' The necklace and the two wads of notes lay in two separate pockets, untouched.

There was no reply from the girl's family to his mother's message. Worse still, every day after school Murat went to the school gates but never managed to meet Sevda. When they walked past one another in the bazaar his uncle refused to acknowledge him. It seemed the whole world – his cousins, his sisters, Sevda – was angry with him.

One day, a small girl approached Murat at the school gates where he still went every day.

'Sevda sent you this,' she said, holding out a piece of paper soaked with sweat from being held in her fist, and ran away.

Sevda wrote that she had to see him. She would wait for him to come to her aunt's house in secret. He must not let anyone see him.

Murat ran to the address she had written on the paper. When he rang the bell a young woman he'd never seen before opened the door.

Looking around her she ushered him inside, clearly very agitated. She was behaving like a member of a secret society. In the living room Murat saw Sevda curled in a ball on the sofa, covered with a blanket. Her right cheek was severely bruised and her right eye so swollen she couldn't close it. His heart sank. What had happened to the girl he loved?

Looking with her one eye at her aunt, whom she realised was determined not to leave them alone, Sevda made a frightened gesture to Murat to come and sit beside her. Abruptly she asked, 'Who is your father?'

Murat felt he was about to drown, as though someone had tied a stone to his foot and thrown him into the water. His head was spinning, but he answered Sevda, 'I told you, Ibrahim the Guard.'

'My mother says your mother is a bad woman and that you're a bastard. They'll never give me to you. I told you to take me away. You didn't do it, and now it's too late. They've taken me out of school and my older brother beat me up. They're forcing me to get married. Your mother has deprived me of my education. What kind of a mother is that? Everyone knew, except me. You didn't tell me. You deceived me!'

Murat looked at the woman waiting before them, then looked at Sevda again. He thought he would never speak again.

Murat didn't know how many times he'd walked the length of Urfa's main avenue. He couldn't go on living. All his dreams about Sevda, his marriage, even the market stall, were dashed. Everything had suddenly turned into a stinking pile of rubbish. The feelings of hatred and shame that he'd been struggling for years to suppress suddenly coursed through his body like poisoned blood. For eight years he hadn't spoken to his mother, had tried to avoid being face to face with her, had fought to forget what he'd seen, had pretended not to understand the things his grandmother had said, but no one had been aware of the battle taking place inside him. They'd made excuses for his behaviour. Now all his endeavours were turning into nothing, like ice melting in the heat.

For the first time it dawned on him that the secret he'd thought so well guarded was, in fact, juicy gossip on everyone's lips. Nothing was secret, particularly in the centre of Urfa. The neighbours would never leave them in peace. Until today he had pretended not to understand those who had been sticking needles into him with their innuendos. But now it was impossible for him not to feel the pain from those needles. Because now it was the people who meant the most to him who were sticking them in. He couldn't go on like this any longer.

After changing his mind a thousand times, Murat finally made his decision. It was wrong, but he would do it knowing it was wrong. Knowing full well he would regret it ... he would spend the best years of his life in prison, all his dreams and ideals would go to waste, but knowing and accepting all of this he would do it.

He returned home towards dawn, when his father would also be returning to sleep. For a while Murat listened to the house from outside. If he heard any sounds or movement he would turn back without entering. But the house was plunged into deep silence. Slowly he glided inside. He went into the room where his father lay sleeping, snoring loudly. He picked up the gun that his father had tossed carelessly beside him.

His father used to put the gun in his hand when he was a child, saying, 'Come on, my son, don't grow up to be a coward. Fire it. Fire it!'

Murat hated this game, which was more diverting for his father than for him, and this was the first time he'd touched the gun since then. He tiptoed out of the room, again in silence. Suddenly he saw his mother standing before him. Her face was tense, but more out of anxiety than fear. He heard her whisper, 'My son.'

Murat walked into the kitchen. His mother sensed that something wasn't right and followed him. He held the gun against his own head.

He saw his mother standing there, looking at him with an expression he would never forget, powerless to do anything. He lowered the gun. He felt his mother take a deep breath.

She whispered, 'It's because of that girl, isn't it my son? It's because of that girl. I'm going to make sure you get her, don't you worry.'

'It's because of you. You've committed a great error!' cried Murat. 'It's because of you! You're guilty. You know what you did!' He didn't say the rest.

Hanim bowed her head in shame. 'I know what I did, my son, may God forgive me.' She fell silent again, took a deep breath, then whispered, 'Shoot, my son. It's my destiny.'

Murat remembered firing three shots one after the other. For years he would be haunted by the thought that his mother had bowed her head and hidden her eyes from him to make it easier for him, to stop him from losing courage. To make the job of her son, whom she loved more than anyone, easier, she didn't flinch, she didn't try to escape, she didn't struggle.

She fell headlong onto the kitchen floor and a pool of blood flowed from under her. Murat put the gun in his pocket and walked outside with robotic movements. Despite all the noise no one had woken. Later, Murat would realise they'd all been awake but pretended not to be, to avoid having to witness anything.

Walking at a military pace, Murat went to the market place. They were just beginning to set up the bazaar. He went to his uncle's shop. The tea boy had come, but his uncle wasn't around yet. Murat collapsed into a chair and accepted the tea the boy brought him. He had no idea how long he waited. When his uncle finally set eyes on him, he didn't say a word. It was as though he knew everything that had happened.

'I've done what you said, Uncle!' said Murat, with simulated pride.

A shadow suddenly clouded his uncle's expression. 'What did I

say, Murat? Pull yourself together. What did I say? What was there
to say? What have you done?'

'I killed that woman.'

His uncle's face grew more and more cloudy.

'Go, my son. Go and tell the police. Why did you get blood on
your hands? This is unbelievable. Go on, my son, don't just stand
there!'

Murat was devastated. His uncle, who had urged him to kill his
mother, had turned his back on him. He left the market place and
walked into the police station which was directly opposite.

The policeman at the door straightened his gun and blocked
Murat's path. 'Where do you think you're going, friend?'

'I've committed murder. I've come to give myself up.'

'Go inside. The inspector will take your statement,' said the
policeman, showing no surprise.

Murat walked up the steps, and turned round before entering. He
looked down at the town stretching away before him.

In the spring of 1999 all the trees in Urfa were in bloom.

All his uncle's calculations turned out to be wrong. Because Murat
was already twenty when he killed his mother, he wasn't eligible for
a reduced juvenile sentence.

Not a single person went to visit him. No one praised what he'd
done. He heard much later that because Sevda's good name had been
sullied, they'd disposed of her by marrying her off to a man old enough
to be her father. Murat was plunged into profound solitude. No
lawyer wanted to defend him. But with the jewellery and money his
mother had left for his wedding he managed to find a lawyer. On the
grounds of his lawyer's claim that he was suffering from a behavioural
disorder, the court sent him for psychiatric assessment. But he was
deemed mentally fit and sentenced to twenty years' imprisonment
for first-degree murder.

Once his sentence was passed, the weight lifted from Murat's shoulders. He was now left with just himself. He understood that his sisters and father had washed their hands of him and would never forgive him. But he too had long ago given up expecting their forgiveness. He had no further scores left to settle in the world. He devoted himself to religion. He despised the other prisoners, who had no idea of self-respect and honour. They could defend themselves with neither religion nor family honour. They raped any new prisoner if he was weak, or became his slave if he was big and powerful. He would never become one of them. By his own will he chose a deathly solitude.

Because Murat had been found guilty of an honour killing he was accepted as a serious criminal and, as such, according to prison customs, respected. Murat hated being respected by these people and being considered one of them. As far as he was concerned he was nothing like them. Along with a few street urchins, he was the only prisoner who didn't receive any visitors.

He spent most of his days deep in prayer and self-interrogation. He devoted himself to reading religious books, although he didn't look like someone who had filled his life with religion. Perhaps he wanted to throw off the burden of his crime and free himself from the tears that came in his sleep. Whatever his motives were, he certainly considered his cell to be a holy place for withdrawing from the world and fasting.

Over the course of my interviews with Murat, there were two questions to which he wouldn't reply. One was: 'Why, when he had made such a point of avoiding calling her "Mother", had he done so twice during our interview?' The other matter I was curious about was why, when talking about his mother's adultery, had he never used the word 'adultery' but chosen 'error' instead, underlining it several times.

I contented myself with what he'd told me. I left those questions

I thought he didn't want to answer in the secret chambers of his heart. But I wanted to hear him express the profound repentance I perceived throughout the time we were together. Had his feelings changed since committing the murder? It was quite obvious that they had, but I was hoping that hearing it from his own lips would add resonance to his regret.

'Let's end this interview with any final comments you may wish to make,' I said.

He nodded his assent, and said, 'The conclusion is a mother can't be bad. I don't need to explain how sacred the person who brought me into the world is. But people also think this: when a father does the same thing, pardon the expression, when he womanises, you forgive him, you don't take it as a personal offence, you say, "He's a man, he's my father, it's completely natural." But when your mother does it you can't accept it. And when people get to hear of it you can't accept it at all. You lose all respect in the eyes of society and feel oppressed. You feel very lowly among them, as though you're something inferior, insignificant.

'I was involved with someone too, even though she was married. I asked her why she was unfaithful to her husband. Because I know her husband, he's a very good man, home-loving, devoted to his wife, does everything he can to earn his living. She replied directly, "Because he doesn't take any notice of me, or pay any attention to me." When I asked another woman I knew who was unfaithful to her husband she said, "The brute beats me. I do it for revenge."

'Because this kind of thing has happened in my family too, it's very easy for me to understand the causes. My father's insensitivity and lack of attention towards his wife, and his ignorance and that woman's lack of education and need for love and attention ... I'm sure my father only found out what was going on after all this happened. And because where we live is very conservative, it isn't easy to get divorced. Even if a woman lives her whole life under oppression, even if she's beaten, hungry, wretched she still doesn't get divorced. It's easy in the western part of the country but people in south-east Anatolia are violently against divorce. Whenever there's a divorce the question on everyone's mind is: "Why did they get divorced?" When someone says, "They couldn't get on," everyone says, "Why couldn't they get on? The woman must have been guilty of some error!" Some women are murdered by their families even though they haven't done anything wrong. One girl was murdered just because she telephoned a radio station.'

He didn't seem to be talking to me anymore, but to his own heart. His voice rose and fell according to the degree of his repentance. After each sentence he looked up at the strip of sky that was visible through the crack in the ceiling.

'What should we do?' I asked him. 'What can we do to prevent this nightmare that has such tragic consequences for both the person who dies, and the person who kills?'

'As long as the mentality doesn't change, no matter how severe the penalties – and the new penal laws are very severe – no matter how heavy the sanctions, this kind of thing will carry on. Because the person who does it has no idea of the terrible loneliness and the personal tragedy he will face afterwards. The only thought in his head is his belief that once he has done it, everyone around him will accept that his honour has been cleansed.

'People who are faced with this kind of problem should consider it very carefully. You too die with the person you kill. She is sure to appear before your eyes every time you lie in your bed. This is an eternal punishment. In other words, you will have hanged yourself with your own hands.

'This is a big responsibility. The person you have killed has the same blood as you. Your mother, your wife, your daughter, your sister. When you consider it logically there's always an alternative. If you haven't lost the use of your reason you can always consult someone and find some solution. People's mentality has to change first, and the only solution to that is economic and cultural.'

He fell silent, I thought he wanted to be rid of us and the cameras as soon as possible and be left alone with his regrets. But then he carried on.

'If I had another opportunity, the only thing I would do would be to move away from where I lived. I would choose another, better life for myself, with better conditions, in another country, far away.

'I definitely won't go back there once I'm released. Because I couldn't live there anymore, even if I wanted to. The few times I've gone back to Urfa, on leave, people point me out to each other, saying, "There's the man who killed his mother," among them some I know very well, who goaded me on to do it at the time.

'Maybe in Istanbul, or Ankara, or Bursa, wherever I'm fated to be, I'm going to turn over a spotless new leaf and start a new life from zero, without getting mixed up in anything unlawful, abiding the law. At least that's what I'm hoping for.'

'Inshallah,' I said, wishing him luck with all my heart.

We started to pack up the recording equipment but suddenly a foolish, unplanned question that I regretted the moment I had asked it, spilled from my lips.

'Are you religious?'

Throughout the interviews it had been perfectly obvious that he was. I was annoyed with myself, but I'd asked the question and I couldn't take it back. Murat could see that I was aware of my blunder.

'Don't worry, if what you are asking is why my religious beliefs didn't stop me from committing the murder, I'll tell you. For someone who is oppressed, public censure carries more weight than religious commandments.

'Why do you think I did it? Because I'm very proud? Because my self-respect is so important to me? No, the main reason was to make the people who knew this secret hold their tongues, to shut their mouths. I did it so they would say, "Even after so many years the man went ahead and killed his own mother, he cleansed his honour."

'You'll ask, has your honour been cleansed? No, it's much worse now. I've become a murderer. I've murdered my own mother. I've lost my entire family and all of my friends. I don't know where I'm headed in the next life. Allah knows it, but the most likely place for me in the next life is hell.'

3

CAVIT BEY AND MEHMET SAIT

It was the era when gangs of street children stoned cripples; when disabled children were hidden away in the most secluded corner of the house; when no one would touch the Alevis' *aşure* puddings because they were considered unclean; when we all fancied ourselves as pure-bred Turks and pure-bred believers; when we heard that women were raped in the houses where leftists hung their hats. I am talking about a well-to-do district of Istanbul only a few decades ago.

It was an era in which no one had ever heard of television, no one but a few select families owned a telephone and anyone who suggested that there might be such a thing as a mobile phone in the future would have been stoned to death for devilry. When I think back to those times, as I write about Cavit Bey, it strikes me that the world has never changed so rapidly before. But it was only forty years ago.

Strangely, I feel a deep nostalgia for those days: for the family house with the courtyard it shared with several single-storey houses, where so many different, impossible-to-blend identities were kneaded together; for the games the children used to play after school as though they had lost all concept of time; for an incredible street liberty in which we were only ever summoned home to have our dinner. I even miss Cavit Bey. Cavit Bey and his family, who had sought refuge in Istanbul for reasons I never discovered, lived in the house opposite ours, with a wide window above the metal front door.

Cavit Bey was the only man in the street who wore a tie. He left every day wishing everyone a good morning, and returned in the evening before any of the other fathers. But every night, after an early dinner, Cavit Bey, father of three, beat his wife. We could set the clocks by these beatings. Cavit Bey was famed among the children because the nightly beatings of his wife created a flurry of activity in the neighbourhood. These flurries were as much of an ordeal for the neighbourhood as they were for his abused wife and their children. But in the eyes of us children, the domestic violence that had become a nightmare for the grown-ups gave Cavit Bey fame. Because they came home late we paid no attention to any of the other fathers, we didn't even know the names of many of them.

Saadet Hanim, Cavit Bey's wife, would come flying out of the door of their house screaming and run to hide in one of the other houses, in fear of her life. For us children it marked the beginning of the evening's fun. I say 'fun' because the moment the neighbours rallied to the aid of this battered woman with blood pouring from her nose and mouth, they forgot all about us children and, with this sudden fortuitous freedom, we could do whatever we liked. No one took any notice of us.

Cavit Bey, who never usually went out without a tie, would chase after his wife dressed in his burgundy striped pyjamas and slippers. Most of the time he wouldn't have sated his hunger for violence and would say to the neighbours protecting his wife, 'Let me vent my rage, or I'll end up with blood on my hands.'

Their three children would huddle together and, in the dim evening light, they looked to me as though they were a single child.

They couldn't meet anyone's eye. They were the children of a mother who was constantly beaten, and a father who cursed all the time and had to be pacified by neighbours.

Cavit Bey and his family looked different from the rest of us. Beside the predominantly dark-skinned residents of the neighbourhood they were a distinctively fair family. Some of the neighbours believed their fairness was the cause of Cavit Bey's anger.

Every night, after each beating, my mother, who was the most talked-about Muslim in the neighbourhood for having read the *Qur'an* from beginning to end even though she kept her head uncovered, read prayers with Saadet Hanim to calm Cavit Bey's wrath. The wretched, abused woman stared vacantly while my mother sprinkled her with the water she had prayed over, and blew prayers into her permanently bruised face. The smile that lent Saadet Hanim's blank expression a strange melancholy was never missing from her lips.

I never found out whether Saadet Hanim complained about her husband's physical abuse, or regarded it as one of the unavoidable facts of her life. It seemed to me that she was more concerned about the violence bothering the neighbours and that was what led her to seek spiritual solutions. During the five years we lived side by side I never once heard a single word of criticism of her husband pass her lips, not even a slight hint.

Cavit Bey's family moved away – I don't know why – during a period when I was well on the way to becoming an ardent adolescent leftist. I never saw any of them again. In the years that followed I never encountered any more battered wives, other than in American movies, but I was aware of violence dancing around me like a ghost; I knew that a veil fluttered before my eyes and obscured my vision of the lives that existed on the other side.

But by the time I was fifty, I was much more concerned with domestic violence and I hated my inability to do anything to prevent it. I went to Adiyaman closed prison to speak to Mehmet Sait, who took pride in having killed his sister. I hadn't chosen to see him: he had invited me himself. He was an ardent defender of murder. He regarded honour killings as necessary for repairing the moral decline of society.

He was wearing a red polo-neck sweater and navy-blue tracksuit bottoms. His worn trainers looked too small for him, as though he had borrowed them from someone else. He had plump, full lips and a jet-black moustache that gave him a youthful appearance. He had several bald patches and he was considerably overweight.

Without allowing me to explain what I wanted to do he declared, with great self-importance, 'I applied to see you myself. I hear you're against us defending our honour.' He looked at me. 'Nothing stays secret in prison,' he said, 'but you listen to me and come back down to earth.'

My instincts told me his arrogance was just for show and that, like a Russian matryoshka doll, there was someone different beneath his bravado. But he said, 'I'm not afraid of anything, and I'm paying for what I did. I don't mind you using my name or filming the interview.'

I peered under the cover of the file I hadn't had yet read because I had only just received it. Mehmet Sait was twenty-nine years old, and four years before he had killed his sister. He caught me looking at his file.

'Files don't write the truth,' he said. 'But I'm going to tell you the exact truth. Files can't see reality. Our life is reality. Our community won't accept this kind of thing. This generation won't allow things like this. Women's teachers should defend morality instead of trying to fill our heads with modern ideas.'

Assuming I was still reading the file, he said, 'You either believe me or the file!' and stormed off. I ran into the corridor and caught up with him.

'Of course I want to hear your version. Otherwise I would have made do with the file, wouldn't I?'

It was unheard of for an 'esteemed visitor' to chase after a prisoner in a prison, but neither the guards nor the prisoners watching dared to intervene.

'Let's go out into the courtyard. I'll tell you whatever I feel like getting off my chest while I'm pacing up and down,' he said.

We went out into the prison courtyard – me hot on Mehmet Sait's heels and my cameraman hot on mine. No sooner had we taken our first couple of steps than a thunderous storm of torrential rain broke out. Mehmet Sait didn't appear to notice.

As he was pacing vigorously back and forth he said, 'You want to make us modern, don't you?' Without waiting for my reply he continued. 'For us your modern airs and graces are ignorance. Instead of telling our women, "Do this, these are your rights," you should teach them to obey our customs and traditions. The people who don't, who tell our women to break with our ways, are the real murderers. The real murderers are the ones who call themselves modern. Okay, we're the ones who pull the trigger, we're the ones who serve the sentence, but you're the ones who cause the murder.'

He had decided I was his enemy. It was as though he was speaking to an opponent. His red woollen sweater was soaked through with rain. The raindrops that landed on his moustache and on his thick eyebrows gathered on the end of his chin and then streamed down in a straight line. The courtyard was a fifty-metre long, twenty-metre wide concrete yard. This pacing back and forth was a strange way of walking that only those who have spent a long time in prison can keep up with. Like a dancing partner he never touched, he dragged me along behind him, making all the decisions about where we would turn, where we would speed up and where we would stop. While we were pacing, the sounds of our footsteps mingled, while the lack of coordination in our pace betrayed our awkwardness. My cameraman struggled with the deluge, while walking ahead of us backwards, trying not to miss a single image.

After a long silence Mehmet Sait continued, 'The girl says "I couldn't care less what you think pal, I've got the state behind me!" The state can say, "I'll cure you of this ignorance and turn you European." But she's not a part of the state, she's a part of me. They don't think about that. They don't say, "Look here friend, how could a man kill his own blood?" We're not talking about a complete stranger. She's your own life, your own blood.'

He interrupted his outpouring to take a breath. 'She's your blood! BUT, when push comes to shove, you kill her, my friend. When push comes to shove, you kill her.'

He ended his speech by punching himself hard in the chest and when he eventually realised that he was cold, all three of us were soaked, and we had attracted a good deal of attention from the prisoners watching us through the ward's steamed-up windows. As we were going in, Mehmet Sait stopped and said in a menacing tone, 'Her children are my children. You write that down in your papers, journalist!' With my head bowed, I promised I would.

According to legend, the city of Antep gets it name from the vow of repentance (*tövbe*) of a judge called Ayni, who regretted his misdeeds as he grew old. His act of repentance was so renowned that the city became known as Ayni Tövbe, which was later shortened to Antep. Ironically, the city of Antep, named after repentance, is famed for being the most hedonistic city in Turkey.

Zehra was born towards the end of the 1970s in a district of this city of repentance which I shan't disclose. She was the seventh of nine children of a poor but respected seller of medicinal herbs. Her favourite brother, Mehmet Sait, who would one day be her killer, was born three years later.

Zehra grew up in a family in which her father secretly cooked for them. When he was a child his father had sold rice with chickpeas on the streets and at night the whole family would assemble to help with its preparation. When he had wanted to follow in his father's footsteps Zehra's grandfather had opposed his wishes and opened a herbalist's shop for his son in a humble district of the town. But for Zehra's father, whose childhood had been spent in his family's lively kitchen, cooking had always been a joy. And so, when her father closed his shop on Sundays and spent time at home with his family, the children begged him to cook for them. At first the ageing herbalist would play hard to get, but then, to please his beloved daughters, he would go into the kitchen which was always piled high with spices, dried vegetables, nuts, pomegranates and sumac. Towards evening, among the culinary miracles he had performed, there was always a tray of buttered rice with chickpeas.

When they reached adolescence, Zehra's older brothers began to object to her father's gentle, compliant behaviour towards his daughters. Her mother had come to her husband's home as a distantly-related bride from the furthest village of Antep, on the border with Urfa. She was a serene, pious woman, who prayed five times a day. Among the relations it was whispered that their mother was older than their father which the children knew wasn't true because their mother's date of birth was after their father's. As an adolescent Zehra would learn from the relations' gossip, which she was now of an age to understand, that her mother's birth had not been registered until six years after she was born. But when she did find out she saw nothing strange about her mother being older than her father. Even if her mother had been younger than her father she would always seem older; she did not possess their father's gentleness, nor his warmth towards his children. Her boundless piety came between her and her children: while telling her beads and praying on her knees on her prayer mat, moving her lips as she recited a whole reading of the *Qur'an* with her eyes closed, the all-pervasive presence of God barred the children from bonding with her. Zehra thought God did not approve of joking and laughter; and she thought her father did not approve of this oppressive sobriety.

Zehra's mother's austerity was not born purely from the solemnity of her faith. In contrast with her father's poverty, Zehra's mother came from a wealthy, notable family who supported Zehra's family and made it possible for the impoverished herbalist to provide for nine children. Every year all the family's winter provisions, from lamb sausage, to pickles, jam and tomato paste, arrived from Zehra's mother's village.

And so, even on the days when Zehra's father didn't sell a single spice, he didn't give in to melancholy because her mother had relieved him of the burden of feeding his family. The gossiping relations whispered that Zehra's father had married an older woman for her money. Zehra, who knew nothing about money and property, found these insinuations tedious, but was too well brought up to answer back.

Zehra would go to the grave without ever discovering that the food, drink and bangles sent by her mother's relations were a kind of bribe to compensate for having deprived her mother of her rightful inheritance. Zehra's religious uncles knew that in Islamic countries daughters could not inherit property and they believed that what they were doing was in keeping with the *Qur'an*, but they knew that withholding a person's rightful inheritance was unjust in the worldly view of things, so they tried to salve their consciences with generous food parcels and gold bangles.

Like a tree that grows towards the sun, the three daughters recoiled from their pious mother and grew up resembling their cheerful, light-hearted father. They dissolved into helpless laughter at the slightest provocation and were frequently punished by their older brothers. Not even the hand-printed embroidered head covers that their mother imposed on them from a young age managed to dampen their spirits.

For their part, the sons, who adhered to the conservative traditions of their household, grew up to be pale and sullen, like flowers left in the shade. They disapproved of their sisters' giddiness and urged them, at their mother's insistence, to behave properly, given that their father wasn't in the least concerned about such things. They tried to knock some sense into them, sometimes by beating them without their father's knowledge, sometimes by forbidding them to leave the house.

And then, one by one, the eldest sons and daughters married and left to live in their own homes. The relations on their mother's side helped the boys set themselves up as small-scale tradesmen, thus ensuring they would have a means of supporting themselves. Once the older brothers set up their homes and families in their own right and became respectable businessmen, and the older sisters left the family home as model housewives, Zehra, who was approaching twenty, became responsible for all the jobs in the home which her older sisters had done. Her mother had become even more devout, hosting *Zekeriya* meals composed of forty-one different dishes of dried fruit and nuts and salads, to thank Allah for granting a wish, and large-scale *mevlits** in her home. Although Zehra had no enthusiasm for any of the other aspects of religion, she loved these ceremonial gatherings.

It is the women who host *Zekeriya* meals, which begin with roasted pistachio nuts. They sprinkle black cumin seeds everywhere, to bring abundance, and place salt behind the door to protect them from the evil eye. The women humbly perform their *namaz*, amid the appetising aromas wafting from the cloth spread on the floor with

---

*   A long, religious poem in Arabic outlining the life of the prophet Mohammed, recited after deaths, anniversaries of deaths and on happy occasions such as births, usually attended by relatives, friends and neighbours and followed by a meal.

dried mulberries, grapes, cherries, plums, dried apricot pulp, figs, dates, walnuts, all kinds of *böreks*, sumptuous *dolmas*, *köftes*, butter, rocket, fresh garlic and onions.

As Zehra watched the women who came to her house for their *Zekeriya* meal perform their *namaz* and repeat the *zikir*, she couldn't imagine them allowing a single morsel to pass their lips. When they sat down to eat after the *namaz* the guests would pick up their first bite with their fingers, murmur long prayers and make wishes which they claimed they would not disclose to anyone but which, in reality, they told each other as they ate, later. After repeating, 'If my wish is granted I pledge to host a meal like this one next year during the holy month of *Sha'ban*,'* they would set to work on the food, with a vigour ill-befitting the spiritual atmosphere of a few moments before.

At *mevlits*, during the recital of the *Qur'an*, enormous pots of *helva* bubbled in the kitchen and little syrupy balls of *lokma* fried. And after the *mevlit* the food, blessed with sacred prayers, was served. At *kandils* (Muslim holy nights) the same dishes were prepared in giant cauldrons in the evening and distributed to the poor and needy in the neighbourhood while they were still fresh and hot. Zehra loved the aspect of her religion that involved lavish entertainment and made her forget about their poverty. Her enthusiasm earned her the prestige of being thought the most skilful cook in the district, the likes of which could not be found at anyone else's *mevlits*, *Zekeriya* meals or *kandils*.

Zehra ran the entire household and was like a mother to her younger brother and sister, the two remaining children at home. Her sister knew that Zehra gave Mehmet Sait preferential treatment, but this was a sacred convention in their community. A boy was always worth more than a girl. The community would place bets on the sex of a young bride's unborn child, becoming very extravagant when

---

*   The eighth month of the Islamic lunar calendar, a month of fasting and
      worship in preparation for Ramadan.

they guessed she would mother a son. Once the babies were born the gifts varied, depending on whether the child was a girl or a boy. It was customary to give baby girls the smallest gold coin, a *çeyrek*, or quarter, and baby boys a *yarim*, or a half, which was worth twice as much. And that is why it was only to be expected that Zehra should spoil the last-born, most precious son in the family; indeed, it would have been strange if she hadn't.

In fact, Zehra's weakness for Mehmet Sait didn't stem from the fact that he was a boy, but from the fact that he had the freedom which only boys could enjoy. She liked the way he could come and go as he pleased without having to justify his movements to anyone. And in return Mehmet Sait worshipped his older sister, who faithfully reserved the chicken's thighs, the crispy edges of the *böreks*, the most perfectly baked portion of *kadayif** and the tastiest morsels of everything for him.

Although no one said so to her face, Zehra was generally considered to be an old maid, beyond marriageable age. There wasn't an unmarried girl of her age left in the neighbourhood. But Zehra's mother was pleased that Zehra did not have any suitors. She thought it a blessing that, in this putrid world, girls who weren't pretty were preserved from the evil eye by God. Praising a girl's beauty was regarded as disrespectful, but praising her plainness was a compliment. Since childhood Zehra had grown used to being complimented on her plainness but deep down in her heart she suffered grievously for thinking herself ugly, and although outwardly she gave the impression that she was content to receive so much praise, inwardly she knew that the praise for her plainness was hypocritical. When the time came for the women – who attended their *Zekeriya* meals and raved about Zehra's culinary skills – to select brides for their sons, they

---

*   A very fine vermicelli-like pastry used to make sweet pastries and desserts. It is sometimes known as shredded phyllo.

always chose the attractive girls with nice figures. Despite having so many talents Zehra had not received a single suitor.

She was so demoralised by being thought ugly that she was determined to make up for it with her unrivalled culinary skills. She prepared exquisite meals that were legendary in the neighbourhood. It was unheard of for a girl of twenty to be able to roll out her *baklava* dough as thinly as an experienced woman of forty who had perfected the art. But Zehra could do just that, and every time her father tasted one of her dishes he declared he could never bear to let her marry anyone, and pretended not to hear his wife's protests as she sat quietly in a corner repeating the *zikir* and telling her beads.

Zehra began to believe that she would spend the rest of her life in this house and that she would never have any children. She felt a bashful curiosity about the opposite sex, of which she had no experience whatsoever. She yearned to be able to take part in the whispered, giggling conversations shared by the married girls who were much younger than she was.

Zehra's dejection at being excluded eventually ended. Through an intermediary, a distant relation asked for Zehra's hand in marriage for her son. They held a sombre, modest wedding at home, tied a red sash around Zehra's waist and put a gold necklace around her neck. They distributed large copper pitchers full of sherbet and cauldrons full of rice with chickpeas in the neighbourhood, and recited a *mevlit*.

Zehra's older sisters and sisters-in-law accompanied her to the ritual bathing at the *hamam*. To keep up appearances, a group of men – none from the bride's family – took the groom out too, parading him through the streets and singing folk songs until dawn. Mehmet Sait made a scene at the wedding and spoiled it for everyone: he was furious about his sister leaving home.

But with her habitual docility, Zehra quickly adapted to her new home. She lived close to her parents' house and would occasionally drop by and help her mother with her chores. Her husband was a penniless man who worked with his three brothers as a solderer. His earnings were barely enough to feed them, and Zehra quickly realised that her new life would be a miserable one. She couldn't claim to have lived a life of opulence at her parents' home, but at least they hadn't depended on anyone, and they had enjoyed considerable abundance there, whereas in her husband's home she was surrounded by genuine poverty for the first time.

Ten months after her marriage Zehra gave birth to her first daughter, and ten months after that her second daughter. A year and a half after that, she gave birth to her third daughter, and with the birth of each child the family became more destitute and more dependent on the charity of others. And then, before he had a chance to see Mehmet Said married, Zehra's father died.

When Zehra went to Mehmet Sait's wedding she was no longer a giddy girl who covered her mouth with her white head cover to hide her giggles; she was the despondent mother of three wailing children. Worse still, after an argument with his brothers, her husband had lost his job at the shop and now sat at home in a wretched, miserable state. At Mehmet Sait's wedding no one showed any interest in Zehra's troubles, they were too busy enjoying themselves. They fired into the air, the men showing off to each other with their guns. Zehra sensed how pitiful her husband and children must appear at her brother's wedding and it pained her heart.

Zehra's husband was an unhappy young man who irritated others, and who grew more irritated himself the more he sensed he was annoying others. In the absence of gainful employment he transferred all his energy into sex. He harassed his wife continually, as she was looking after the babies, cooking, going to visit the neighbours. He incorporated violence into sex, as punishment for not having given birth to any sons. Zehra's husband blamed their poverty exclusively on her having had three daughters in quick succession. He claimed that the girls had brought bad luck on the family. If they could have had just one son, the family's grim fate would have changed. Good luck shone on families with sons.

When her husband's harassment changed from sexual abuse to violence, Zehra began to hate being alone with him even for a moment, but her hatred was not enough to protect her from him. And the neighbours' charity, the secret handouts from her mother and the money her husband earned from his temporary jobs were not enough for them to get by. Each year Zehra's husband became more aggressive than the last, but now, when her husband began to beat her, Zehra would break free of him and counter his attack. Having withstood so many years of brutal violence she was now able to defend herself, relatively speaking, but it hardly mattered anymore.

And then, paradoxically, as her husband's bouts of violence and rape eased off, Zehra became more aware of her own unhappiness. When he had beaten her she hadn't had a chance to think about their impoverished circumstances, or their children. Zehra had kept her suffering secret from her family, but by the time her life had calmed down she was at the end of her tether and the roles in her own family reversed. Now it was no longer her husband but Zehra who nagged and humiliated, although she was often beaten for it. She yearned desperately for the humble home of her childhood. She missed her former life in which she transformed a tiny income into miracle feasts for guests. Day and night she fantasised about going back.

In fact she could have returned. Her mother was by then very old and lived all by herself in a large house. And with the food parcels that arrived from the village she was able to get by modestly without depending on anyone. If Zehra took her children and went back to her father's home she could enjoy life again, and be a better mother. She dropped hints about her plans to her elder brothers and was shocked by the violence of their reaction. They were adamant that they did not want a divorced sister living back in their parents' home.

'The only way you'll leave that house is as a corpse,' said the eldest.

And so the door of hope slammed in Zehra's face. She realised she was doomed to endure her life as it was. She would live out the rest of her days with these wretched children and this penniless man. After her brothers' reaction, Zehra walked around in a daze. She stopped cleaning the house or cooking for the children; she didn't even go to see the neighbours. Hour upon hour she tossed and turned in bed, submerged in nightmares and her loneliness.

At first, Zehra's husband didn't seem to care that she had broken off all ties with the world. The children spent their days at the neighbours' houses and the neighbours in turn sensed that something was amiss, but they didn't want to meddle in a husband and wife's business. In the end, the inevitable storm erupted. Zehra's husband attacked her. He dragged her out of bed and began to rain blows on her head and face. Zehra screamed for her life. If she could only reach the door she would escape to the neighbours' and be free from this man's clutches. But Zehra's husband beat his wife as though he had gone out of his mind, all the while cursing her at the top of his voice.

And then, suddenly, he let go of her. He collapsed onto the couch and began to sob.

'They forced me to marry you,' he said. 'While they were putting pressure on me to accept you, they promised they would provide for the whole family. They went back on everything they said. You're nothing but a burden to me. You brought cursed daughters into the world. You didn't bring the prosperity of even one son to the house. You've ruined my life.'

Zehra looked up at her husband in astonishment from where she had been cowering on the floor. This was the first she had heard of any of this. She had had no idea that there had been a bargain to make her husband accept her. He covered his face with his hands and continued to curse his fate.

'My mother told me, "If you marry an older woman she won't obey you. The man of the house won't rule his roost," she said. I didn't listen. Damn me for not listening. It's your age that's brought such bad luck on my head!'

Zehra sat absolutely still. She knew that, compared with other girls of her age, she had been married late, but this was the first she had ever heard of being older than her husband. Tongues had been wagging for years about her mother being older than her father, but it had never occurred to her that that might cause bad luck. Her wretched, prematurely aged husband looked much older than she did, but it would seem that a woman being older than her husband was ill-fated. Somewhere among her thousands of other prayers her mother had squeezed in the words, 'Girls repeat their mothers' destiny.' After so many years she had been proved right. Apparently she had shared her mother's fate without having noticed.

Looking at her husband with contempt, Zehra straightened her hair and clothes. She put on her head cover and, gathering up her daughters, who had remained huddled together in shocked silence during all the commotion, Zehra dressed them. Not even the fear of her older brothers could stand in the way of the long-standing resolve that had been building up inside her: Zehra was leaving that house. She headed straight for her father's house; a voice inside her warned that it would be wiser to send word to her brothers, and wait for them to come for her. But, in her haste, Zehra ignored her better instincts.

When she knocked on the door of her parents' home, her devout mother, prayer beads in hand, the *zikir* on her lips, admitted her daughter without a word. Zehra would never know if her mother was pleased or unhappy about her coming. The paternal hearth that she had dreamed of for so many years was no longer the same place she had left. Zehra crept into the house like an uninvited, burdensome guest but the children, who had no idea what was going on, ran into the kitchen and set to work devouring their grandmother's *böreks*.

Zehra's mother didn't ask Zehra what had happened, she guessed, and, breaking her vow of silence, she had a heart-to-heart talk with her daughter. After that conversation, the first ever to have paved the way for a friendship between mother and daughter, Zehra cried for hours. Learning that her mother, whom she had always assumed was indifferent to what was going on around her, bore the same scars as herself, was a bittersweet comfort.

'I too was married to a younger man in exchange for money. I never knew happiness either. I too was nothing to look at and beyond marriageable age. But I found peace by devoting myself to religion. For years I prayed to God to make fortune smile on my daughters. But He didn't answer my prayers, darling. Daughters relive their mothers' destiny. Dry your eyes, let's hope it will all work out for the best.'

And then Zehra witnessed her mother lying for the first time, in order to protect her. The elderly woman didn't tell her sons that her daughter had come back home for good. She pretended that she had asked her to come and stay for a while because she hadn't been feeling well, and needed her daughter to take care of her. It was as though she had sensed what would happen and, being powerless to prevent it, wanted to at least delay it.

Zehra was grateful and over and over again she performed the ritual *namaz* to give thanks to God. And just as she had in her childhood, she devoted herself to the household tasks and the cooking. To prevent her brothers from realising what the true situation was and flying into a rage, she would send them some of whatever she had cooked, to give the impression that she was a capable, devoted housewife. She prepared the most delicious desserts and cakes, things that she hadn't been able to make in her husband's home, for her young daughters, and dressed them in clothes that, though worn, were spotlessly clean. The unlucky little girls' misery was slowly coming to an end. Zehra's children were well fed and content. They hardly ever cried anymore.

Mehmet Sait found out that his sister had left her husband from the newly-appointed apprentice, in his workshop. The apprentice had heard from his brother-in-law's nephew. The news had spread through the neighbourhood like a virus and Mehmet Sait went into a frenzy. He telephoned his brothers and informed them of what had happened. He had no idea what to do. They told him to 'do his duty'. As far back as he could remember this was the first time any girl in their family had gone back to her parents' home.

Abandoning his workshop Mehmet Sait roamed aimlessly around the town, like a vagabond. He knew what 'his duty' was. Only the previous week, in the most crowded district of Urfa, a father had slaughtered his daughter like a lamb because she had dishonoured him. But in his own family there was no father. It fell to the youngest brother to cleanse the family's honour. That was the custom.

The family could not tolerate a woman who deserted her family home without her husband's consent. In the eyes of the city a divorced or widowed woman was no different from a prostitute. In cities where relationships between girls and boys outside marriage were forbidden, most adolescent boys enjoyed their first sexual experience with a widow or divorcée, but before a week was out these secret assignations were the main topic of conversation in every coffee house in the district. There was not a single widow or divorcée without a slur on her good name.

Mehmet Sait rushed home, ignoring the look of apprehension on his wife's face. There was an unlicensed gun in every household in the city. Seizing his, Mehmet Sait stormed off to his father's house.

Zehra was cleaning. In fact, since the day she had arrived, she had been cleaning the already spotless house from top to bottom, as though it were an act of purification to cleanse her of all that she had had to endure. The moment Mehmet Sait walked in through the door he marched up to his sister. He was livid. When he entered the house and saw his sister so happily engaged, his fury rose to a peak. He grabbed her and made her sit on the couch. He was hoping to hear her say, 'It's not true, I haven't left my husband.'

Their mother, swathed in white, sat on the edge of the couch without moving a muscle, like a ghost transformed into a statue. Zehra bowed her head. Her brother was no longer the loving child she had doted on and protected. He was a fully grown, hot-tempered, fierce man. She shrank back as far as she could. She wanted to speak, but no words came out. Catastrophe filled the room, like fog.

Mehmet Sait shouted, 'How could you walk out on your home, you've shown us up in front of everyone! We're part of a community, if we become ridiculous, if my neighbour won't call on me, if no one will greet me, if no one will give me their daughter or marry mine, then what am I in this community? What?' he yelled.

And then his voice became hopeful, his manner persuasive. 'Go back home and we'll forget all about this.' But, because Zehra did not reply, he became angry again. 'Deserting your home has brought shame on us. What did you have to walk out for? What you've done will drag our good name through the mud.'

Zehra eventually summoned words. 'I wouldn't go back to that house if you killed me, Sait!' she said. This, naturally, was not what Mehmet Sait wanted to hear. Nor had it ever crossed his mind that any woman in his family would stand up to him. He shook his sister, slapped her, and demanded that she retract her words. When he saw his sister sprawled out on the ground, for a fleeting moment he felt a stab of pain in his heart, but then he imagined the adolescent boys who would soon be enjoying her sexual favours. He envisaged his sister's name being bandied about the coffee houses with lewd innuendos, and saw red again. He continued to beat her.

At one point Mehmet Sait saw his mother's imploring gaze fixed on him and although this matter went beyond the respect he owed his mother, he made an attempt to control himself.

'Pack your things,' he said, 'I'm taking you back.'

Zehra dragged herself along the ground, oblivious to the violence, and fell at Mehmet Sait's feet.

She said, 'He doesn't want me anyway, because I'm older than him. Have you no dignity as a brother? You're sending me back to a man who doesn't want me. I won't go back even if you kill me!'

Mehmet Sait knew that the repeated words, 'Even if you kill me' were a challenge; but he also knew that Zehra assumed he wouldn't do it. From that day, what stuck in his mind was her challenge. His own blood, his own life, had scorned him and undermined what he was capable of doing.

He asked himself over and over again if he had really wanted to pull that trigger. He knew he didn't. He didn't want to do it, but he did want to show Zehra that he could do it if he wanted to. Zehra never knew these things. She died on the spot. Two gunshots, one after the other, remain in Mehmet Sait's memory. He remembers his two little nieces cowering behind their grandmother's snow-white clothes, and that she was rooted to the spot. And he remembers that the baby, who was not yet able to walk or crawl, was terrified by the gunshot and screamed for all she was worth. But Mehmet didn't cast another look in the direction of his sister slumped on the ground; he simply left the house, closing the door behind him.

That day and that moment would not only be the last time he saw his sister, but also his mother. Silent tears wet the serene face of his passive, elderly mother for perhaps the first time in her life.

When Mehmet Sait gave himself up at the central police station, the police treated him kindly, saying he was a victim of fate.

'These things happen, it's destiny,' they said.

People who commit murder because of family matters are respected in every sector of society. To set them apart from true criminals they are referred to as victims of fate, and neither Zehra's family nor her husband accepted responsibility for Zehra's funeral. The hapless woman was buried by government officials in a cemetery for the homeless one silent afternoon. But rumours about her continued to fly for a long time afterwards. The city of repentance buzzed with the news of the honour killing.

The murder trial went on for a long time. Mehmet Sait was sentenced to life imprisonment, but discovered, from the calculations of more experienced prisoners, rather than those of his lawyer, that he would serve a maximum of ten years before being released.

Mehmet Sait didn't show any emotion when he received his sentence. He had saved the honour of a large family, and because of that everyone treated him with due deference. They congratulated him at the hearings, in the prison ward, during visits, and held him up as an example to adolescent boys, telling them he had rendered a valuable service.

'Ten years will pass in the flash of an eye, may God rescue you,' they would say, by way of consolation.

Mehmet Sait instructed his wife on the first day she came to visit him.

He said, 'Her children are my children. You'll take care of them, feed and clothe them.'

He asked his older brothers to do the same. He made them promise not to differentiate between their own children and the orphans. He had his nieces' few remaining possessions taken from the house of their father – who had suddenly disappeared – to his own house. But some time later Zehra's estranged husband returned, with a new wife, and reclaimed his, in his eyes, cursed daughters from the family.

According to reports the youngest daughter, Melek, whom he hadn't seen since she was crawling, didn't recognise her father and, fearful of the strange man, cried for days. Mehmet Sait sent word to him from prison. If he didn't take Melek back within two days, no matter where he escaped to, he, Mehmet Sait, would find him on the very first day he came out of prison, and kill him. The threat worked. The little girl was handed back to the house of her mother's killer.

Mehmet Sait never saw his mother again. She neither came to visit him nor sent her blessing in return for all the news he sent her. The woman who believed only God could take away the life He bestowed did not make her peace with her son. Quietly, unobtrusively, she departed from this world.

Whenever Zehra visited his dreams Mehmet Sait would wake up in dread in the crowded loneliness of the prison ward, knowing that all the eyes of the other prisoners under their quilts were on him. In his nightmares his sister would appear as just a silhouette, keeping her face averted from him. The strange thing was that Mehmet Sait could no longer recall his sister's face; it had been blotted from his memory.

In the prison wards, the more his world expanded after hearing each prisoner's story, the more convinced Mehmet Sait became that the morals of society were in total decline. Girls were flouting customs and traditions everywhere. He decided that television had corrupted well-brought-up country girls, making them want to ape the morally degenerate girls of Istanbul. The words bandied about by women writers and defenders of women's rights emboldened girls and led them astray. They were the real murderers. In the mornings Mehmet Sait would hold meetings in the courtyard with all the prisoners in his ward, cautioning them against the traps set by the Europeans to make honourable Turkish families resemble their own debauched families. Nevertheless, his status as an influential and powerful moral leader by day could not protect him from the nightmares that haunted his nights.

The visitors entered as we left Adiyaman prison. After an extensive body search, the prisoners' relations went into the visiting cells. Mehmet Sait smiled at us from behind the wire mesh of his visiting cell. The tense expression he had worn when I first saw him had changed. I got the impression that after so many years, even the little he had managed to get off his chest had done him good. A young woman, her hair securely tucked under her head cover, and five or six children, the exact number of which my cameraman and I couldn't agree on, crowded before his window.

He must have told his visitors about us because the young woman and the children turned to look at us. When Mehmet Sait saw we were looking at them he placed his right hand on the window and proudly pointed to the youngest child.

I looked at the child he was indicating. A dark-complexioned girl with tangled hair and chapped red cheeks was jumping up in her torn plimsolls, in an attempt to reach the window. She was trying to show Mehmet Sait her new beaded bracelet.

Mehmet Sait said, 'Her uncle's one and only *Melek* (angel). Tell the visitors who you love most in the whole world?' The shining, jet black eyes turned to look at us, and then the girl put her tiny finger in her mouth to moisten it and, leaping up suddenly, stuck it on the glass. 'MY UNCLE!' she said.

Only an angel could love her mother's murderer and I wondered what would happen when she moved on from angelhood to womanhood. Sorrowfully we hoisted our equipment onto our backs. Then I felt someone's eyes on me. I turned and looked. I had not been mistaken. A sad-looking man I had never seen before was looking at me. He wore a familiar, mournful smile on his lips and I felt strangely connected to him.

'Do you remember me?' he said, in a way I thought too refined for our surroundings. He hastily corrected himself, as though he had said something wrong. 'How would you? It's been so many years. I'm your neighbour Cavit Bey's son.'

Suddenly a terrible curiosity took hold of me. I was ashamed of the feeling and, trying to compose myself, I said, as though we bumped into each other every morning, 'How are things? Do you work here?' I addressed him with the formal 'you' because the years had wiped away any familiarity between us.

'No,' he said. 'My older sister killed her husband five years ago. She was transferred to this prison last year. I've come to visit her.' He mentioned this as though it was the most normal thing in the world.

I took several paces back, as though a fierce fire had been lit between us.

'And if you're going to ask about my father,' he said (but I hadn't; I couldn't), 'It's been a long time since we lost him. My mother also died last year. And if you want to know about us, violence has never left us alone. We've never been happy.'

4

NURAN

Avcilar is the northern gateway to Istanbul. Anyone entering from Europe will be faced with derelict buildings which are still in ruins after the massive earthquake in 1999 on one side of the motorway, and well-to-do housing developments like Bahçeşehir and Esenkent on the other.

The people from the housing developments do not mix with the people of Avcilar, and the residents of Avcilar avoid the residents of the housing developments. They are strangers who live side by side; neither group is interested in how the other lives, and each is strongly prejudiced against the other.

The housing development residents think the *gecekondu* peasants of Avcilar – with the exception of the Bulgarian immigrants – don't belong in Istanbul and should be sent back. The Bulgarian immigrants are different. They are mild-mannered, have small families, keep their *gecekondus* in pristine condition, have well-kept gardens planted with flowers and work hard at whatever jobs they can get. The people from the east, on the other hand, are a violent-tempered race whose huge families live in cramped, subhuman conditions in dilapidated shacks. Their children do not go to school, their women go about wrapped in *çarşafs* to conceal their bodies from men, and their men idle about in the coffee houses all day, thinking themselves too good for any job.

This is how the well-to-do neighbours think as they gaze out on the *gecekondus* dotted here and there on the land opposite theirs, but a large number of the housing development residents aren't originally from Istanbul either. Many of them arrived as immigrants in the last fifteen or twenty years, but by investing their capital from the east in middle-income enterprises in Istanbul they have acquired middle-class status on the outskirts of the city.

The *gecekondu* dwellers believe the men in fancy cars and the young girls on bikes who inhabit the housing developments have been Istanbul natives since time immemorial. Because they do not observe the *kaçgöç* rules prohibiting a woman from showing her body or from openly socialising with men, the *gecekondu* dwellers regard them as sinners and deviants from the true path, even though they have not renounced the faith. The housing development residents look down on those in the *gecekondus*, while the *gecekondu* dwellers curse those in the housing developments. They put avoiding each other and not getting defiled by one another's sins before every other consideration.

When my cameraman and I set out for the address we had been given in Avcilar, it didn't occur to us that the camera would be of no use. The day after a three-minute television broadcast of one of the stories we had filmed in a prison, we received a call from someone who wouldn't give his name. He wanted to tell us about an honour killing he had witnessed. If we went to such and such address he would recognise us and come and talk to us. The truth is, because I never imagined this cloak-and-dagger-style rendezvous would lead me to the most horrific story I had ever heard, I was not especially excited by it.

The voice on the telephone belonged to a male with an eastern accent and it was easier to discern distrust, irritability and a determination to make us bend to his will in his voice than it was to discern any grief.

When we got to a mud track in Avcilar that was inaccessible by car, we began to ask for directions to the coffee shop that the caller had mentioned. A shabby-looking adolescent boy appeared by our side. He hadn't been shaving for long and his face was pock-marked with acne. I took him for a local who would direct us, but the moment he began to speak I recognised the voice on the telephone.

Pointing to the bulky shoeshine chest in front of the coffee shop he said, 'I just have to go and get that, then we can leave.'

We had to move our recording equipment into the passenger seat to fit the shoeshine chest into the boot and then the young boy jumped into the car and waited for the cameraman to pull away. I asked him where he wanted us to go. He didn't want to go anywhere, he just wanted to speak to us.

My cameraman and I thought for a while and then decided to go to a nice café we knew in Yeşilyurt. The young boy had not told us his name and, assuming he didn't want to reveal it, I didn't ask. But when he still couldn't bring himself to initiate conversation, I asked him how he would like me to address him. Surprised, he retorted, 'I have got a name, you know!'

'But I don't know it,' I replied.

'Harun,' he said. I was about to find out that males from eastern Turkey are generally shy about revealing their names at a first meeting.

Once we had sat down in the café and ordered, Harun listed his conditions. We couldn't use his name. We couldn't take his photograph, and because he didn't want to even see the camera, the cameraman took it back to the car. All Harun wanted was to make his repentance known, like the prisoner he had seen on television who had killed his mother.

'Are you a murderer too?' I asked him.

He paused, bewildered, and a long silence followed as he considered how to respond. Eventually he made a mental calculation and replied, 'As good as.'

At every one of our subsequent meetings, all my questions left him perplexed. Somehow he could never find the right words to reply. But then he was a boy of barely eighteen, innocent in so many respects. He had not even done his military service, he'd never been anywhere except Avcilar and his village in Van, had not read a single novel in his life and had never touched a computer. In order to earn a reasonable income he had to clean at least twenty-five pairs of shoes a day. His older brothers also cleaned shoes, but despite the muddy conditions in the area, most of the time he was hard pushed to clean twenty pairs a day whereas one of his older brothers, who polished shoes in front of a hotel in Ataköy, never shone under fifty pairs a day. He said that when he had a bit more experience he wanted to set up his shoeshine chest in front of the hotels in Taksim. He had never seen Taksim, but he knew it was the stamping ground of the wealthy. He would need a long time to save up the key money for a shoeshine chest in Taksim. But saving the key money alone wouldn't suffice. He needed to buy the consent of the parking-lot mafia who had parcelled out the streets of Taksim. His eldest brother had said he knew someone who could sort that out for him, but then this tragedy had struck and he was imprisoned.

He believed God had put a curse on his family. He wanted to tell us his whole story but he had one more condition. Because he wouldn't be able to work while he was with us, he wanted the money he would have earned if he had worked. He couldn't return home without his daily income from polishing shoes because his mother had no other means of support.

As I was handing him an envelope containing a little bit more than the fee he had requested as payment for his first meeting with us, I was too ashamed to tell him that it didn't come to even a quarter of our bill at the café.

Nuran was the only daughter and the last of six children in an immigrant family which moved from Van to Avcilar. There would be no more siblings because her mother, Zahide, had had to have a hysterectomy two years before.

Nuran had not yet turned six when they arrived in Istanbul, but she remembered sitting beside her mother, riding on a big bus for the first time and noticing that practically all the passengers were men. The bus they boarded in Van one evening arrived in Istanbul the following evening. For Nuran and her brother Harun, who was a year older than her, this bus journey was their happiest childhood memory. Whenever the bus stopped to refuel, the men got out and ate cheap motorway service meals, but she and her mother stayed on board and ate the exquisite food their relations had packed for them. But because Nuran had no idea how awful motorway services food tastes, she longed to sit and eat at the tables. Her father sent Harun to Nuran and her mother with tea and *ayran*, the delicious, refreshing yoghurt, salt and water drink, from the small, brightly-lit restaurant.

It was a windy night, but Nuran didn't feel the cold on her trips to and from the toilet, guarded by Harun, every time the bus stopped. The brother and sister were endlessly entertained by the booming male voice which announced where the bus had started its journey and called out the stops through to its final destination. At every announcement they pressed their faces against the steamed-up windows and tried to guess which of the names written on the buses had been announced; they mimicked the voice. Neither of them could read or write and because their mother could neither speak a word of Turkish, nor read or write in the only language she did speak, Kurdish, they couldn't ask her either, and so they could not confirm whether they had guessed correctly. Nuran imitated the arrivals, while Harun imitated the departures.

'Passengers travelling on the Özvan bus from Van to Istanbul, we are about to depart, please take your seats.'

'The captain of the Özelazığ bus travelling from Istanbul to Elazik is going to make a short stop, welcome to our service, we are pleased to offer you a cup of complimentary tea.'

Although their father barked at them to stop from time to time, unless they were sleeping the announcement game kept them entertained until they arrived.

Once they had settled into the converted *gecekondu* on the third floor of a ramshackle apartment block with a rug Laundromat at its entrance, Nuran's father gathered his children around him and made them perform *namaz* to give thanks for their new situation. Nuran understood then why they had migrated from Van. Her father, who despised the Kurdish war, had fled those troubled lands to prevent his sons' hands from getting soiled with blood.

At the end of the summer he enrolled each of his sons at the school, but he didn't want Nuran, the only girl of the household, to be educated. Nuran used to put on the blue uniform of Nevin Abla's daughter, their downstairs neighbour. They were the same age and Nuran would put the daughter's satchel over her shoulder and pretend she was going to school. Zahide, Nuran's mother, couldn't bear it and begged her husband at least to let the girl go to primary school for a couple of years. In truth, Mehmet Mirza was not the sort of man to pay any attention to what his wife said, but the upstairs neighbour, a teacher, had threatened to report him to the authorities if he didn't send the girl to school. Mehmet Mirza didn't mention this threat to his wife but, telling her he had only agreed for her sake, he enrolled Nuran in the same class as Harun. In this way the boy would be able to keep an eye on his sister. Mehmet Mirza knew all about the wickedness that went on in schools and he didn't want a single member of his family going anywhere where the Devil roamed.

Mehmet Mirza purchased some shoeshine chests with his meagre savings and, with the help of his more experienced relations, started work in the affluent areas of Istanbul. While his four eldest sons worked in four separate areas, he did shifts shining shoes with each of them in turn. Neither he nor his sons were educated, nor did they know any trade except farming. Their only means of putting food on the table was by shining shoes.

Mehmet Mirza's children revered their deeply religious father, and they carried out his every command with blind obedience. Their mother was a silent woman who yearned passionately for her village, and spent her days cooking, washing and knitting. She had a mournful voice and Nuran always knew when her father had come home because her mother would suddenly stop singing her tearful folk songs. The sound of a woman's voice is *haram* (forbidden by religion) according to many interpretations of Islam, so Mehmet Mirza neither allowed the television to be switched on at home, nor did he permit singing. The only reason he'd bought the television in the first place was so that they wouldn't appear destitute to the neighbours.

When the family began to feel the pinch and it became difficult to buy wood and coal in winter, Zahide began to work in the slipper workshops that employed some of her female relations. Once a week, taking Nuran along as her interpreter as soon as she came home from school, Zahide would set out to collect the slippers from the slipper factory two streets away. She would pick them up, together with the patterns she had to sew onto their uppers, the sequins and the beads, and return home. The owner of the workshop, Zuhal Hanim, was moved by the plight of this immigrant woman who didn't speak a single word of Turkish and so brought her adorable little daughter with her, and he gave her more slippers to work than anyone else.

For Nuran, her mother's trips to and from the workshop were

a source of entertainment. She would tug at the shawl the size of a tablecloth her mother wrapped around her brown *çarşaf* and laugh impishly when Zahide scolded her in Kurdish. But Zahide was a timorous woman who existed only as an appendage of her husband. She lived in mortal fear of word getting back to him about these antics of Nuran's that were so outrageous in a girl.

The melancholy silence of a hospital ward descended on the family of six children when Mehmet Mirza was at home. In the early evening they would hurriedly eat the traditional Van dishes their mother prepared and, as soon as they had performed the evening *namaz*, they would withdraw meekly to their beds. Their father believed that conversation, leisurely eating and impertinent laughter at the table were grave sins.

Nuran despised her father's rules. At school her teacher had said anyone who laughed just once would be as healthy as if they had eaten a kilo of chops. She had never tasted a chop but, being fond of meat dishes, imagined they were something good. When her father wasn't at home they took no notice of any of his rules, and she and Harun had the time of their lives rolling and tumbling and wrestling. What Nuran loved most was going to see the neighbours because, at their houses, she could watch as much television and laugh as much as she liked. But her days of happiness were short-lived. At the end of the third year of primary school her father took Nuran out of school. She could read and write, and he thought there was no need for her to know anything more. But he had misjudged the speed of her learning: Nuran still couldn't read by the time her father took her out of school, nor could she recognise numbers properly.

For days Nuran cried in secret. If Mehmet Mirza had seen her crying about not being allowed to go to school he would have punished her. Her older brothers didn't go to school, Harun had left by choice and Nuran could not go to school by herself, it was out of the question. She couldn't even go to the shop on her own for a simple shopping errand that she could have done in minutes, if she ran. Even for just a few loaves of bread or a few kilos of onions her mother would put on layer upon layer of outdoor clothing and accompany her.

Nuran got into the habit of waking up early and watching enviously as her peers from the upstairs and downstairs apartments went to school. Once the students were out of sight she prepared the family's breakfast and, after the male members of the family had left, she sat beside her mother and embroidered beads and shimmering sequins of every imaginable colour onto the slippers.

Nuran liked embroidering birds best of all. She embroidered sparrows' feathers in green and yellow sequins and gave them beaks of red beads. She was very curious to know who bought the slippers she made and whenever she escaped to Nevin Abla's house to watch television, the first thing she looked at was the feet of the models and film stars she saw on the screen. She wanted to see if they were wearing her slippers. She hadn't seen any so far, but she was convinced that one day she would.

When Harun returned home, exhausted, in the evenings, Nuran would tease him, making sure her father couldn't hear, saying, 'Guess what! That woman in the soap opera was wearing the slippers I embroidered today!'

Harun didn't believe his sister's banter as he scrubbed his blackened fingers with a brush, but after a few minutes Nuran would become so believable that he would have to convince himself she was joking.

At the beginning of the week Nuran and her mother would return to the workshop, hand over the finished slippers and collect a fresh batch to embroider. Between them they embroidered sixty pairs of slippers a week and earned six million lira. Nuran never saw any of the money. Her mother would take it from Zuhal Hanim without looking at her, her head bowed as though she were doing something shameful, and as soon as she was out of the workshop, she would put it in the purse she attached to the breast of her winding *çarşaf* with a safety pin.

On the occasions when Zuhal Hanim said there weren't any slippers to embroider, Nuran's mother returned home grief-stricken, weeping while she sang her most mournful folk songs. These were the only moments in which she and Nuran bonded as mother and daughter. What united them during these profoundly intimate, private moments was their desperate yearning for their village. For Nuran the village signified going out dressed exactly as she pleased, going visiting to admire the trousseaux of prospective brides, and baking bread collectively in the village *tandir*.* In short, the village meant freedom. As for her mother, Nuran never found out what it meant for her but she understood from the lyrics of the Kurdish folk songs that it was something very close to her heart. It was on these rare occasions that Nuran loved her mother, these infrequent moments when she lay on her mother's knee listening to her songs and they wept together, sharing the grief of the financial hardship they suffered for not having any slippers to embroider.

Once those moments passed Nuran's mother turned into that shrinking woman again, particularly when her father was at home; the woman who strove to do everything that would please him, without taking her eyes off his feet. Zahide never went to visit the neighbours, or her family. Crowds of relations often descended on her, chaining her to the kitchen, but the neighbours never went to see Zahide either. If it hadn't been for Nuran's boisterousness the neighbours would never have believed that there were any women in that apparently all-male household at all.

When she returned home after her hysterectomy Zahide was confined to her bed for a long period, and so the running of the house fell to Nuran. But the moment her father was away she would pull off the

---

*   A shared wood fired oven used by a number of families in a village.

headscarf he forced her to wear, complete all her chores at the speed of light and rush outside to join her peers in the street while her mother lay in bed, semi-conscious.

Of course it took no time at all for her to be found out. Nuran's father arrived home unexpectedly one day, dragged her into the bathroom, beat her black and blue, and then slashed her leg with a knife.

'Remember this scar the next time you put on a short skirt,' he said.

Harun buried his head under a cushion to drown out the bloodcurdling screams from the bathroom, and thought how hard it was to be a girl. When Nuran's father came out of the bathroom he ordered Zahide, who was lying placidly in her sick bed, to go and bandage the girl's leg.

But not even the knife wound succeeded in making Nuran religious. She continued to pull off her headscarf the moment her father was away, and to play hopscotch with her friends, despite the limp she developed after her father's attack.

When Nuran was not able to leave the house she would go out onto the balcony and she and the downstairs neighbour, Nevin Abla, would pour out their troubles to each other from their balconies. Once she dangled her leg with its deep scar over the balcony railings and said, 'My father punished me for going out into the street.' The neighbour was horrified and could only whisper, 'Don't ever go out into the street again whatever you do, my little Nuran; if you really need to get out come to our house.'

Harun knew that the reason his father's tyranny was getting worse was because Nuran had just turned fourteen. She had developed into an attractive, statuesque young girl, and looked older than her years. She had snow-white skin and bright green eyes. She wore her thick black hair in a waist-length plait. Harun believed that what made her so beautiful was the ever-present smile on her lips. In fact, she still

looked more like a naughty child than a young woman. To anyone
not familiar with the difficulties in her life, Nuran could have been
mistaken for a carefree daughter of a liberal family.

Zuhal Hanim gave this mischievous child a pair of slippers as a gift,
but the very first time she put them on her father beat her and threw
them into the bin, saying he knew what wearing such fancy slippers
would lead to. The following evening he brought home a pair of plastic
men's slippers and tossed them at Nuran. She would wear those from
now on. With socks! His religious beliefs prohibited an adolescent
girl from revealing so much as the tip of her fingernail.

The morning after the incident with the slippers Nuran watched
from the balcony until her father and older brothers were out of sight
with their heavy shoeshine chests and, ignoring her mother's protests,
went to the slipper workshop. Zuhal Hanim was taken aback when she
saw the young girl there for the first time without her mother. When
Nuran said breathlessly, 'I'm going to run away, I can't take my father's
bullying anymore,' she said, 'No, please don't, whatever you do, my
little Nuran! Your father will kill you. Get that idea out of your head
now.' But her instincts told her the girl wouldn't listen to her.

That evening Zuhal Hanim made a proposal to some relations of
hers who were looking for a suitable girl for their son. She knew a
pretty, capable young girl. Would they be interested in going to see
her? Zuhal Hanim praised the girl so warmly that the young boy's
mother was even more curious to meet her than he was. It was no
easy task finding someone decent for her son among all those city
girls of dubious morality. They decided to go to see Nuran. But first
they were going to seize the opportunity of one of her visits to the
workshop to arrange for the boy to see her from a distance. And
indeed when the young man saw Nuran a few days later he was very
taken with her. She was young but very vivacious. Zuhal Hanim was
delighted. The marriage would be a gift for Nuran; it would change
her destiny. Zuhal Hanim would set Nuran free and save her life. If

it weren't for small good deeds like these, she felt, there was no point in being a human being.

But Zuhal Hanim's relations rued the day they went to ask for the hand of the daughter of such a conservative family. There were light years between their world and that of this family that wouldn't allow men and women to sit in the same room. Moreover, Mehmet Mirza was deeply suspicious about how they knew Nuran, and subjected them to an interrogation worthy of the police. Before an hour had passed the guests left the house under a dark cloud of despondency. Little did they know that upon their departure Nuran received the worst beating of her life.

The following morning the day began in the neighbourhood as usual. Children set off bright and early for school. Commuters pushed and shoved their way onto buses crammed to twice their capacity. Shopkeepers rolled up their shutters with a murmur of *Bismillahirrahmanirrahim*', praying the day would bring good custom.

While Nevin Abla was doing her morning cleaning she heard her upstairs neighbours' door slam violently. When she opened her door and looked up she saw Nuran running down the stairs dressed in her plastic slippers, a thin blouse and a long skirt with an elasticated waist. Although she realised that something was up she said, 'What's your hurry, my little Nuran? You should have put on a jacket, you'll catch cold.'

The girl, her eyes on her mother who was talking to her from upstairs in Kurdish, said in a fluster, 'I'm going to the village, my father doesn't know. Please, don't tell anyone.' When the neighbour looked up at Nuran's mother with a worried expression, Nuran said, 'Never mind her, she doesn't understand Turkish!' and bolted outside.

Nevin Abla heard Zahide muttering in Kurdish at the top of the stairs for a long time before she eventually closed the door, and then the apartment was profoundly silent.

In the days that followed Nevin Abla took her neighbour *böreks* and desserts several times in an attempt to find out what had happened to Nuran, but to no avail. It was always Harun who opened the door; he would take the neighbour's offering silently, with his head bowed, and close the door. It had been a week since Nevin Abla had last seen the girl, but in her place carloads of Kurdish-speaking people streamed into Zahide's apartment and the crowds spilled out onto the stairs.

Eventually the multitudes stopped arriving, the cars no longer appeared and life in the neighbourhood continued as before. No one remembered Nuran or wondered what had become of her. The pace of city life in the new millennium is too tough to allow anyone to indulge their curiosity about a young girl who has disappeared, at least not for very long.

Not knowing Istanbul at all, Nuran had no idea where to go. She wanted to go to the station to get a bus to Van, but she had no money for transport. She approached Zuhal Hanim, but the woman's heart leapt to her mouth when she saw her with no coat and no socks on. She pressed ten million lira into her hand and urged her to go back home straight away. She felt terrible about bringing so much trouble on Nuran's head by sending suitors to her home and decided to protect the girl, but without ever interfering in the family's affairs again.

Nuran was crushed when the person she trusted most in the world told her to go back home. She realised she wouldn't be able to turn to anyone she knew. They were all afraid of her father. It was still very early but she knew she had to get away from the neighbourhood before her father and brothers returned.

Nuran went to the playground at the primary school she used to attend and waited for the students to come out. Perhaps she could persuade one of the local girls to let her stay at her house. She waited for hours but didn't meet anyone she knew, either at playtime or after school had ended. It was as though the ground had opened up and swallowed everyone she knew. Nuran waited despondently for the last student to leave the playground and then, without knowing where she was going, she started to walk. A stranger's hand touched her shoulder from behind. She spun round, her heart pounding. It was her primary school teacher. When the woman saw the desperate state Nuran was in she understood that something very serious was the matter. When she found out that Nuran had run away from home she became very alarmed and, slipping a little money into the girl's pocket, persuaded her to go back home immediately. And to ensure that she did go home she accompanied Nuran as far as her street corner.

But Nuran had tricked her. She had no intention of going home. No one could understand what hell her house was. Nuran pretended to go inside but she hid in a little alcove until her old teacher had turned back, then, the moment the teacher was out of sight, Nuran began walking in a direction she wasn't familiar with. She had quite a lot of money in her pocket now. It would be enough to get her to Van.

Eventually, after asking around and changing buses several times, she reached the bus station. The vastness of the place made her dizzy. The only bus company she knew was Özvan, but she couldn't pick it out among so many names. She knew it would get dark soon and she began to feel frightened. The streets were no safer than at her home. People began giving her strange looks, and shady-looking youths began harassing her with lewd comments. Nuran changed her mind about going to Van. What she decided to do was to go back home as quickly as possible, to get to the house before her father and persuade her mother not to say anything to him about what she had done. Then she became aware of someone walking beside her. When she turned to look she realised that a young boy, who looked slightly older than her, was speaking to her.

'Which company are you looking for? Where do you want to go?'

he said. He told Nuran that he worked at the bus station; he said she needn't be afraid of him.

Nuran's dwindling hopes were immediately rekindled. The boy seemed trustworthy. He reminded her of Harun. She told him she wanted to go to Van, and that her older brother was waiting for her there. She told the lie about her brother to show that she was not running away, but she was so naïve that she didn't realise that her falsehood actually exposed her vulnerability to the boy.

'You're in luck,' he said. 'Our company's going to Van. I'll get you a ticket and tell the driver to look after you. It's a long way.'

Nuran took the money out of her pocket and handed it to the boy. Afraid it might not be enough, she said nervously, 'I'll give you the money for the ticket now.'

The boy took the money Nuran was holding out to him and counted it, it was fifteen million lira. He took ten million and handed the other five back to her. 'This is enough,' he said. 'I know the driver, I'll get him to give you a discount. You should keep some money on you.'

Nuran began to believe that God had sent her a miracle. Her earlier qualms had vanished and she even scolded herself for losing hope. Here was a kind-hearted person who wanted to help her. Perhaps he even had a sister. Maybe that was how he thought about her. Nuran thought of Harun and her nose twitched. They had grown up like twins and she knew Harun was the one who suffered the most when her father beat her. Yet Harun wasn't free either. Because Nuran was a girl their father was harder on her than he was on her brothers, but they too crept around with their tails between their legs when their father was around, and they never disobeyed a single word he said. They handed their meagre earnings over to him, and he gave them an allowance. They couldn't go anywhere without his permission. In fact, they weren't allowed to go anywhere, full stop. The only place they could go in the whole of Istanbul was to their relations' houses, and the only people they were allowed to speak to were their relations' children.

To her amazement Nuran found herself telling this complete stranger about Harun and her other brothers. She wanted to stop but seemed to have lost all self-control. Her instincts told her that talking about her older brothers made her look stronger. But her brain kept insisting it wasn't appropriate to discuss her family with someone she didn't know. Brushing off her misgivings, she kept on talking. Her eldest brother, Alihan, was like her father. Like him, he was hard, bad-tempered and intolerant. But although they had never said anything about it to each other Nuran knew it wasn't easy for Alihan either.

Nuran said that her father was stricter with his sons when it came to religion. Her brothers could not skip Friday prayers, *Bayram* prayers or *taraweeh* * recitals. They hadn't continued their education, but they knew all the prayers by heart. They had grown up as religious as Nuran herself would have loved to be but could not. Her brothers disapproved of anything forbidden by religion, but religion prohibited all the things that Nuran enjoyed. It disapproved of laughter, going out, playing, watching television, singing, going to school, in short, everything that gave her pleasure.

'This can't be right, it must be a mistake,' she said to the boy beside her. But he didn't reply.

Nuran knew she really did need to stop talking now. She tried to shift the conversation to her companion by asking, 'What's your father like?'

But instead of replying to her question, the boy kept Nuran distracted with trivial chitchat while walking her in a semi-circle around the huge bus station. Nuran was completely worn out by

---

*   A special prayer recited during the month of Ramadan in which one *juz* (1/30) of the *Qur'an* is recited each night so that the entire *Qur'an* will have been recited by the end of the month.

the time the boy disappeared into the ticket office of one of the companies, telling her to wait for him. It was dark by then, and all the lights in the station had been switched on. Fear started to gnaw at Nuran's insides, but when the boy came out he was holding a ticket. Nuran chased her apprehension away and thought that nothing could stand in the way of getting to Van now. She had no way of knowing that what the boy was waving at her was actually a blank left luggage receipt. She had never bought a ticket before.

'Did you have enough money?' she asked.

'Don't you worry about that,' said the boy. 'Your bus is leaving late. Let's go to where I work and wait there.'

All her suspicions now allayed, Nuran followed the young boy. They passed secluded, dark corners, wandered around the back of the bus station and went into a place that looked like a warehouse. It was pitch black outside, but the warehouse was even darker. Nuran wanted to be in the safety of the lights of the bus station, but she didn't dare open her mouth to say so. She knew she had already said far too much.

They sat on the ground. The boy took off his jacket and gave it to her to sit on. For some time they remained silent and then Nuran became aware of a hand groping her legs. She was afraid, but she sat completely still, as though turned to stone. She had no idea what to do. The hand groped its way further up her leg and then the boy pushed her to the ground and started to thrust himself inside her. Nuran suddenly realised how much he stank and she thought she would die of fear and disgust, but she couldn't bring herself to scream. The guilty, her father had said, could not scream, and Nuran was guilty and her father was right. The streets were full of evil. And this foul-smelling man lying on top of her and hurting her was the Devil. God was punishing her for running away from home.

Tears streamed down Nuran's face because it hurt so much. She couldn't imagine how she would explain all this to her father and she knew he would kill her. All she wanted was to go home. She abandoned forever the idea of the ticket to Van, of going to the village, and everything she had dreamed about just that morning when she ran away from home. She would never disobey her father again, she would never hanker after anything sinful again. For years she had dreamed of a life beyond the confines of her home, but the day that dream looked as if it might come true she yearned desperately to be back at home. She felt a warm substance trickling down her legs. Thinking she had wet herself in front of a stranger she cringed with shame; she wanted the ground to open up and swallow her.

The boy rolled off Nuran and lay down beside her, but he kept his hands on her body. When he thrust himself inside Nuran for a second time, grunting, a few minutes later, it hurt much more than before. Nuran could not remember the exact moment when he got off her and left the warehouse in silence. She lay there on her back in the pitch darkness. The inside of her thighs was sticky and she had unbearable pain in her breasts and groin. Judging from the wet sensation in her mouth she imagined her lips must be bleeding too. Sometimes feeling drowsy, sometimes lying wide-eyed, Nuran remained in that position until morning, while engines from some mysterious source roared outside. During the rare moments when she dozed off Nuran had nightmares. She dreamed that her father wanted to kill her and that she was begging him to spare her life. Each time she woke, in a cold sweat, the reality of finding herself still alone in the pitch-black warehouse filled her with more dread than the nightmare.

When a sliver of daylight found its way into the warehouse, Nuran was thirsty, cold and even more terrified. Although it was not yet completely light she managed to catch a glimpse of her legs in the pale light that filtered into the warehouse. They were covered with dried bloodstains. Nuran stood up and smoothed her ruffled hair and clothes. All she wanted to do was to go home and beg for her father's forgiveness.

The warehouse door opened and some people came in. They were porters and they were startled to see Nuran. She told them she had lost her way and had spent the night there. One of the men took her outside and told her which bus she needed to get home.

When Nuran eventually arrived home after a journey of several hours, she tiptoed into the apartment building she usually burst into. She didn't want anyone to see her in her dishevelled state. Praying that her father and brothers would not be there, Nuran knocked on the door. Zahide opened it, her eyes swollen with crying, and Nuran threw her arms around her, weeping. But Zahide, who knew what fate was in store for a girl who had failed to return home at night, pushed her sullied daughter away from her.

When Harun put his head round the door and saw his sister in her dishevelled state he was stunned. 'You look like a beggar!' he exclaimed. But he couldn't hug her because Nuran's father, his face expressionless, stood behind him.

None of the family had gone to work. All the relations were in the house as well as all the family members. They locked Nuran in a room. No one in the family was permitted to speak to her. But, because someone had to find out what had happened, Nuran's eldest aunt took it upon herself to ask. She entered the room and asked Nuran what had happened. Stammering, Nuran tried to explain, but was unable to reply to many of the questions.

'What's the rapist's name?' asked her aunt.

'I don't know,' said Nuran. And she genuinely didn't.

As her aunt was leaving the room Nuran heard her say, 'She won't tell us his name.' She didn't remember anything after that because she fainted with terror.

Mehmet Mirza had difficulty fitting everyone into his house. Although they stayed until the early hours, the relations from Kartal, Tuzla and Türkoba returned to their own homes, but all those who came from their distant village in Van had to be accommodated. They were all men and, as tradition dictated, they could not stay in a house where there were unmarried daughters: as the family saw it, fire and gunpowder could not be placed together. Furthermore, regardless of any potential threats to their honour, it was imperative to ensure the daughters' names were not linked with any gossip about such a sensitive issue. Mehmet Mirza had a tough job segregating men and women in the houses of his Istanbul relations, and then sharing the guests out among them.

Owing to the magnitude of the tragedy no one went to work, the shoeshine chests lay abandoned on the balcony of the household whose income was small at the best of times. When things get tough it is customary for relations to help each other out, although Zahide was still the hostess, and so, no matter how much the relations' daughters and daughters-in-law helped out, she had to contend both with her grief and with the burden of feeding and attending to so many guests. But a seemingly endless supply of *böreks* and *dolmas* rained down on Zahide's household.

Night after night the older women and men excluded the young women and discussed what they were going to do among themselves, but they could not reach a verdict. The final decision lay with Mehmet Mirza, but he simply listened to the others, he wouldn't tell them what, if anything, he had decided. His eldest sister proposed making Harun kill Nuran, saying he would get off with a light sentence, because he was so young. One of his nephews volunteered to kill her himself: he said he could kill her in a park and leave her there without anyone from the family becoming involved, and no one would know who was responsible. Alihan said it was his duty as the eldest son to clean up this business. The youngest nephew, who had come from Van, insisted that marrying her to an old man from the village would be a better option than killing her. That way no one would get into trouble and they would be rid of the girl forever. Mehmet Mirza listened in stony silence.

For a week Mehmet Mirza performed *namaz*, read the *Qur'an* and prayed to God for an answer. And he cried like a baby. Throughout his life nothing *haram* had ever passed his or his children's lips; he had never looked at another woman with lust, never coveted anything that was due to another and he had fulfilled every one of the commands of Islam to the best of his ability as a faithful devotee. He didn't know why God had punished him.

'Why did you send me this devil for a child, my Allah?' he asked. 'I never disobeyed any of your commands. Why did you paint this stain on my forehead?'

Eventually he pulled himself together and summoned his wife, his sons, his brothers and his nephews after the afternoon *namaz*. Thirty-two people sat cross-legged in rows in that tiny living room, as though listening to a sermon.

Mehmet Mirza said, 'This job is my responsibility.'

He said that it wouldn't be right to ruin his sons' lives: they were young, and they were also the breadwinners, and if one of them went to prison Zahide would die of grief.

Although Alihan attempted to protest, Mehmet Mirza gave him a look that ordered him to obey. It was clear he did not want anyone to contest his decision.

'I'm going to clean up this business myself,' was his final word.

Everyone bowed their heads in silence. Harun felt his heart constrict but he knew his sister was an eternal sinner. There was nothing he could do. Even if he could do something it would be wrong to collude with a sin.

'I'm going to stay at Fatma's tonight. I'd like my nephews to drive me there before it gets too late,' said Mehmet Mirza, beginning to tell his beads. Everyone knew what that meant. They weren't going to kill Nuran in this cramped apartment block where it was easy for all the neighbours to hear what was going on; it would be done in her aunt's *gecekondu* where there was a garden with a wall all the way round it.

The family had informed the police on the day Nuran ran away from home, but they hadn't told them that she had returned. The brothers waited for a moment when there was no one in the street and then they bundled Nuran into the car in silence. Just as no one in the apartment block saw Nuran return after her flight, no one saw her being driven away from the house.

Nuran knew what lay in store for her and she was terrified. Her nightmare was coming true, but she lacked the strength to beg her father for forgiveness. But even if she had managed to find the strength, her father would not have spoken to her, or even looked her in the face, as tradition dictated. Where he came from they believed that anyone who looked a defiled person in the face would become defiled too.

Nuran was hauled out of her father's house like a piece of unwanted baggage and dumped in her aunt's house. Her aunt and her children had gone to Nuran's house and only her aunt's husband remained. Mehmet Mirza broke off the cord from an old iron. He slit it with a knife and pulled out the electrical wires. His daughter was kneeling before him, staring at her father in wide-eyed terror. She knew she was going to die but she didn't think her father would be capable of killing her. In God's eyes, she thought, her fear should be enough to atone for all her sins.

Mehmet Mirza knelt down behind Nuran. He placed the wires around her neck and Nuran knew that no miracle would save her. But still she begged her father, in genuine fear for her life. 'I'll do anything you say. Forgive me father. Don't kill me.'

Mehmet Mirza didn't listen to his daughter. He was afraid that if he did his resolve might weaken and he would end up sparing her. When she was still a small child he had taught her that she had to grow up to be virtuous like her mother; he had wanted to make it

clear that she carried the family's honour in her body. But the girl had
never understood that being a girl was a shameful thing.

Mehmet Mirza thought about Nuran's sins, and so made himself
deaf to her entreaties and then, abruptly, the girl fell silent, her frail
body twitched for a few seconds and then she lay still. For some time
Mehmet Mirza waited, kneeling in the same position. When he let go
of the wire the lifeless body in front of him fell with a thud. The girl
seemed to have shrunk after her death and he was free of the Devil
in his family. He knew that he had saved his sin-susceptible daughter
from committing other, more terrible sins.

They wrapped the girl's dead body in a sack that her uncle had
prepared. It served as her shroud. Then they carried her to the car.

'We should take her as far away as possible,' said his sister's husband.
'Then suspicion won't fall on us.'

The two older men got into their nephew's car and told the young
boy to drive to the forest where they picnicked in summer.

'It's the middle of the night, uncle, let's not do it now,' said his
nephew. 'There's a lot of traffic control at night, and we'll get caught.
Let's leave it till morning. No one will take any notice of us then.'

Mehmet Mirza nodded and told his nephew to take him home.
They went home in silence, with his daughter's body in the boot.
When Harun opened the door to his father, he knew his sister was no
longer alive. He couldn't ask him anything, and neither could anyone
else in the family. They slunk off to their beds in silence. Mehmet
Mirza knew his daughter's body lay in the car that was parked outside
the apartment and before falling asleep he recited the *Surah al-Fatiha*,
so the girl's soul would find peace.

Towards noon the following day they set out, equipped with
spades. They went to the remotest forest, on the Asian side of Istanbul,
on the Black Sea border. Although it was February and it should have
been getting warmer, it was in fact still cold and the forest was almost
deserted. Except for the odd giggling couple in a parked car, there was

no one around, and the couples in their cars took no notice of the two old men who were digging a hole. They were obviously forest workers, judging from their clothes. The couples could never have imagined that while they were making love away from the eyes of their families, a young girl's body was being buried right beside them.

Life had returned to normal on the third floor of the converted *gecekondu* apartment block in Avcilar but Mehmet Mirza no longer worked, or even left the house. His sons went to work, but he and Zahide spent the day repeating the *zikir* and awaiting the return of their children. Their relations had also stopped coming, and the family was left to deal with its secret alone. The atmosphere in the house had been oppressive before, but it seemed to Harun that their home was now clouded with the secret of death, and it was choking the air from their lungs.

And then the doorbell rang very early one morning. It was the police, and they had come in connection with the missing girl. A body had been found in the forest at Beykoz, they told Mehmet Mirza and Zahide gently, trying to soothe them. There was a possibility that the body might be Nuran's, and they wanted Mehmet Mirza to identify it. Mehmet Mirza accompanied the police to the morgue at the Institute of Forensic Medicine and said that yes, it was his daughter, Nuran.

But Mehmet Mirza's apparent indifference to his daughter's death baffled the police and made them very uneasy. Even if Nuran had run away from home, she was still his daughter and it was surely natural that he would want to know who had killed her. So, after making investigations in the neighbourhood, the police focused their attention on the family. One evening they questioned each of the sons separately. Harun was the first to break down. The police handcuffed him straight away and took him before the public prosecutor. He was placed under arrest and transferred to prison. Harun's arrest was followed by that of his elder brothers, his uncle and finally his father.

Harun found out from his father that his mother and aunt had also been arrested and sent to a women's prison. Harun was devastated: every last member of a family that had never before walked through the door of a police station was now behind bars.

The hearings went on for more than two years and even though Mehmet Mirza took full responsibility for the murder, the judge would not be persuaded that he had committed the crime alone and would not allow the others to go free. The evidence had been pieced together from testimonies given by all the members of the family and so the court sentenced Harun's father, his eldest brother and his uncle to life imprisonment. The court acquitted his mother, his aunt, his other brothers and himself, and allowed them to go free.

The four young men who had not been imprisoned were thereafter responsible for supporting not only their mother, but also their father and brother. Nuran was dead, Harun's father and elder brother were in prison, and the family's existence, which had been wretched to start with, was now in ruins. Harun was filled with remorse and his heart was weighed down with grief. He wanted to tell someone how much he missed Nuran, and when he heard the deeply repentant prisoner who had killed his mother on our television programme, Harun decided to contact us.

I could not offer him any comfort.

Before he left he put a crumpled, faded receipt on the table, beside the coffee cups. It was a blank left luggage receipt. Harun had kept the only thing Nuran had left behind. I wondered if Harun's burden had been made any lighter after he'd told us about Nuran's fate, but when he hung the thick strap of his heavy shoeshine chest diagonally over his shoulders and walked away, it was clear that no one would ever be able to lighten his burden.

Never again would I witness so much grief in any one person.

5

AYSEL

We drove towards the city centre along the Istanbul–Edirne motorway: it was littered with rubbish that made a terrible smell inside our car. We discovered later that a battle about rubbish collection was going on between the municipality and another authority which, until it was resolved, had turned the city into a rubbish dump.

It occurred to us that if the city was in such a mess, the situation in the prison we were driving to would be much worse so, when we saw the prison building in the middle of a wide, well-kept piece of land on the outskirts of the city, we were pleasantly surprised. We thought we had arrived at a rehabilitation centre, rather than a prison.

The prison was also a farm, and the director of the prison had stipulated that we must go on a tour of the farm in return for permission to interview Ilyas. While the director showed us around he said proudly, 'Customers have to stand in long queues to get the milk, butter and eggs produced here. Our products are famous.'

At last the director took us to a large garden at the back of the main building where a small, fair-haired prisoner, who was obviously intimidated by the director, brought us *ayran*, and some food and fruit on a wide tray. We knew that the director of the prison was putting on a show for us, but we were impatient to find out whether Ilyas would agree to meet us. He was the last prisoner on our list.

Then the director surprised us by pointing to the prisoner who was serving us and saying, 'This is Ilyas. I will leave you alone in the garden if he agrees to talk to you.'

My cameraman and I looked at the prisoner again, more carefully this time. Neither of us had suspected that he might be Ilyas. We had expected a dark-haired, well-built man, because recent press coverage of convicts had been dominated by such men, but Ilyas did not suit our image of a person who might have committed the crime described in his file. For a moment I wondered if the director of the prison had made a mistake, but he hadn't. If I had met him on the street, I would have judged Ilyas to be a soft-hearted and sad person fallen on hard times; this man, Ilyas, had murdered his sister.

Before I began this study I doubted the way some prisoners defined themselves as 'victims of fate'; I thought they were simply refusing to face up to their crimes. But when I met Ilyas, I began to understand how the city's badly-run judicial system, rather than simple ill-fate, had a great impact on people like him. While interviewing Ilyas I began to feel like an accessory to a crime, rather than a mere interviewer of a criminal.

Ilyas bowed his head when I asked him whether he wished to talk to us.

'You know best,' he said.

But it was, of course, his decision, and it took him a long time to make up his mind. Finally the prison officials left us alone and, while I leaned against a walnut tree and the smell of grass and acacia wafted through the garden – which was only cultivated for the benefit of important guests, not for prisoners like Ilyas – he finally came to a decision. He would talk to us.

He began by telling us that he was born in two different places.

Both in the middle of the district of Pinarhisar in the city of Kirklareli, as well as in the district of Uskudar in Istanbul.

He kept saying, 'I was originally born in Uskudar, at the hospital called Uskudar Zeynep Kamil. After I was born, I lived in Istanbul, in Umraniye. But I was also born in the town of Pinarhisar, in this region.'

When we had given up trying to make out exactly where Ilyas had been born, a prison guard who'd overheard Ilyas joined our conversation. He told us that Ilyas's real birthplace was Uskudar, but that he had been trying to explain that his family's birth records were registered in Pinarhisar.

This intervention helped Ilyas become less timid, for which I was grateful. I didn't want his shyness to turn my interview into an interrogation, and I asked him to sit cross-legged like me, and not so respectfully, on his knees. I tried to explain that I thought of us as equals. I said that if he sat cross-legged he wouldn't get cramp, and eventually he did sit cross-legged, although he wouldn't lean against a tree like me, for fear of being disrespectful.

He allowed us to use his name, his real identity and his story and he said we could film his face. He said, while signing the consent papers, 'Perhaps, if you broadcast my story, it will help some of those who see it not to do what they are planning to do. And so my sins might be forgiven.'

Ilyas had been in prison for seven years but, ten months earlier, he had been transferred from the central prison in Istanbul to this agricultural prison in Edirne. Bowing his head resignedly, he said, 'We are as happy as we can be here.'

A little while later, thanks to a jug full of *ayran* and a tray full of food sent by his cellmates, Ilyas obviously felt easier with us. Eating together is often the best way to break down social barriers.

Ilyas had been given responsibility for the sheep at the prison farm. He had become a shepherd and the dairy products that 'his' sheep produced had boosted his confidence and made him feel successful in a way that he could never have achieved when he was a free man. Because the *ayran* that we were drinking had been made from the milk which came from the sheep he fed, and from the yoghurt produced by him from the sheep, he felt less inferior as he watched us drink it. And so, as we talked of the sheep's milk, cheese and *ayran*, Ilyas's confidence grew and I knew that, if I steered the conversation gently, Ilyas's pride in his sheep and the food they produced would help me find a way to his heart.

Often, when Ilyas couldn't stop his tears, he asked us to turn off the camera, and so my cameraman did so, not turning it back on until Ilyas's stopped crying. This means that, when you watch the film, you could be misled into thinking that Ilyas was a happy man; but if you look closely you will see the tears that filled his eyes. Even if you never see them spill over, they are always there.

Ilyas was over thirty-five, but his fair hair made him look much younger. And like many of those of Thracian origin, he dropped his aitches. Even the fact that he'd grown up in Istanbul had not affected his accent. His family, even though they had migrated from Pinarhisar to Istanbul, had never left the small enclave where they'd settled and so Ilyas would never have heard, or been affected by, other accents.

The society Ilyas grew up in was a closed society which did not indulge in candid conversations. He was uncomfortable with direct expressions and his pale face grew paler at some of my questions and the answers they required from him. But the smile on his face never once relaxed when I apologised for asking a direct question. He would simply say, 'Don't mention it, don't mention it at all.'

My cameraman loaded and reloaded his camera and when Ilyas's tragedy, the tragedy of an ill-fated life, had finally been revealed to us on an ironically beautiful spring day, we left more touched than we had ever been by the story of a murderer.

Ilyas's family was among those gentle Thracian emigrants who settled in Istanbul. His father used to work at a factory belonging to the Koç Holding. Those were the years when labourers' wages had not yet exceeded those of civil servants. Workers then didn't belong to the middle class in Turkey.

Ilyas's family were tenants on the ground floor of a three-storey, illegally-built building in Umraniye. They didn't have the guts to build an illegal house of their own. Instead, they had become tenants in slum houses built by those who had migrated from the east.

Ilyas's father was an easy-going, peaceful man. He was a law-abiding and loyal husband who went to work before sunrise and returned home before sunset – a man who neither drank nor gambled. But, as if to make up for the lack of such vices, he smoked so much that people said it caused the gap between his front teeth, which gave him an unpleasant, almost sinister aspect. Because of this, none of the family ever picked up the habit even though everyone in the neighbourhood smoked.

Ilyas and his five siblings grew up hearing their father lamenting hopelessly. He would say, 'Ah, I should have built a slum house just here. Today I could have received permission to build three more floors. I would be a rich man.'

Ilyas was astonished to see that a man who regretted not building a slum house would look out at the ever-multiplying slum houses all around them but still couldn't find the courage to build one himself. Yet he didn't dare question his father. In a neighbourhood teeming with law-breakers they were a timorous family that never considered breaking the law themselves.

Ilyas's father retired before he was fifty, but by then he looked so old it seemed as if he might die the very next morning. He admonished his children from the moment he woke up until the moment he went to bed, 'My post-retirement money wasn't even enough to buy a house. We are still tenants, but I raised you without any disgrace. Building a slum house is nothing; what is important is to ensure that the family lives decently and harmoniously. I raised you on this principle. Look at this neighbourhood: everybody has more than one slum house but there are many rumours about their daughters or daughters-in-law. My daughters are sparkling clean. Because if a family is not decent, if is not led by a man, then it is doomed. But I stand by you, and the honour and dignity of our family are well secure.'

When his father died of cancer, Ilyas realised that being a good family was useless. They had taken his ailing father from one hospital to another but no health care institution in Istanbul would accept him. Ilyas's father passed away at home on the eighth day of the eighth month of the year nineteen eighty-eight, on Ilyas's thirteenth birthday. One month later, their grandmother, who buried her son before herself, couldn't accept such divine injustice and followed him to his early grave.

At least this was what Ilyas construed, hearing the conversations of those who came to offer condolences.

On his mother's instructions, Ilyas followed in his father's footsteps. He sensed that fate was treating him unfairly, but he couldn't express it in words. One year after his father's death, Ilyas started work at a textile factory and his wages were a substantial supplement to the family pension. But they were still tenants.

Ilyas's three older sisters were married consecutively. Curvaceous blondes in a neighbourhood of dark, fat Kurdish girls, they were all married to local young men without difficulty. And then, only Ilyas and two siblings remained in the house.

Ilyas was married, silently, to a deaf and dumb girl before enrolling in the army for his military service. Disabled children and stray dogs were objects of derision for the neighbourhood children. The children would play wildly and unfettered all day: they would put nails in the ears of the stray dogs they caught, or follow the disabled around throwing stones at them. In such a neighbourhood, Ilyas's wife had

had her share of such cruelty. For years she had been chased, stoned and called names, but fortunately she had managed to escape with only light scars on her face, mere traces of the stonings. By the time she married Ilyas and was older, she was no longer of interest to the children.

She was, however, of interest to Ilyas's mother: she was diligent, meticulous and clever. She was not disrespectful like other girls in the neighbourhood; she was decent. Moreover, the girl lived with her mother in a house they owned (albeit a slum house). Ilyas moved in with his wife and mother-in-law, several blocks away. His own mother had always said, 'If a person is not a tenant and owns the house he lives in, he subsists even by eating onions and does not have to struggle to make a living. The thing that hampers one's livelihood is the rent.'

Ilyas was enrolled into the army as soon as he got married, and it was the first time he'd seen the East. He felt the deadly frost and saw the declining cities from which his immigrant neighbours and his brothers-in-law in Umraniye came. During his military service, Ilyas cursed himself for not having attended school and not having a proper education. Soldiers who graduated from high school immediately became sergeants and those who had driving licences became private drivers for the generals; they enjoyed privileges he could only dream about. But as he neared the end of his military service, he concluded that it was a significant experience for everyone no matter how they got through it. He took no leaves of absence, but had them counted towards an early discharge instead.

When Ilyas returned home, his father's boss employed him. The factory manufactured colourful, expensive sweaters and cardigans. He started to live just like his father. He went to work and then returned home. He did nothing else. He brought knitwear to his wife and his sister, who liked dressing up. He tried to please them. His only luxury was playing football with his neighbours on a synthetic pitch at weekends.

The first disaster in his dignified but poor life occurred nine years after his father's death. The youngest of his older sisters, who had just married, was gruesomely killed while her husband was out. Ilyas, who had never before come across a murder or any kind of crime, had never spoken to the police or seen the inside of a judicial court, couldn't bear to look at his older sister's corpse when he went to the morgue to identify her. He fainted in front of the policeman, falling to the marble floor. The policeman reproached him and said, 'If you ever experience a foul indignity in the future, how will you be able to clean it up if you can't even cope with this?' His sister's burnt corpse haunted Ilyas for months. He saw her in his nightmares.

The murderer, improbably, was a young girl who had been a close friend of his older sister. She was the adolescent daughter of a neighbour who coveted a set of five bracelets that had been given to Ilyas's sister at her wedding. The neighbour's daughter had waited until Ilyas's sister was alone at home, and then she'd stabbed her seven times. Ilyas noticed the oddity of the numbers: they made him nervous.

To avoid the murder being discovered, the murderer had removed the bracelets and wedding ring from his sister's arm before she wrapped the body in a thick blanket and burnt it by spilling gasoline over it. Fire had overwhelmed the house, burning the apartment building almost entirely, with the dead woman inside.

If it hadn't been for the neighbour's daughter's rush to sell the wedding ring bearing the name and the wedding date of the deceased, no one would have realised that the poor woman had been killed nor that the murderer was a close friend. But she was impatient and sold the wedding ring and bracelets to the only goldsmith in the neighbourhood just days after the murder. The goldsmith remembered the woman to whom the thin gold ring, which had been bought from him for a happy occasion several months before, belonged.

The police arrested the girl. Although she confessed, Ilyas could hardly believe that a human being could kill another human being, let alone that a young girl could kill her closest friend. That kind of ferocity was inconceivable to him.

During the condolence visits Ilyas met neighbours with whom he'd previously had little contact. As the neighbours arrived bearing trays piled with food, they kept telling Ilyas how concerned they were about his unfortunate sister. But the expressions of sympathy were immediately followed by elliptical comments such as, 'God takes the good early and leaves the bad.' Ilyas understood that 'the good' meant his deceased sister, however he didn't understand who they meant by 'the bad'.

Ilyas kept hearing these comments during the lengthy condolence season. But he discounted them since he never thought anyone in his family could be deemed bad.

Then, on a day off, Ilyas did something he rarely did: he stopped at the neighbourhood coffee house. He had planned to drink one or two glasses of tea and leave, but the youngsters in the coffee house spoke to him scornfully. Though he was uncomfortable, Ilyas pretended not to be. He didn't want to get into trouble. But when he stood up to leave, a strapping layabout blocked him and said, 'Are you operating the house in the neighbourhood? If you are, you cannot do it without benefiting us!'

Ilyas understood that he meant extortion when he said 'benefiting', but he couldn't work out what he meant by 'operating the house'. Ignoring his provocations, Ilyas silently left the coffee house but he immediately went to his sister and told her what he had been through. He said, 'What the hell did the bastards mean?' His sister angrily replied, 'Take it easy, brother, don't pay attention to the gossip of complete strangers. Let each care for their own daughters' decency. Nobody's knows what people do in private. Don't worry about it.'

Having had no doubts until then, Ilyas became suspicious after his sister's response. It was clear that her honour was in question but how and because of whom?

Because his own wife couldn't hear or speak, he couldn't ask her to canvass the neighbourhood and find out what people had been saying. And his mother-in-law was a reclusive woman who wouldn't get involved in her neighbours' gossip. (And even if she had become involved, she wouldn't have wanted her family to be disgraced along with Ilyas, if there had been any truth in the gossip.) But the gossips didn't test Ilyas's patience any further. It suddenly emerged that Ilyas's sister Aysel was regarded as a prostitute by the people in the neighbourhood.

Rumours flew but despite the doubts he harboured, Ilyas battled each gossip valiantly. He didn't want to believe that there could be an indecent girl in his family, and he didn't have any proof that his sister was debauched, so he turned a deaf ear and dismissed the gossip, saying, 'These are slanders, with no truth to them. Everyone should mind their own business.'

Yet each rumour made its mark and Ilyas became even more reclusive as the pity felt by the neighbours towards his family, because of the recent murder of his sister, vanished. The poisonous gossip turned Ilyas into a hunch-backed silhouette of his former self, even though he was never convinced that his sister had ever strayed. Ilyas was considered worthless in the neighbours' eyes, because he didn't take any notice of the flood of gossip about Aysel.

The neighbourhood children who had once attached tins to street dogs' tails and sneered at his wife, now set their sights on Ilyas. Although the children failed to understand the meaning of the gossip, they realised that Ilyas was pathetic, and somehow deserved to be tortured. As time went by, fewer and fewer acquaintances greeted him in the streets, until finally Ilyas was completely shunned and so was his whole family.

That Aysel was thought a prostitute stemmed from the family's links to Pinarhisar. The gap between the lowly, Thracian minority immigrants whose daughters were considered sluts and the Kurdish majority whose daughters were veiled and whose men killed to protect their honour gradually widened.

Although Ilyas pretended not to hear, he writhed under the insulting stares of his neighbours, who belittled him and considered him a coward. He grew sick of their stares. He only wished to be left alone with his newborn son and his wife. He failed to understand how Aysel's behaviour divided the neighbourhood so easily, as if a watermelon had been cut into pieces.

Ilyas didn't dare ask Aysel if she really was a prostitute but he began to treat her badly as well. He heckled her on every occasion and he was as hostile to her as the neighbours were to him, while Aysel swore that her blondeness excited the envy of the ugly girls in the neighbourhood and that was all.

Ilyas hoped for a miracle from God, but God did not grant his wish. And it was impossible to leave the neighbourhood because Ilyas couldn't afford to on his salary, nor could they desert his mother-in-law. Ilyas's mother-in-law had become the mouth and ears of her daughter. Besides, she looked after the baby. When the baby cried, his mother-in-law would attend to the baby's needs and calm him. Ilyas understood that the old woman held herself responsible for her daughter's condition, and therefore dedicated her whole life to her daughter and grandchild in a way quite unfamiliar to Ilyas.

His mother-in-law had married her uncle's son. Three of her children died before they were a year old and only the last baby had survived. Ilyas's mother-in-law had been devastated when the doctors said that the reason her lastborn could neither hear nor speak was because of her marriage to a close relative. She had tried hard ever since to overcome her daughter's disability. But Ilyas never minded his wife's disability. She was just as dextrous as her mother and she was a lively woman who lived by unerring intuitions that he found miraculous. Besides, Ilyas didn't like talking at all. He could have lived happily if it hadn't been for his neighbours.

Ilyas's isolation from the community was punctuated by overnight attacks. In time all the windows were broken but as his wife couldn't hear, she wasn't scared, although when she woke, she was saddened to see the mess. But his mother-in-law and child woke up frightened by each attack, and they couldn't be calmed for some time. Ilyas stayed up late to guard against the attacks, but those who broke their windows didn't even bother to conceal their identities. They were Kurdish youngsters who claimed responsibility for the decency of the girls in the neighbourhood. They openly stated that they wouldn't permit any indecent girl to live in their neighbourhood. For fear of being associated with immorality, Ilyas's kind neighbours, who were also Thracian immigrants, gave Ilyas's family the cold shoulder too.

Ilyas slowly realised that the roots of this nightmare could be traced back to the time when he went to do his military service. When he was enrolled in the army, rumours had started because there was no man in the house to guide the women. As Thracians were not accustomed to living together in extended families like the Kurds, their remote relations didn't look after the girls in Ilyas's absence.

Eventually, when people in the neighbourhood started to spit in his face, Ilyas couldn't stand it any longer. He decided to confront Aysel and get to the bottom of the matter. But Ilyas also had a genuine belief in the power of numbers. When going to work in the morning, he had thought, 'Today is the day when my father died and the day I was born. The eighth day of the eighth month of the year nineteen eighty-eight, may God save us from calamity.' He reassured himself and said, 'What else can happen to destitutes like us? Calamities strike the bigwigs. What are we afraid of losing?' But he was about to pay a high price when he realised that calamities befall the destitute as well. It seemed that the God he believed in had ordained his downfall.

On that inauspicious day, Ilyas played football on the synthetic pitch and had just returned home when he found Aysel there, caring for the baby. She stank of booze. It was the first time Ilyas had seen anyone in his family drunk, and even worse, it was his sister. Aysel told Ilyas that she came to her brother's house because their own mother would be worried if she saw her dead drunk. Ilyas saw that his mother-in-law was watching them anxiously. His wife didn't quite understand what was happening but she sensed that something was wrong. She told Ilyas through sign language not to get angry.

The feelings of shame which Ilyas had been harbouring for months suddenly burst out. He harshly took his son away from Aysel and gave him to his mother-in-law. He didn't want the innocent baby to be frightened. He said to his sister, 'Isn't it enough that you've disgraced us in the eyes of the neighbourhood? Now you're disgracing me before my mother-in-law.' Aysel took a roll of money out of her bag and held it up. 'Money makes up for everything,' she said. 'Let me pay for whatever you need, brother. This world belongs to those who have money ... nobody opens his mouth at the sight of money.'

As his sister swayed with the money in her hand, Ilyas felt as if he was swaying too. He thought that he was a hopeless loser. His mother-in-law told Ilyas that the girl was drunk, and suggested that he talk to her in the morning after she'd sobered up. But Ilyas didn't listen to her.

He demanded again, 'Sister, why do you drink? Does it befit your decency?'

She shouted back at him, raising her head from the sofa. 'Am I going to ask you whether I can drink or not?'

Ilyas cursed his sister, saying, 'Be far away from me and close to God.' He turned away and, as in the hush before the storm, the family watched television without speaking. Ilyas's mother-in-law took the little boy to lull him to sleep and retired to her room. His wife retrieved him from her mother's room around midnight and then put him in their own bed because she believed that he should experience the love of the whole family. But before this, Ilyas's wife took Ilyas forcefully to bed, as if she wanted to protect him. Everybody retired early. Aysel lay on the sofa, sleeping and snoring, and still stinking of booze.

And when his wife took the little boy from her mother's room and brought him to theirs, Ilyas silently got up. He couldn't sleep anyway. He entered the dining room and fell into a chair. He held his head in his hands. Looking at Aysel's bloated face, he began thinking about his wife, his mother-in-law and his sister and how hard it was to have his life so attached to them all, and why he failed to achieve happiness. He needed so few things to be happy and yet God withheld even those tiny wishes. He felt himself rebelling against God. He thought about all those crooked, fraudulent people who lived in nice houses and didn't struggle to earn a living while he and his family didn't disobey any of God's commands but God gave them nothing. The only thing he wanted was to have the people in the neighbourhood lose interest in Aysel, to forget about her. But they didn't. They even talked about her to those who wanted to forget.

Ilyas longed to hear his sister say that all the rumours and stories about her were lies. But even if she didn't, he wanted to say to her, pleasantly, 'Go to sleep. I'll see you in the morning and we'll talk then.' But he failed to say even that. And as he sat there he remembered the delicious food Aysel used to cook, especially the fried meatballs she made for the evening meals during Ramadan. The sole source of entertainment for the family had been those evening meals when people cooked the best food and prepared the best meals. And Aysel had been the queen of Ramadans.

As he thought about this, Ilyas's heart softened, and a voice in his head said, 'Ilyas, you have a family to look after. Your wife cannot speak, your son is too small, your mother is ill, and you're responsible for all of them. Don't worry about all those empty words, mind your own business, be responsible, struggle to make your living. You cannot prevent people from talking. In time, if you manage to save some money, you can leave this gossipy neighbourhood, your son can grow up in a better place. You can forget about all of this – you won't even remember.'

But another, different voice in his head provoked his way and said, 'Coward. You're disgraced. Aren't you a man? How will you face the people in the neighbourhood? And even if you can, how will you face your son? Don't you think he will condemn you when he grows up? Those stories about your sister are true. Look, she is lying here dead drunk. How will you ever hold your head high in society?'

And so it was that, suddenly, Ilyas leaned over Aysel, put his hands round her throat in a vice-like grasp and squeezed. But it was as if he was still sitting with his head in his hands and the hands that strangled Aysel didn't belong to him. He would never know what led him to do it because he was afraid of hurting, let alone strangling, anyone.

When Ilyas released Aysel's throat, which was beginning to swell and discolour with thick purple bruises, she had stopped shaking. There hadn't been any noise and Aysel hadn't resisted, as if she had been willing to die.

Ilyas looked at the doors that led from the living room to the bedrooms where his wife, son and mother-in-law were sleeping peacefully. He listened for a while to see if they had woken up, but there was no sound or movement: the sleepers were unaware that their lives had just changed irrevocably.

Ilyas opened his sister's bag. A wallet, a lighter in the shape of a woman's breast and a packet of cigarettes fell out. Ilyas opened the packet and saw those thin cigarettes that female villains used to smoke in movies and then he knew that he hadn't killed his sister because of some unfounded rumours. She was ruined and she deserved it. Ilyas's anger at the people in the neighbourhood abated. They were right. A family couldn't live with such a woman.

Having never smoked before in his life, and after several failed attempts with the lighter, Ilyas lit his first cigarette with the lighter shaped like a woman's breast. He smoked non-stop until dawn and as the smoke from each cigarette filled the room, Ilyas peered apprehensively at his sister's corpse. He sobbed not because he saw his sister's open eyes and breathless body, but rather because he had failed to prevent her losing her way in life. Occasionally he became angry with the dead woman in front of him for obliging him to kill her, and he punched the corpse hopelessly. He and his wife had sobbed until dawn, just like this, when his son was born and the doctor told them the good news that the child could hear and speak like normal people. Tears, Ilyas realised, didn't discriminate between happiness and sorrow.

When the morning call to prayers started, Ilyas stopped crying. He had a strange feeling of tranquillity. The corpse, himself and God were alone in the room. God was helping him to calm down. He held his hands towards the sky and prayed. It was too late for him to pray for good fortune, but he thanked God for bestowing a bright and happy future on his little son. He certainly deserved it.

Ilyas kept praying until the first beams of daylight passed through the cotton curtains and the first noises of the day began to penetrate the thin walls of the house. He prayed for the sinful dead, including Aysel. He tiptoed to his neighbour's house and knocked on his door. When his neighbour opened the door, rubbing his eyes, Ilyas whispered to him, 'Aysel is dead. I cannot telephone because the people in the house are sleeping. Please notify the police!'

The man barely understood what Ilyas was saying, but he grabbed the telephone automatically. Ilyas tiptoed home again and found a cloth to cover his sister's face. He could no longer look at her. Then he began preparing to go to work: he thought he could go to work as usual. He failed to realise that his life was about to be turned completely upside down.

Ilyas was just leaving his house when the neighbours and the police poured into his house. He didn't mind the police, but he was surprised to see how quickly the people in the neighbourhood, who he had tried so hard to forget, had heard about what had happened.

A policeman lifted the cloth from the corpse and started to take photographs. Ilyas fell into the chair once again and held his head in his hands. He didn't know what to do any more.

'She is my sister, she was lost,' he told those who were taking the photographs.

But the police didn't ask Ilyas anything. He went to the bedroom, woke his wife up and told her, in sign language, that there were policemen in the house. She jumped out of bed in horror and, hugging her baby instinctively, she ran to the dining room where she started to cry loudly. Ilyas's mother-in-law didn't come out of her room even though it was impossible for her not to have heard all the noise. But it seemed that the old woman simply wished to lie low until the storm passed.

Ilyas would never see her again.

The police handcuffed Ilyas. They took him out of the house and to the police car waiting outside. The women of the neighbourhood gathered at their windows and said harsh things about Ilyas in a terrible flood of anger. They beat their breasts for the ill-fated, murdered Aysel and they wanted to strangle Ilyas. He couldn't believe that they had loved his sister so much, they had never said so before. It was as if they weren't the same people who had cursed Aysel. A small army of children appeared, beating and pushing each other and running around the car. Ilyas couldn't understand how they had woken and heard about the incident so quickly. He looked at his house for the last time. He was leaving the neighbourhood he hated for good. He would never see his wife or son again.

Ilyas was taken to the murder unit at the police station. There, in the custody cells, Ilyas realised how many crimes had been committed in that city. There were perverse men who cut their own bodies; drunks with blood all over their faces; gypsies arrested for theft; women drug dealers and prostitutes; various kinds of people who drifted through the night and into the morning, sometimes soliciting the policemen, sometimes swearing at them impudently and noisily. But Ilyas didn't resemble any of those people and the more experienced policemen saw that he didn't and immediately took him to make his deposition. Ilyas was dispatched to the public prosecutor before noon.

Ilyas made the simplest and most accurate deposition that a criminal could make. He completed his deposition in three sentences and after he signed each typed copy, the policemen took him to the public prosecutor in Uskudar. He didn't understand what the prosecutor said, but he realised that he had been arrested when he was handcuffed again. The procedures that determined the path of the rest of his life were smooth and systematic and if it hadn't been for the traffic congestion in the city, Ilyas's transfer from public prosecutor to prison would have taken little more than five minutes. But because of the traffic, he was delivered to the prison in the evening.

The prison guards received all Ilyas's belongings in a fatherly manner and they had him x-rayed for security reasons. They said, 'May God rescue you,' to him and took him to the prison ward where he would stay during his court trial. When he entered the ward, he was surprised once again to realise that all the other prisoners were aware of his guilt. He couldn't grasp the speed of communication among people.

No one disturbed Ilyas out of respect for his privileged position – here was one who had defended his honour. They expressed their condolences to him and then stood aside. Unfortunately Ilyas didn't have a bed because each convict had to bring his own bed with him to prison. He was given a mattress by a senior prisoner and when he lay down on it, on the concrete floor, he fell asleep hoping that when he woke everything that had happened would simply prove to be a nightmare. But Ilyas had to face that what he had been through was real, when he woke up feeling deeply guilty and saw his sister's swollen purple face looking through the prison ward window. The moment of his sister's death was etched into his mind from then on and he knew he would relive it forever.

The court trial lasted for one year. During that period Ilyas usually stayed in his bed in the ward, except for court hearings. He couldn't get used to walking in the prison yard in groups composed of several people who trod its length from end to end. He preferred spending his time cleaning the ward, or staring at a fixed point for hours. His most precious time was when he lay in bed with his eyes open, staring at the ceiling. That was when he saw his two dead sisters, one of whom was burnt and the other strangled, gazing down on him from the ceiling, hand in hand.

The Bar of Istanbul assigned a lawyer for Ilyas free of charge, but the attorney told Ilyas that there was nothing he could do. Ilyas was sentenced to penal servitude for twenty years. However, nothing, neither the penalty imposed by the court nor his broken life, hurt Ilyas as much as the unspeakable pain he felt when he learned about the forensic report. His sister, about whom so much had been rumoured for months, had been a virgin. Ilyas's lawyer objected to the forensic report but the conclusion of the second report was the same. On that day Ilyas understood that he ruined his whole world for nothing. His sister had been a virgin 'prostitute'.

Ilyas realised that it was the neighbourhood they lived in that was the real murderer. The neighbourhood shared their greatest loves as well as all their troubles at holy nights and at feasts, but they hated anyone who was in any way different. Ilyas thought that if it had been possible to live an isolated life his family's tragedies would never have happened.

In prison, Ilyas was only visited by his brother. The rest of his family ignored him. His brother told Ilyas that rumours were still rife in their neighbourhood and that no one believed that Aysel's virginity was real. People accused the family of bribing the authorities to obtain a report verifying Aysel's virginity in order to save their honour. Ilyas was deeply saddened because it seemed that even Aysel's death couldn't put an end to the rumours.

As soon as the court order was ratified, Ilyas was sent to a prison in Bandirma. He stayed there for five years and four months. When Ilyas was sent to Edirne prison on probation his son was nineteen years old. His wife, who had never visited him in prison, sued him for divorce.

At Edirne Ilyas worked hard, just like any ordinary free citizen. He took his sheep in and out of their shed after counting them over and over again; he put them out to pasture; he milked them and watched them lamb at Edirne prison. At the same time he tried to find ways to dissuade his wife from divorcing him. He asked his brother to contact the *hodja* in the neighbourhood to request his help, but the *hodja* refused to help, saying that he disapproved of trying to persuade the wife of a prisoner against divorce. Ilyas gave up trying and decided to accept whatever life offered him. It was then that he attained the spiritual peace of mind provided by surrendering to God. He decided to be the best shepherd in the prison house. And being engaged with animals began to assuage his sins, while the affection he felt for the animals gradually cured his injured soul and lessened his guilt.

He would get up at seven every morning and have a breakfast that consisted of a glass of milk and a piece of bread and cheese. Then he would put fodder in feeders and take them to the shed. There he would separate the sheep from the lambs, releasing the lambs into the shed while turning the sheep out to graze. He had to make sure the sheep finished grazing before noon because they couldn't graze in the midday heat. At noon, Ilyas would return to the shed with his sheep and he would let them stay with their lambs until mid-afternoon. After the lambs had drunk their mother's milk, Ilyas would graze his sheep once more, returning with them late in the evening.

He would herd his sheep singing folk songs instead of playing a shepherd's pipe. If the song he sang was a melancholy one, the sheep would graze towards the meadow. If the song was of a fast rhythm, the sheep would return to the shed. Ilyas gained a reputation in other prison houses for having trained the sheep with his folk songs. The prison vet began to ask Ilyas to perform his folksongs when important guests arrived.

Growing up, Ilyas had had many dreams, but he had never dreamt of being a destitute shepherd in a prison house. He had had quite easily attainable dreams. He had been planning to save up to buy a small knitting machine for the house where he and his wife, whose skills had improved considerably, would have knitted many beautiful and colourful sweaters and cardigans. The income they would have made from selling their products in the neighbourhood would have been more than enough.

But none of their dreams had come to fruition. Ilyas hadn't planned to have another child. He had planned to use all his modest assets for his son, to ensure that he could become a dentist in memory of Ilyas's father who had died from tooth cancer. But while he was in prison, missing his family, Ilyas also realised that his father had been wrong. Ilyas wished he'd left the neighbourhood after the first rumour began to circulate about Aysel. He realised that, because he had been a tenant, he could have left the neighbourhood. A tenant was at great liberty, but a house-owner was a prisoner. If you were a tenant, you could live wherever you wished.

If only, Ilyas thought, they had moved to a different neighbourhood, a place where nobody knew them. He wouldn't have had to suffer the shame that grew inside him. He could have talked with his sister and removed her from harm's way. Time would have cured their troubles. But they hadn't given themselves that time.

Ilyas spoke as if he had forgotten that the camera was there. He wiped away the tears that streamed down his face and picked up the empty *ayran* glasses from the grass.

'Could you please visit my wife to ask her to forgive me?' he asked quietly, without looking at us.

And then he suddenly changed his mind. He seemed to remember something sad as he saw the dates on the film cassettes.

'No,' he said, 'I don't want you to. Don't ever do it.'

And then he stood and slowly walked towards the sheep sheds, with his head bowed, and without saying goodbye.

It was the eighth day of the eighth month.

6

NAILE

Bahri knew that the coffee-house preacher was a significant person. Every Friday he went to listen to the sermon that he preached in the coffee house instead of in the mosque. Because Bahri often forgot what was said, he wanted to take notes, but he did not dare attempt to do so in the coffee house because he knew that it would be misunderstood. It was considered a queer and suspicious thing to sit in a coffee house and scribble. Nobody in this town had anything to do with writing, except the teacher. And whenever Bahri wanted to take notes, he had neither paper nor pencils on him. It had been so long since he dropped out of school that if ever he saw paper and pencil he stared at them as if they were inventions which he knew to exist, but which he himself had never touched.

Each time he repeated the preacher's words to himself when he returned to work, but he never managed to remember them all.

'If you put a leg of lamb in front of a wolf, would the wolf say, "No, I won't eat it"? It would swallow it in the blink of an eye. Who is guilty? The wolf who tears into the meat offered to it, or those who whet its appetite? You can say that the wolf is wild; it would eat a whole lamb if given the chance. Then look at the cat at your door. If you leave meat outside, the cat will come and eat it. Who is responsible for this, the cat or the meat?

'I will not answer this question. You will work it out yourselves. A man who does not think is no different from an animal. You will think, so that you will remember that you are a human being. You will think, so that you will find the truth.

'The man who lets his daughter go out with her head uncovered and wearing make-up is no different from the man who lays the lamb before the wolf. If a man who commits no sins raises his child as a sinner, he himself becomes a sinner. Letting our daughters make up their faces and display the intimate parts of their bodies is a disaster for coming generations, and not just for them. The girl who thinks of putting make-up on her eyes and revealing her intimate parts is going astray! She is lost! The real danger is that her daughters will also be sinful. God ordered women to cover themselves as the first trial of fidelity and virtue. Covering and chastity go together hand in hand.'

Bahri nodded with satisfaction. His mother and four sisters never once put on make-up or revealed their intimate parts, let alone permitted anyone to see even one strand of their hair. The family was raising chaste girls for society. Bahri felt a wave of affection for his sisters who had not behaved in a way that would defile the dignity of the family. His middle sister was sick, and his father had taken her to a doctor. Bahri hoped that, with God's will, there would be nothing seriously wrong with her. Before he left the coffee house, he prayed to receive the preacher's spiritual healing so that his sister would have a quick recovery. He set off for home. He was curious to find out whether the doctor had cured Naile's aching head and stomach pain.

Her father was walking so fast that Naile had trouble following him. The mud oozing through the hole in her shoe dampened her woollen sock and irritated her foot. Nobody would have guessed that she was just fifteen under the *ihram* she was wrapped in from head to toe. They would think she was the ageing wife of the dark, elderly man walking briskly in front of her.

After dragging themselves through roads mired with newly melted snow, they eventually arrived at the hospital. The small town hospital was full of chronic invalids, coughing and wailing elders and screaming babies. The sullen nurses and the swarthy male attendants came and went, trying to avoid eye contact with the pushing and shoving crowd. It resembled a field tent with people running hither and thither under bombardment more than a hospital in a town that had had no war for over a hundred years.

Yusuf turned and looked for his daughter, but he could not recognise her among all the women in dark *ihrams*. Naile saw her father looking for her and stepped forward. Yusuf beckoned his daughter to follow him without altering his solemn expression. He shoved and pushed his way through the crowd and advanced towards the door where a burly attendant was standing. It was Alim; he was from the same village and promised that he would take them straight to the doctor. Yusuf gave Alim the malodorous bag of herbed cheese he was hiding under his arm. It was a small gift in return for Alim's favour. A second, larger bag was for the doctor. Yusuf prayed with all his heart that there was nothing seriously wrong with his daughter.

Naile went through the half-open door and followed her father without saying a word. They went into the room at the end of a dark corridor where Naile saw a doctor's examination room for the first time in her life. On one side of the room, which was divided by a dirty white plastic curtain, there were a desk, pharmaceutical cupboards and a jumble of tools that Naile had never seen before. On the other side of the room there was a narrow bed with a dirty white cover and poles with stirrups attached to their ends. A sullen young man in a white jacket sat at the desk. A young nurse who stood beside him watched them enter the room.

With a grin on his face, Alim pointed at Yusuf and Naile who were waiting timidly by the entrance. He said, 'Doctor, I have brought your patient.'

'Leave us alone,' said the doctor.

'Let me tell you my daughter's symptoms first,' said Yusuf. 'She has stomach aches and headaches all the time, doctor. The child is ailing with this chronic illness. I hope that you can heal her.'

'We shall see,' said the doctor.

Alim hurried Yusuf out to prevent him from saying anything more.

The nurse led Naile behind the curtain and told her to take off her clothes. After a long hesitation, Naile first removed her *ihram* and then her hand-knitted sweater. She pulled down her skirt which had an elastic band at the waist. She felt embarrassed when she took off her shoes and saw that her wet socks were the colour of mud.

'Of course you will have stomach and headaches if you walk around in wet socks like this,' muttered the doctor while he stood beside her. He started to run his hand along Naile's naked back, then along her stomach and her throat. He asked her questions and made the nurse repeat them when Naile did not respond. Besides the embarrassment Naile felt at being naked in the presence of the doctor, she did not know how to reply to such intimate questions and was becoming annoyed. She quietly whispered in the nurse's ear that she had begun menstruating. When the doctor asked the date of her last period, she could not reply, not because she was shy, but because she really did not know.

The doctor asked Naile, 'Did you have an *imam nikah*?'* The girl drew her legs into her stomach, and covered her face with her hands. She was extremely upset. Somebody had guessed her secret, which she

---

*   The *imam nikah* does not count as a legal marriage.

had hidden for a year. She didn't know what to do. When the nurse insisted that she should reply, she said, 'Doctor, don't tell my family that I'm married.'*

The doctor beckoned to the nurse without responding to Naile. The young woman put Naile's feet in the stirrups. Naile felt as if she would faint in that position, entirely naked in front of the doctor and the nurse, with her legs suspended and spread apart. She had spread her legs with pleasure for Aziz, but this made her feel ashamed.

Then Naile felt cold metal moving inside her. She was so nervous that the doctor had to tell the nurse to tell Naile to relax. When he was finished with his examination, the young man told Naile to get dressed and when Naile was dressed again, feeling cold both from shame and from her wet socks, the unsmiling doctor said, 'We two will talk directly. Since you are going to be a mother soon, there is no need for an intermediary. We will see each other often from now on.'

He repeated what he said when Naile did not respond.

'You understand that you are pregnant, don't you?'

Naile nodded, but did not utter a word. The doctor stared directly into her eyes and said, 'You're pregnant. It seems that there is no problem with the baby, but next time you should come with your husband and not your father.'

Naile nodded again. She was not reacting to what the doctor was saying. 'Doctor, the girl is not married in the eyes of the law,' said the nurse.

The doctor became angry. 'Since you have the courage to become pregnant without being properly married in this town, you should be brave enough to talk to me,' he said. 'At least I won't kill you,' he went on. 'How old are you?'

When he didn't get a reply he continued, 'When your father comes

---

* Sleeping with another man is considered shameful – so that even when there is no marriage, religious or otherwise, the other man is referred to as a 'husband'.

in, we will have to tell him that you are pregnant. He will be able to see your condition for himself in a couple more weeks. What are you thinking of doing? Who is the father of this baby? Talk to me, so that I can help you,' he insisted.

Naile didn't say a word. It was as if an unseen hand had sealed her lips for eternity. The doctor couldn't even make out if she was sorry, or if she had just discovered that she was pregnant and, if so, whether she was in shock.

In his helplessness, he told the nurse to let Yusuf in. He didn't know how to talk to the man. Naile immediately got up from the chair she was sitting in and put on her *ihram* when her father and his villager attendant entered, and waited beside the door with her head bowed.

The doctor looked once at Alim and then at Yusuf with discomfort. Yusuf put the bag of herbed cheese on the desk. He said, 'Doctor, my wife made this for you herself. Our herbed cheese is very popular here.' The doctor didn't like the nauseating odour rising from the bag, but he remained silent because he did not want to stray from the point by discussing the cheese. He didn't know if he could speak in Alim's presence, but he thought the problem might get worse if he sent Alim out. Besides, if this man reacted unexpectedly when he learned of his daughter's pregnancy, Alim would know his temperament and, perhaps, be able to calm him down.

'Thank you for the cheese,' he said uncomfortably. 'Yusuf Efendi, has your daughter had an *imam nikah*?' Yusuf immediately understood why he'd been feeling uneasy for days. He had suspected this, but he'd hoped it would not turn out to be true.

He took his cap off for the first time since he'd arrived at the hospital. When Atatürk changed the regime and banned wearing anything but ordinary hats, the former Ottomans and the new Turks, who weren't used to having bare heads, started to wear caps imported from Europe. However, while the residents of the cities got used to having bare heads, the villagers liked wearing caps which, although initially worn as symbols of modernity, eventually became the uniform of conservative villagers and townspeople. At this moment, his cap, which Yusuf was squeezing like a ball in his hand, represented the impending family disaster.

'Your daughter is about twenty to twenty-two weeks pregnant, Yusuf Efendi,' said the doctor.

Alim, who was just standing there, suddenly started to wail frantically, making things worse. He stopped immediately, as if a button had been pushed, when the doctor looked at him harshly. Yusuf became hopeful at the word 'weeks'.

'If it is only a few weeks, just give her an abortion and solve the problem,' he said.

'That isn't possible,' said the doctor. 'Twenty weeks is too late in the child's development for a legal abortion. Since your daughter is in love, it is better to find the father and let them marry.'

Yusuf didn't want to talk to his daughter, and didn't even look at her. She was soiled. She was a cruel daughter who had brought shame on the family.

The doctor called Naile. He forcefully made her remove her *ihram* so that he could see her face. 'Tell me who your husband is and let us marry you,' he said. He hadn't been working in Osmaniye long, but he had learned that here the words 'boyfriend' or 'beloved' were definitely not used; the word 'husband' was used instead.

When Naile still didn't utter a word, first Yusuf and then Alim started to kick the girl in their fury. 'If you don't tell us here, only your dead body will leave this place.'

The doctor was stunned. He hurriedly got up to prevent the girl from being kicked, but Naile had begun to talk. The doctor, who thought that the problem would be solved in some way or another when the girl opened up, realised that he couldn't have been more mistaken. Naile had been with Aziz, who was her aunt's husband.

Moreover, she thought of herself as his second wife and said that he'd promised to marry her in a religious ceremony. The doctor repeatedly asked her if her aunt's husband had raped her. Naile said that they loved each other, and that he didn't know about the baby. The doctor was astonished by Naile's self-confidence, composure and the bravery she showed in defending the man she loved. He wasn't expecting this from a girl who appeared so helpless when silent. This remote suburban town was full of surprises. He felt great affection for this young girl who seemed to be so deeply in love, and who had such strong convictions.

Eventually, Yusuf recovered himself and took his cotton handkerchief from the inside pocket of his vest where it was fastened with a safety pin. He unknotted it and removed some money from the ball of notes, which were wrinkled from being knotted so tightly in the handkerchief. He held them out to the doctor. He said, 'Doctor, you must know the right people. Let us hospitalise her and tell people that she has an acute ailment. After she gives birth, I will come and pick her up. We will give the baby to an orphanage. Let this matter be closed. If I take this girl back as big as she is with child, our family will shoot her. Her aunt's home would also be destroyed. Maybe the girl is lying; maybe the one who got her pregnant is not her aunt's husband. But, doctor, you can help us. We need a solution.'

The doctor did not know how to extricate himself from this bizarre situation. He was an only child. He was born in Izmir, had studied in Izmir and had passed his internship in Izmir. He fell in love with one of his colleagues in Izmir but when he was appointed to this suburban town, for the obligatory term of service for all doctors, he realised that he had no idea about life in small towns: until then he thought that the whole country lived the way they lived in Izmir. He couldn't even guess at the nature of the women who were hidden beneath their *ihrams* through which only one eye could be seen; he had never before experienced what it was like to trudge along roads in mud up to his knees; he had not lived through merciless snowstorms; he had no experience of village girls becoming pregnant at the age of fifteen. He did not know about honour killings, or smelly cheese with herbs, in fact he had absolutely no experience of the way these people lived, except that it was beginning to dawn on him that they lived as if they were in the nineteenth century, not the twenty-first.

The doctor put his head between his hands. He wanted to help, but he did not know how. 'Put your money back in your pocket,' he said. 'If you want, I could write in her records that she was raped and then, perhaps, an abortion will be allowed.'

Yusuf, supposing that the doctor found the money too little, drew a few more notes from the wrinkled bunch. 'We are in your hands, doctor. Don't think that we are poor by looking at our clothes. We are villagers, and that is why we wear these clothes, but I have three more daughters like this one. The one who is older than her is still single. I could sell her to one of the landowners and get a good dowry. There's no need for you to be shy about money.'

'Put your money in your pocket,' said the doctor, 'this is not a matter of money, Yusuf Efendi. But let's see how we can save the girl and your family.'

Yusuf was offended by the doctor, who refused the money he offered. 'Well, then,' he said, 'we will do what we can. Just don't tell anyone. We'll say that she was raped by a coward.' Then he remembered the other witnesses in the room and turned to Alim.

'Now Alim, keep your mouth shut; because you know well that this could be our end.' Alim made the sign meaning a promise: he put his right hand on his mouth and then on his heart. While Naile was wrapping herself in her *ihram*, Yusuf slapped her face with all his might. 'I shall never again hear you mention the name of your aunt's husband. Somebody abducted you six months ago in broad daylight and got you pregnant. Now start walking!'

When they were leaving the room, Yusuf tried to slip some money into the nurse's hand in the hope that she would keep her mouth shut, but the nurse turned her back and started to fiddle with the bottles in the medicine cupboard.

Upon returning home, Yusuf told his anxiously waiting wife that Naile's illness was acute; she should not do housework, and she should be taken to the doctor often. When he was leaving to go to the coffee house, he insistently warned his wife not to let Naile go anywhere alone.

Although Hediye had some suspicions about her husband's unusual instructions, she did not want to annoy the man who was already so worried about the girl. She did not believe that Naile was having head and stomach aches. She was sure that she was plotting something and would elope with someone soon. She hated Naile's silent but rebellious attitude, which was different from her other daughters. She hated her disappearances from the house, her frequent visits to her aunt's house, her keeping her *ihram* on even in the house, and covering herself even in the presence of her brothers. She was sure that Naile would bring evil on the family, but all she could do for the time being was be watchful and careful about the people to whom Naile spoke.

Yusuf had neither the time nor the inclination to keep an eye on his daughter. He left with the morning prayers, collected milk from nearby villages and delivered it to the producers' cooperative with Bahri. His tasks were finished before noon prayers when he would go home, eat his lunch, and then go out to the coffee house. He would return home at evening prayers and would go to bed early. Hediye found it difficult to understand why Yusuf didn't like Aziz who, as far as she was concerned, behaved like a father to Naile and watched over her as Yusuf should have done.

Neither their daughters nor their sons had had any education, but they all knew how to recite the *Qur'an*. Nobody prayed except Yusuf. The others prayed and fasted during the month of Ramadan and afterwards went back to their normal lives. But all the girls wore *ihrams*. It was not because Hediye was religious; she wanted the girls to be covered to keep them chaste. But she did wonder why the more emancipated girls in her suburban town got married and went away, while not even one of her covered daughters was yet married. And despite the fact that Yusuf had announced to the relations the amounts of the dowries he wanted for each girl –such announcements also meant that the girls were now at the proper age for marriage –, none of them even had any suitors.

Hediye was planning to marry the two elder girls to her nephews but, since the boys were working in Germany, it was difficult to realise her plan. Hediye's two elder sisters were also in Germany and they had planned to marry one of their daughters to Bahri and take him back to Germany, but Hediye had refused because the girl did not want to come to her town. She was happy to send the girls away, but not her son. Moreover, Bahri had not yet completed his military service. If Hediye could marry her daughters to her elder sisters' sons, she could host a magnificent wedding for Bahri with the dowries they would bring. Hediye knew that the important thing was to get the girls married and, more urgently, to marry off Naile.

But Hediye felt that Naile was cursed. She had brought bad luck since the day she was born. Hediye was not exactly sure when she became pregnant with Naile, but she believed that it was one of the evil moments when Yusuf Efendi had come to her bed without ablution. She wanted to send Naile away as soon as possible to relieve her house of her curse.

Hediye realised that something terrible had happened when her elder sister Raziye stormed into her house. Naile had been at her Aunt Raziye's for a week to help paint the walls but when one of Raziye's neighbours, Alim's wife, asked her if Naile had given birth to the baby yet, Raziye discovered that Alim had told his wife that the doctor had examined Naile in the town hospital, and that he had heard that she was six months pregnant. Alim's wife said that she knew who the father was, but would not tell because she had promised not to.

When Raziye hurried home to confront Naile, she had removed her *ihram* and even her head cover, which she usually kept on at all times, and was lying on the couch with her swollen belly exposed. Even worse, Raziye's husband Aziz was at home and so he would have seen Naile's belly. Raziye beat Naile, but Aziz interfered and calmed Raziye down by saying, 'Don't beat her. She did an ignorant thing. Let it be between us and let's not let others know about it.' Raziye tied Naile's hands and feet, and went to her sister to ask what to do. She told Hediye that, according to Alim's wife, Yusuf knew about the pregnancy.

Hediye fainted when she heard the news, and when she came to her senses, she started to wail, beat her knees and curse her daughter. Raziye had difficulty calming her sister but she said that if she continued crying and screaming, the boys would realise what had happened when they came home. She and Hediye had to decide what to do.

Hediye sent her youngest son to the coffee house to bring Yusuf home, and then she put on her *ihram* and hurried with Raziye to her daughter. Hediye beat Naile and tore her hair, and then brought the rolling pin down on her back. Hediye broke four rolling pins on her daughter's back but Naile was made of steel: she neither uttered a word nor revealed the identity of the bastard's father. Although Aziz interfered occasionally and tried to calm Hediye down, she swore that she would not leave without learning the name of the father of the bastard in her daughter's womb. When Yusuf did not come, Hediye and her sister dragged Naile, with her swollen face and mouth and paralysed feet, through their neighbourhood to her home.

When they got there they found Yusuf squatting beside the wood stove and smoking. His expression was sad. Hediye attacked and insulted her husband, the man whom she had obeyed for twenty years. She said that Naile had denigrated the honour and the dignity of the family. She said that, from now on, it would be impossible to look their neighbours in the face and it would be impossible to find Bahri a bride. She said that if Yusuf had known that Naile was pregnant for two months, why had he kept it a secret from her? And he hadn't even bothered to come to Raziye's house to bring his daughter home. Yusuf, who until then had silently listened to his wife, suddenly stood up and punched Hediye in the face. The accusation that he hadn't gone to Raziye's house was the last straw.

'Not only I, but you also will never go there again,' said Yusuf. 'Naile will never go there again. None of you will ever go there again.'

'What is wrong with my sister and her house?' said Hediye. 'First look at your slut of a daughter. Look at your daughter's belly!' Hediye struck Naile's belly with a rolling pin yet again, but Yusuf could not stand it any longer. 'Ask your daughter who the father is, ask her!' he said.

Hediye screamed, 'I've been asking for three hours. I've been hitting her with this rolling pin but your slut has sealed her mouth! When Bahri comes home, I'll ask her again what she's got sealed inside there.'

Yusuf rose and seized Raziye's arm. He said, 'The baby in the girl's womb is from your cheating husband.'

Raziye hesitated for a moment, and then began to beat herself frantically, pummelling her head with her fists. 'It's not enough for you to be a slut,' she said, 'but you have to slander others as well. There is evil in you, you are going to go to hell, you whore!'

Aziz was summoned and Yusuf spat in his face, but Aziz said that Naile was lying. He told them about the sacrifices he had made to make Naile behave decently, and he denied laying a finger on her. This made matters even worse for Naile: each family member beat her again, for lying.

And then a decision was made: they would call the uncles and aunts in Germany and a family council would convene. Until then. Naile would be held at home, secured by a rope tied to her ankle. There was one month to go before she would give birth to the baby.

Hediye told the neighbours that Naile had been raped by a stranger and advised them to guard their daughters. Yusuf took Naile to the town hospital again where she gave birth to a daughter that evening. The beatings had obviously brought on her labour, but Yusuf did not even look at the baby and prevented Naile from seeing her. The baby was left at the hospital to be given to a state orphanage. The family could not accept a baby without a father.

The next day Naile's fate was to be decided. All the relations who lived in Germany had arrived, but when Yusuf went to the hospital to discharge his daughter, he discovered that the doctor had forbidden Naile to be given to her family. He had informed the police and the office of the public prosecutor, and said that he suspected that the girl would be the victim of an honour killing if she was returned to her family.

By the evening, when the family had found out that the doctor would not let Naile go, the whole tribe, including Hediye's relations who had just arrived from Germany, invaded the hospital. They threatened the doctor, but they got nowhere, because the doctor was certain that Naile would be killed if he let her go with them.

The next morning Hediye took Yusuf to the public prosecutor's office. She begged the prosecutor to return her dear daughter. She said that; nobody was going to lay a finger on her and that Naile needed to rest at home to recover from childbirth.

The prosecutor believed her when she said that no harm would come to the girl, although he made them both swear not to harm her with their hands on the *Qur'an*. Then the prosecutor instructed the police to let Naile go back to her family.

Naile was discharged from the hospital at noon. The worried

doctor called the prosecutor, but the prosecutor calmed him down saying that there was nothing to worry about. He said that the family was obviously so religious, and that even if they were fools to themselves, they could never fool Allah.

Naile was brought home in the afternoon and immediately locked in a room with her hands and ankles tied. The whole family, and even some neighbours, formed the family council. There was no need for a long discussion. They decided that the identity of the father of Naile's baby should be revealed; and that Naile would be shot in the street as an example for other girls.

Everyone agreed to this, except Yusuf. Despite what he had lived through for the previous three months he did not want his daughter to be killed. His relations immediately cursed Yusuf by breaking all the windows of his house with stones. (In villages like Naile's it is an old tradition to stone the houses of those who do not cleanse their dishonoured daughters.) Hediye told Bahri to lock his father in a room and while Bahri was doing that, she took Naile outside. Then Hediye told Bahri to come outside and do what he had to do. She told him to be quick. She wanted him to do what he must do in daylight, so that everyone could witness the killing.

Bahri stopped at a spot on the street where he was sure to be seen from all the houses. He walked a few steps away from his sister and fired three times. His first shot missed, but the shot to her head was enough to kill her.

The young men, along with the married and old women who watched the murder through their windows and doors, applauded Bahri's bravery. Aziz and his wife Raziye were at the forefront of the approving mob. But the old men and the young girls bowed their heads in grief.

Hediye ran and caught her son. She embraced him affectionately. She slipped a knotted handkerchief into his pocket and said, 'My brave son! Now run away and never come anywhere near us, otherwise the police will catch you. We shall call you when everything calms down.'

Bahri slowly walked off as the sun set.

The unclaimed body of a young mother lay in the street where she'd fallen.

Hediye had the walls of the house whitewashed and announced that their honour was restored.

The relations from Germany left, but Bahri could not bear to live as a fugitive and turned himself in after a month, although he refused to admit that the murder was the decision of the family council. He said that he'd done it himself and, during the hearings, Bahri told the judge that he'd turned himself in because Turks could not live in dishonour. He said that if a Turk's honour was slighted he could not utter a word, even if he was sworn at or cursed.

The prosecutor ordered that the father of the baby be identified. The only suspect was Aziz, and tests were completed which confirmed that Aziz was the father. But the doctor was sure that Aziz would be killed if his paternity became widely known in the town, so he requested that the information should not be used in court.

Aziz admitted, in a private hearing, through tears, that he and Naile had been in love with each other, and were together for more than a year, but they couldn't reveal their love for fear of being killed. Yusuf despised Aziz, but accepted that it would be senseless to commit a second murder and kill the father of his sister-in-law's three children. Moreover, this would neither bring his daughter back nor restore their honour.

In the court records, it was written that Naile was raped and Yusuf and Aziz swore, with their hands on the *Qur'an*, that they would keep the secret of Naile's child's true paternity.

Bahri was sentenced to sixteen years imprisonment but, because he was a minor, the sentence was reduced to ten years.

Afterwards Hediye and her sisters came to an agreement about a wife for Bahri. Hediye's elder sister would not find a husband for her youngest daughter, she would wait until Bahri had served his sentence. Both youngsters knew that it was now impossible for them to marry anyone else. And it would be impossible for Bahri to emigrate to Germany, since he would be an ex-convict, so the relations decided that, the bride would emigrate from Germany to their town where they would open a store for Bahri and then the newly-weds would get along just fine together.

And Hediye believed that she understood the saying of the Prophet about there being a good outcome from every evil. If all this had not happened, Bahri wouldn't have become engaged to his cousin so easily. Her sister's daughter, who'd been brought up in Germany, might even have refused to marry Bahri and fallen in love with an infidel. Although there had been a death, in Hediye's eyes their lives had been saved. Their family would have collapsed if she hadn't made this deal with her sister, because they couldn't request dowries for their other three daughters after what had happened to Naile. When a girl is dishonoured, all the other family members are under suspicion.

The municipality buried Naile in the anonymous cemetery. And although Yusuf said to his wife, 'The girl is dead now. Let her rest in peace,' Hediye sent her relations to erect a painted black stone on her grave.

Bahri had told us that he would not give us an interview without the permission of his family, so Yusuf accompanied us to the penitentiary.

We met a child in the visitors' room, not a furious, self-confident man. He had luxuriant black hair and the round face unique to easterners. He was wearing an old woodcutter's shirt and shoes with holes. He gave the impression that he was extremely poor. He was holding the largest of his prayer beads between his middle and index fingers and he turned the rest around his middle finger. This turning of the praying beads lent him a mystical air, but it was obvious that he was feeling insecure and timid, as if he had been jailed by mistake. And he was very young, he was only nineteen.

Without looking at me he started by saying, 'This event goes very deep.' Then he raised his head, 'Why does a person live? For honour, dignity and for his daily bread, for example,' he said, waiting for my confirmation. He acted as if his father was not present.

'Everything families like us attempt to do ends up in failure,' he said. 'Our families neither have jobs to make us happy, nor money like those working in Germany. Should we give up our honour and dignity, too? Our society expects morality from women and dignity from men. A society with immoral women and dishonest men has strayed from religion. If I must rot in prison to save our honour and dignity, let it be so. I will rot instead of the society.'

He continued, 'The authority of our family over the girls would have been shaken,' he said, 'if I hadn't shot Naile.'

Like all the others I had interviewed, I thought that he was trying to mitigate the gravity of the situation by using the word 'shot' instead of 'murdered'. He turned to my cameraman, probably because I am a woman.

'Could you accept it if your sister became pregnant out of wedlock? If she went to the bed of a man without asking you, wouldn't it be as if she was telling everyone what she took the family for? Can you control the other girls if you don't shoot the one who has proved herself immoral? And if you don't shoot the immoral one, you jeopardise the morality of the others. All the girls in your family will be soiled. In such a situation you can be as innocent as anything, but you are committing a sin by letting others commit sins.'

'Now, you assume that I have punished a sinner, don't you?' Bahri was looking at me now, but he answered his own question. He said, 'No, I prevented my other sisters from committing sins. I've fallen, but they're saved. It doesn't matter how long I am imprisoned,' he said. 'I'm innocent in the eyes of Allah.'

His voice weakened once more. He lowered his head again and whispered, 'My aunt's husband is the one who led my sister astray.'

He turned his back without telling us that the conversation was over and walked out of the visitors' room into the darkness of the prison. He never said a word to his father.

We picked up our belongings, but as we were preparing to leave, Yusuf said, 'Neither Hediye nor Bahri is speaking to me, because I hid from them that the girl was pregnant for two months.' Then he murmured sadly, 'And it seems that the boy knows who the father of Naile's child is. When Bahri is released, he is going to shoot that scoundrel. Our home will crumble once more.'

7

NIGAR

*'If, one day, you no longer hear my voice with the winds,
the rivers and the birds,
Know from the sounds of the winds, the rivers and the
birds,
That I have died.'*

— FROM AN ANONYMOUS SONG

In Batman, south-eastern Turkey's most conservative city, the suicides of young girls were causing alarm. Even in this male-dominated society, where the murders of dishonoured women were not a cause for concern, the fact that deaths among young girls had become unstoppable was shocking.

In one month, seven young girls had committed suicide in an almost identical fashion. Batman's residents were angry; they held the dead girls responsible for ruining the city's image.

As the government (which is considered reformist, under pressure from the West) increased sentences for honour killings, rumours spread that in order to protect their men from prison, families were forcing girls who had lost their chastity to commit suicide. But the allegations had not been proved.

I've been to Batman several times but, I confess, I never once thought about the plight of the local girls; while there I was preoccupied with talking to representatives of Turkish Hezbollah, who are more famous than the city itself. Because they remained invisible, the women were ignored. City life was devoid of women. Although the suicides were on the national news, almost daily, the predominant feeling in the city was one of normality. It was hard to believe that beneath this quiet surface there were dozens of young girls who, brimming with anger, vengeance, and love, were turning their backs on life.

Barely a month before I arrived in Batman, Nigar Demir had ended her life by drinking quantities of bleach. We were on our way to her father's home. He had told a colleague of mine, a writer for the local paper, that he desperately wanted to see me.

We stumbled along on the pitch-black, muddy streets. My colleague, who was acting as our guide, was greatly amused at our inexperience. When we finally crossed the neglected yard of a large, dimly lit house and rang the doorbell, our guide whispered that the upstairs lights were not on because the household was in mourning: Nigar had died in one of the upstairs rooms. Lights were only on in the living room and kitchen.

As we took off our muddy shoes and entered the living room, our guide murmured that this was the first time that men and women had sat together in this house. The segregational rule had been broken because Nigar's father had rebelled against it. However, besides the tearful aunts and female cousins, the only man in the room was the grieving father. The other men of the house had disappeared and the only other men were our cameraman and guide.

Nigar's father, like all local men, spoke to strangers with a bashful smile. This smile was a combination of respect, timidity, warmth and restraint, and despite his grief, Nigar's father's face still wore that expression. He said, 'Everyone suffered their woes in their own way. Wanting to abide by their religion, families wrongly sacrificed their daughters. But Nigar had decided that, from now on, she would dedicate her life to showing that these actions were not in the *Qur'an*.'

The conversation deepened and the female relatives began to serve food to us; they were generous in spite of their bereavement. As they came and went, everyone spoke of Nigar: with her thick, jet-black eyebrows and her big, jet-black eyes, people who saw her always did a double take. And when she wore her headscarf with red flowers, she became even more attractive – a mysterious charm was added to her beauty.

And so Nigar's family told us her story.

Nigar was remarkably good at housework. She'd taken on the responsibility of cooking at an early age, and she grew up preparing – like all Anatolian women – poorly presented but delicious meals. To Nigar, decorating the food the way she saw it done on television would have meant tampering with God's gifts and after being scolded by her family for the few experiments she made, she renounced novelties in the kitchen.

She would get up early and, after cleaning the house and before the noon prayers, the evening's meal would already be on the stove. In the afternoon, Nigar would grab her needle and white lace spools, and weave lace for her trousseau under the blazing sun. Other girls looked enviously at the laces she wove, and wanted them. Nigar would raise her head from her lacework and say, 'I won't give my trousseau to anyone. When I get married, I'm going to hang them in my home.'

On the television, the Prime Minister was talking about Batman, but that was not why Nigar had turned it on. She was waiting to see how the village chief, who had fallen in love with a destitute young girl, would arrange his wedding on her favourite show. Strangely, ominously, the Prime Minister appeared before Nigar and began talking about the city in which she lived.

The Prime Minister said, 'In previous years, it is true that Batman had a poor reputation, but the people of Batman never deserved this. There are many respectable, compassionate people who are ready to put the past behind them. The people of Batman don't want to remember those bad times; they want to draw a line through the past and connect, work, and create with today's values. In solidarity, rich and poor are attempting to overcome that negative atmosphere. This is a victory of our government.'

Nigar thought, 'The people of Batman want to live in the present. What a lie! They want the present to be worse than the past.' There was a huge gap between what the Prime Minister was saying and what Nigar knew that Batmanians wanted. She wondered which residents the Prime Minister was referring to: her peers, who were daily committing suicide, or the men who, running back and forth between mosque and coffee house, never once paid any attention to the pain the girls were in?

Nigar heard footsteps outside and, so that she wouldn't be seen watching television, she quickly turned it off. She had never yet been caught in this forbidden act, but she took all the necessary precautions. She covered the television with its lace cloth and placed the plastic flowers back on top. The television stood in its corner, apparently untouched, and when the cruel sentinels of her unhappiness walked in – her uncles, her father, her brothers and male cousins – Nigar was innocently preparing food. But as she did so she wondered who these men, and the other men in the neighbourhood, were protecting her and the other girls in her family from. These men were a small army, but the men they protected the family's girls from were men just like themselves.

These men, who wouldn't allow their own daughters to be seen, ogled other men's daughters and they made unbelievable marriages. The year before, when his wife died, Nigar's eldest uncle had paid a great deal of money to marry his fourteen-year-old god-daughter. But because she was so young, they couldn't get an official marriage licence. Although everyone in the house treated the little bride with respect, calling her *yenge*,* the poor girl lived in the house like a frightened animal. On top of that it became increasingly clear, despite her loose clothing, that she was pregnant. Her uncle, who had nine sons – the youngest of whom was twenty-five years old – was going to have a tenth child. Nigar prayed that the child would be a boy. If her new young aunt gave birth to a daughter, she'd be treated with contempt.

As the men came into the house, Nigar and the other girls hurried to take off her father's and uncles' shoes. They took the men's threadbare jackets, which smelled of cheap tobacco. Among the arrivals there were also a few men the women didn't know, but this was normal. It was customary to invite guests spontaneously for dinner. The more guests one had, the more highly one was regarded.

The evening rush – for the women of the house – had begun: heating the meal they had cooked that morning according to the men's orders; preparing the trays; handing the trays to their brothers from the living-room door so they could serve the food; frothing coffee and brewing tea; preparing the guests' mattresses while the men sipped tea and watched television. Nigar belonged to one of Batman's wealthier families, but it made no difference: wealth didn't prevent the girls from being treated as household servants, nor did it provide them with comfort. The family earned money but didn't spend it. They lived no differently from the way a poor family lived except that, unlike the poor, they had no trouble. Religion forbade women from living luxuriously. It occurred to Nigar that this religion had been made for

---

*   *Yenge*, in Turkish, means uncle's wife. To call someone *yenge* is a sign of respect, acceptance and warmth.

men; but then she remembered that to think that way was to commit a great sin and she put all bad thoughts from her head.

Men were allowed to watch the same television that was forbidden to women. Television, which ruined girls' moral values, improved those of men by showing them the exemplary state of the world.

Like her siblings, Nigar was not born in the town centre, but in the city's outskirts. The family had built a three-storey house in a conservative migrant neighbourhood in order to live away from the city centre, where, according to the elders, morality was disintegrating. Six brothers and their families lived on different floors of the house. The men would eat together in the living room on the ground floor while the women ate in the gigantic kitchen. Nigar loved the time they spent together in the kitchen. While they made bread, prepared *börek*, or collectively stuffed vegetables with rice, the older women, who were no longer concerned with living virtuously, told dirty jokes or sexual anecdotes from their married days, while the young girls listened, both amused and embarrassed.

Two years before, Nigar had graduated from primary school, but she was then confined to the house to await her fate. Still, she was luckier than her female relatives who had been taken from school before they finished even the third grade. She herself had attended school for five years.

The girls in the family mostly watched television dramas featuring brides. This choice did not come from sexual curiosity, but from the hope that marriage would one day alter their boring lives. Sometimes the girls would remove their thin white headscarves and make veils out of them. Ashamed to admit they wanted to be brides, they merely said they wished to wear a wedding gown. Nigar secretly wove the lace veil she would one day wear and, to protect it from the evil eye, she hid it in her mother's trunk.

Her mother became angry at the time Nigar spent weaving rather than worshipping God, but her most religious, eldest uncle protested that Nigar was better off with her eyes on a needle than on a lover.

That night, as usual, the men were discussing mandatory literacy courses. Nigar's uncle said, 'We'd read if it was a good thing.' As it was rude to argue with the family's elder, everyone listened reverently while he griped about the government. He snapped at the television, 'The country's full of unemployed young men, and they drag girls off to school. First find jobs for all the educated jobless.'

He continued, 'So they learn to read and write, but what happens to those who can read? Their breath stinks from hunger; they come to our doors begging us to find them jobs. If studying is so great, why won't anyone hire these people? First, they don't create any jobs for the men of Batman; then, they pass a law that girls have to study. And they call us ignorant! They're the ignorant ones. Is time so cheap that they should spend it learning something that won't help them? Call Nigar; she'll recite you the *Qur'an* like a *hafiz*.'*

When Nigar heard her father call, 'Come here my girl!' she quickly donned her headscarf and ran to the living room. Her uncle handed her the Arabic prayer book and said, 'Recite this; let's see if you make any mistakes.' In a panic, Nigar recited the prayers. Her uncle was pleased. He smiled at Nigar – he rarely smiled. He must have been in a splendid mood. He asked, 'Did the prayer soothe you?'

Nigar gently nodded. She whispered, 'My Lord soothed my heart, Uncle.'

'See how the *Qur'anic* script uplifts the soul? Now read the infidels' writing.'

Nigar knew she was the apple of her uncle's eye. Especially after two girls in the family had shamefully committed suicide. Terrified of making a mistake in front of the guests and losing his favour, she stuttered as she read the tattered book that was placed in front of

---

* A *hafiz* is one who has memorised the *Qur'an*.

her. After she'd read a few sentences, her uncle interrupted and asked, 'Now tell me, did this uplift you in the same way?'

Nigar answered, 'It did not soothe me, Uncle.'

Her uncle seemed satisfied. He said, 'Now go about your work, my girl.'

Nigar left the room without losing her poise but she knew that whatever the *Qur'an* said, the television said the opposite. Her heart belonged to the *Qur'an*, but, deep in her soul, Nigar wondered about the lives of the people she saw on television. To tell the truth, she didn't like the way the 'television girls' dressed immodestly and covered themselves in sinful amounts of make-up. She wondered whether such girls really existed. She wondered whether they lived in the same country as her. She wondered what their parents said to them when they went home. Television girls were women who could speak to, and be seen outside with, men. Nigar didn't want to talk to men, but she did want to go outside. She didn't want to dress indecently, but nor did she want to be segregated in her own home. She envied only their freedom, not their debauchery. She wanted to emulate them without becoming sullied.

But Nigar would never know such freedom. It was an impossible dream. The year before, when her two cousins Nadire and Halime had committed suicide one after the other, the family had lamented their shame. Halime had pressed her father's unlicensed gun to her head and pulled the trigger; Nadire had hanged herself from a hanging cradle.

In the *Qur'an*, killing oneself was a terrible, unpardonable sin. Nigar knew why the girls had been sinful, but couldn't understand how they had found the courage to do it. Nadire had fallen in love with the wrong man and when the young man's family came to request her hand in marriage, her uncle threw them out of the house.

When Nadire, Nigar and Halime were little, animosity arose between the family and the in-laws. The in-laws had gathered scrap metal from Nigar's uncle's garden; the uncle's youngest son had tripped on the scrap metal and injured his face and eye. The two families got into a huge fight – men, women, rocks, sticks and all – in front of the entire community. Finally, when the neighbourhood imam intervened, they made peace. But it was an artificial peace. In Batman, no matter how enmity began, it was never forgotten. People would pretend to forgive and forget in front of the religious elite, but their enmity was secretly passed on to the younger generations, never to be undone.

But, as if there had never been any animosity between the two families, as if the in-laws had wished to ridicule Nigar's family, they came to ask for Nadire's hand. Because one must never speak ill of the dead, Nigar had never said that she thought Nadire was at fault. How could she have forgotten that hostile families would never allow their children to marry? How had she allowed herself to fall in love with the son of their enemies?

A month after the in-laws had been kicked out of Nadire's home, they married off their son to the daughter of one of the city's wealthiest families. Unable to live knowing that the man she loved was about to marry another girl, Nadire took her life. Nadire's mother was fifteen years older than her. She had married at thirteen, had her first son at fourteen, and Nadire at fifteen. That year, she had given birth to her ninth child, a boy. Nadire hanged herself from her youngest sibling's cradle.

One month after Nadire's suicide, Nigar's other uncle's daughter, Halime, shot herself. But her suicide had been forced. It was discovered that she'd been laughing with a boy at the marketplace. When she hesitated during her interrogation, the family knew she was guilty. They placed a gun in her hand and left the room. The implication was that if she didn't kill herself, they would. But Nigar still wasn't sure if it was Halime or one of the men in the family who had finally pulled the trigger. Nor could she ask her female elders what had really happened. They would never betray their men's secrets.

When the police came to investigate, Halime's father couldn't tell them her name; he had forgotten it. The newspapers publicised this fact and the family was humiliated. Why did the public care that her uncle no longer knew his daughter's name – wasn't her death the real tragedy? The two cousins' deaths were never mentioned again in the household, but the terrible events still terrified not only the girls in the house, but all those who lived in the neighbourhood.

A month before, the governor, whose reputation had worsened due to the suicides, tried to restore the city's dignity. He brought over some famous singers and organised a concert. Of course, only young men – and the children of civil servants and military officers – had been able to go. What local family would allow their daughters to go to a concert? Besides, didn't the *Qur'an* forbid women from letting men hear their voices? Nigar had never seen the governor, but she could tell he wasn't very clever.

The children in the family were forbidden from disclosing the reasons behind the two girls' suicides. The elders said they refused to allow a girl to ruin the family's honour. They were proud that Nadire and Halime had taken their lives instead of running away.

But the girls who remained had to be more cautious. Talking to a boy – even a neighbour – on the street, requesting a song on the radio, going to the movies, wearing trousers to a wedding – anything could signify bad intentions. Nigar knew that a girl in Urfa had requested a song on the radio and dedicated it to all who love and are loved. To set an example, she was killed in front of her entire family. When it was discovered that a girl in Mardin had secretly gone to the ladies' matinee at the movie theatre, she was dragged from the theatre and beaten to death. Another girl, from the neighbourhood, had attended a wedding wearing trousers and no headscarf. Nigar found it unbelievable that such small things could cost a girl her life.

Nigar's uncle highly disapproved of the girls who had committed suicide. He said, 'They disobey the book to attain their loved ones. This is the most diabolical of all religious transgressions. Even penitence won't bring them forgiveness from Almighty God. Virtue is living according to Islam's bidding. One mustn't cross the boundaries of virtue. One mustn't enter places forbidden by God. A man's virtue is reflected not only in his daughter, wife, mother or sister, but also in his neighbours. A good Muslim should protect their virtue as well as his own.'

Nigar's uncle was all-powerful. His power came from the privileges bestowed on the family patriarch by the holy book. Sometimes he got so swollen with pride that, to show the younger generations his 'god-given' strength over women, he'd invent petty reasons to beat Nigar's mother and aunts. Only Nigar and his tiny newly-wed were spared his beatings. Nigar believed her instinct had protected her from being handled roughly; she thanked God for it.

After handing the last cup of tea to her brother that night, Nigar slipped upstairs. She was tired. As the only television was downstairs in the living room, she couldn't watch it, but she could lie on her bed, daydream and rest. She retrieved her lace veil from its hiding place and removed her headscarf. She carefully fixed the veil to her head and stretched out on the bed.

She wondered who she'd marry. She had reached marrying age and, as long as she wasn't married off to an old man like the poor girl who had married her uncle, she'd be freer anywhere than in this house. If she could be the woman of the house, and turn on the television whenever she liked, what more could she ask for? In any case, she wouldn't marry someone who didn't let her watch television. Even if her father tried to make her, her uncle would never make her wed against her will.

The bedroom door swung open. Her brother Bekir said, 'My uncle wants you to come downstairs.' Nigar was caught red-handed with her dreams and her veil. She threw herself from the bed, frantically crumpled the veil and shoved it underneath the bed. She sped downstairs faster than Bekir. She had to prevent him from reaching the elders first. She paused at the living-room doorway to adjust her headscarf. Just as she was about to enter, she saw her mother beckoning to her from the kitchen. An inexplicable feeling of distress welled up in her. This never happened. Her mother would never interrupt when her uncle called for her. Something strange was going on.

Nigar went to the kitchen. Her mother pulled her inside, closed the door, and said, 'There's a man in there who wants to marry you. When you enter, don't raise your head to look at his face. He was impressed with the way you read the *Qur'an*, and wants you. Your father isn't too thrilled, but your uncle gave the man his word.'

Nigar paled with excitement. Her dreams were coming true. But if she showed how happy she was they'd know how badly she wanted to marry.

She asked, 'Why isn't my father happy about it?'

Nigar's mother didn't answer because Bekir had come in, singing sarcastically, 'They sold Nigar for lots of money, they threw me a little change.'

Nigar pinched him to make him stop. But when she saw, through the kitchen door, her uncle approaching her, she let Bekir go.

'Nigar, my child,' her uncle said. 'With God's permission, our *kirve's** uncle has asked for your hand. He saw you recite, and liked it very much. We said okay. It would not be comely to refuse our *kirve*. Your days in this house are numbered. I'll call on you often. None of the girls can take your place in this home, but the wedding is God's will. What can we do? Girls, like birds, must fly from their nest.'

Nigar bowed her head.

Which of the guests was the *kirve's* uncle, she wondered. To be

---

*   A *kirve* is a man who acts as a sort of godfather to boys during their circumcision, and throughout their lives after it.

polite, she hadn't taken a good look at the guests' faces when she had read from the *Qur'an* to them. Which man would be hers? She regretted missing the opportunity to look.

While her head was bowed, Nigar saw a pair of shoes leaving the living room. She thought, 'It's probably him.' The man, whose face she couldn't see, was trying to hang a red ribbon – tied around a gold piece – around her neck and Nigar heard him say, 'This is an engagement gift.'

Nigar lifted her head so that he could fit the ribbon over it. Before her stood a well-groomed, bearded, cheerful man. She realised this was her new father-in-law and he seemed kind. According to custom, you kissed your elder's hand after receiving a gift, so Nigar took his hand but the older man pulled his own hand away violently. Nigar realised that she'd gone too far, had seemed too eager. Her cheeks turned scarlet. The man returned to the living room.

'I knew you'd like him, my child,' her uncle said. 'Kadir is a truly good person. He won't mistreat you like those hooligans who spend all day at coffee houses. He knows the value of women. He's well off. You'll never go hungry; you won't have to live from day to day. In fact, he'll treat you like a rose. As you know, after I buried your aunt, I took their daughter. She has turned out to be a crown on my head. You will be Kadir's crown. Your father said nothing, but it's obvious he disapproves. Who knows why. Don't let him convince you. May God make you smile at your good luck. Now go and rest. Brides are allowed to be spoiled. If anyone tries to put you to work, they'll have to answer to me. You're our guest now.'

Nigar felt as though hot water was being poured over her head. She had become just like the village girl she had once pitied. She'd been given over as a bride to a man older than her father. A lump lodged in her throat. Her eyes welled up with tears, but she knew she must not cry.

She trudged wearily upstairs. Her dreams had abandoned her. So she decided to abandon her dreams and her life. She didn't want to see anyone. Life had tricked her. So much had changed in a single day.

The next morning, because it was getting late and Nigar still hadn't appeared, her siblings went to her bedroom. They found her with eyes that were shut tight, and her face a deep purple. They shook her, pushed her and poked her, but she wouldn't wake up. The red ribbon with the large gold piece still hung from her neck.

Funeral services did not segregate men and women. In fact, women were buried more respectfully than men; women, who'd been considered worthless during their lifetime, became enviously precious when they died. Nigar's funeral, and the services that followed, didn't break with this tradition. Women beat their breasts and wailed. Men engaged in sorrowful conversation.

Nigar's story was repeated time and time again, in different ways. Tales spread about which word, which look, which act had filled her with such pain and hopelessness that it sent her to her death. What event had shaken her so badly that it fatally altered her destiny?

Within two years, a third girl in the family had died. The house was cursed. The Demir family couldn't take it any longer. Without waiting for the forty-day mourning period to end, they sold the large house and the family separated. Nigar's father, who held his older brother responsible for his daughter's death, migrated to Istanbul. He never again wanted to see anyone from the extended family.

The fact that these girls had chosen suicide over an impure life had won the family a great moral victory, but the survivors' hearts would be forever wounded.

8

FADIME AND YETER

To reach Giresun prison, we first had to fly to Trabzon, then rent a car and drive for an hour and a half to the small but magnificent town of Giresun by the sea. But in Trabzon tension was running high: three young members of the association of solidarity among prisoners' families, one of whom was a young woman, had almost been lynched when they attempted to hand out flyers. Journalists were flooding into the outraged city and when people saw my cameraman, it was impossible to convince them that we were not just there to film the current tension in the city.

The crowd demanded that we shoot and broadcast their insults, their rage and all they had to say about honour. As journalists taken hostage by the crowd, we had no choice but to comply. They insisted that they would not allow their city to be defiled and they used the word 'honour' so often that I could not help asking how the city's honour would be defiled if the families handed out flyers about prison conditions. But my question, which they thought insulted their honour, only made their rage worse.

What interested me was the sensitivity of the scale by which honour is weighed. All the prisoners in the prisons I visited, regardless of whether they agreed or refused to talk to me, indicated that it was their honour which decided whether they were accepted or refused by society. In Trabzon that day, the honour of an entire city was apparently under threat. I wanted to understand the definition of honour – this unchallengeable premise upon which every case, from killing a woman to protecting a city, is based. But even my attempt to understand appeared to be an insult to the honour of the people of Trabzon, to whom honour is valued above everything else. They turned away from us in disgust, but my mistake had a benefit: it saved us from delaying our journey to Giresun any longer.

We found a car and set out on a difficult journey, off the main highway. We drove past frail women carrying enormous bales of wood on their backs. My cameraman suggested that it would be perhaps nobler to document these women's doomed lives rather than those of women who were already dead. I didn't know what to say. It seemed to me that in small villages in Turkey, the simple fact of being born a woman was tragic in itself.

At night, when we reached the small bay, which looked like a magical holiday resort, we were still talking about the human habit of turning the beauty of nature bestowed upon us, into hell.

A feast of a breakfast awaited us the next morning at the prison. From locally produced peanut butter to vegetable quiche, freshly picked tomatoes, green peppers and cucumbers, home-made butter, honey and a variety of cheeses, our breakfast lacked nothing, while through the window, the glittering blue of the Black Sea dazzled us.

The prison prosecutor, whose requests I could not refuse after such a breakfast, insisted we were wasting our time by interviewing prisoners. He thought it would be socially more useful if we drew attention to the prison's work therapy programme, or the vocational courses organised for the inmates. Instead of a long conversation with a murderer it would be better, he thought, to show the prison's efforts to provide repentant prisoners with productive vocational skills.

I realised that the prosecutor was attempting to get us to film the prison's kiwi cultivation programme, to which the national press had so far remained indifferent. He wanted to make his efforts public while he had the opportunity.

Although my cameraman resented every distraction, he went along with the prosecutor's request and, as he shot the kiwi production facilities, I got on with the paperwork. The prisoner I wanted to interview was a father from the Black Sea area whose rage had not diminished even after he had killed both his wife and daughter. This was the first time in his life that someone had asked his permission for anything. He did not understand what it meant, and my explanation did not seem to make things clearer to him. He signed the paper I handed over without even reading it. I thought that perhaps he was more concerned with hiding his illiteracy.

Nevzat was in his fifties, and he was small, with thinning blond hair. He had come to Giresun from one of the small towns in the region. Before I could even ask a question about the murders he had committed, he summarised his entire life in a single, brief sentence: 'Daughters are difficult.'

'If God gives you a daughter,' he said, 'let her be decent. And even then, your guts will burst until you manage to marry her off. You cannot just say to Ahmet or Mehmet or whoever "come wed my daughter".'

Nevzat did not understand why a television crew would come all the way from Istanbul to Giresun just for him, yet he was flattered that someone had asked for his permission to listen to what troubled him. It was proof that someone thought him important, even though he hadn't uttered a word about what had happened for years.

'Why are daughters difficult?' I asked him.

He sighed deeply. 'A daughter is a burden on her father's shoulders.

You want to protect her from disaster, but you get struck by disaster yourself!'

Nevzat had already served five-and-a-half years, but he still had seven to go. He told his story calmly, as if he were speaking about someone else. And throughout the interview he never asked for the camera to be switched off, nor did he want to say anything off the record.

He had killed his wife and daughter. I asked him if he regretted it.

'Yes, very much,' he said. He wished he'd known that it would be so difficult to serve time in prison after the age of forty-five. He said that instead of killing them and suffering in prison himself, he should have shot them in the legs and let them suffer for the rest of their lives as cursed invalids. His rage made me shudder.

I was incandescent with rage myself. I wanted to speak; but when I moved my lips nothing came out. I wanted to say to him, 'Sir, I don't want to hear this monstrous talk about making your wife and daughter disabled,' and then leave the room; leave him alone with his curses. For the first time in this series of interviews I thought I was face to face with one of those killers you only see in films.

And then my cameraman stopped shooting and rushed from the room. I followed him. His face was crimson, his forehead covered in sweat. He rubbed his wet palms violently. 'That man is suffocating me,' he said. 'Let's not interview him, he's a monster!'

'I think,' I replied, even though I agreed with him, 'I think we ought to be patient. We ought to go through with this. But we can take a break if you like.'

I told my cameraman that things were often more complex than they seemed at first. I said that there is always another reality hidden beneath the image that a person presents, especially a person like this one. I said that I thought that a grieving father might emerge from inside this ice-cold peasant. My cameraman seemed to believe me and calmed down. We went back in.

Nevzat's file said that he had killed his fifteen-year-old daughter because she talked to her boyfriend on the telephone, and that he'd killed his wife because she'd condoned her daughter's telephone calls. And so, sipping our tea, we began to listen once more.

Although it had been many years since Nevzat and his wife had moved to the city, they had married according to village tradition. They were neighbours in one of the remote districts of Giresun. Both were ordinary young people who had not attracted much attention in the villages they came from, or the neighbourhood they had moved to. Nevzat's wife, Fadime, was an unremarkable girl. Nevzat was an unremarkable man. They were both from average families who had nothing but the income they obtained from the small nut grove in their village. Fadime was small, blonde and ugly; Nevzat was also small, blond and ugly. They seemed more like siblings than husband and wife. Their relationship revealed no spark of passion worthy of neighbourhood gossip. And they weren't even aware of the possibility of a different kind of life.

They had six children: two boys and four girls. Yet they had never once kissed. Nevzat found kissing and hugging immoral. He especially disliked it when hugging and kissing were shown on television. He hated the way privacy was made public. When television channels displayed so much immorality, it was difficult to control the children, to raise them in the traditional ways. He was always saying to Fadime that once they had honourably married off their daughters, they would be the happiest of parents. He had a gut feeling that the sooner he could find husbands for his girls, the happier he would be.

Fadime grew the vegetables they needed – things like beans, eggplant, green pepper and tomatoes – in the small garden in front of their house. At nut harvest time she went to the village with her children where they picked the nuts themselves, which Fadime then sold to the dealer. In these ways she managed to save money, but even so it wasn't easy to manage with six children.

Nevzat and his brothers ran the business they had inherited from their father – a small, mobile street stall which sold clothing accessories. But since one stall could not support so many brothers, they had allotted areas in the villages and towns of Giresun between them: each brother sold his wares in a different area.

The money they made was not too bad and, along with the money Fadime made from the nuts, they were able to send their elder son to serve his military duty. Upon his return they also managed to give him money to buy a van which he drove for a living, and they married him to the daughter of one of their relations who lived in Istanbul. But the boy would have to save for the charges that were required to drive a commercial van along Istanbul's lucrative Bayrampaşa–Aksaray road route.   Nevzat's family had easily overcome the first small-scale threat to their honour. When Nevzat's younger son had returned from military service, his eldest daughter ran away from home. Nevzat travelled to his village to fetch his pistol, and went after his daughter. He thought that his daughter might have been abducted and sold to one of the brothels in the infamous Soğukoluk district of Iskenderun, which he had seen while doing his military service. Nevzat knew that girls were sold there for considerable prices and that a clandestine, organised network forced the girls to work as prostitutes.

He also knew that nearly all the girls were under eighteen and that they almost always returned to the brothels as soon as they were set free. Perhaps by then there was no other place these girls could go, but Nevzat could not even begin to imagine his own daughters in the brothels.

Fortunately he did not have to collect her from one. His daughter's boyfriend's family, with whom she had taken refuge in Istanbul, handed her over to the police because she was underage. Nevzat went to Istanbul with his wife and youngest daughter, Yeter. Following routine procedure, the police first tried to mediate between the two families before handing the girl, who was a minor, back to her father. It worked, and the two families agreed that the young people would be married straight away. The police were happy, and the young lovers were happy.

It was at her sister's wedding that Yeter saw Aziz for the first time.

Nevzat had learned from this painful experience with his eldest daughter, and he told his wife to have heart-to-heart talks with his other daughters to try to understand what they were thinking. When his wife showed no inclination to do so, Nevzat did something very unusual. He asked two of his girls whether they loved anyone. One of them bowed her head and uttered the name of a boy from their village; the other said she did not want to get married. But Yeter was still so young that Nevzat did not feel the need to ask her. Before there was a chance of any kind of scandal, Nevzat saw to it that his daughter was wed to her lover, and that the one who did not want to get married was sent to Istanbul to his wife's brother to nurse the children and help with domestic chores.

Nevzat doted on his youngest daughter. He had wanted her to get an education, but she was not remotely interested. Frequently he told her, 'You know I'm for as much equality as possible. For a son or a daughter. If you go to school, you will be the educated member of the family. You will be our pride and joy.' But Yeter told him that she did not want to go to school, and instead implied that she wanted to get married. Although she was the youngest, not yet fifteen, Yeter was by far the most attractive woman in Nevzat's family.

Nevzat did not force his daughter into education because he also wanted someone to take care of him and his wife when they grew old. Her excessive fondness for the family from Keşanli, neighbours who visited them quite often, concerned him a little but he did not give it that much thought.

One evening when he came home and once again found the family from Keşanli at his house for dinner he turned to Aziz and said, 'Look, you can come and go as much as you like, but I'm warning you that just because you're a bachelor, I don't want you ogling my wife or daughter.'

He said this lightheartedly, but later he thought that God had made him say it. He said to me, with regret in his voice, 'God warned me in my heart but I did not get the message.'

Nevzat didn't remember seeing the thirty-two-year-old son at his eldest daughter's wedding. But he wouldn't have suspected anything even if he had. Neither would he have imagined that the boy from next door would turn up at a wedding in Istanbul.

Aziz had shamelessly replied to Nevzat, 'Your daughter calls me brother. How can one have bad intentions towards anyone they think of as a sister?'

If Nevzat had known how deceitful Aziz's words were then, he would have shot him – that treacherous rapist, as he called him – right between his eyebrows then and there.

When Nevzat arrived home unexpectedly early one day, he overheard a conversation between Yeter and the daughter-in-law of their downstairs neighbour. In a dejected tone, the neighbour's daughter-in-law said to Yeter, 'I married when I was fourteen, Yeter. Stay put and enjoy the leisure of your father's home. You will regret it if you don't.'

'No,' replied Yeter, 'I am obliged to get married.'

Who she loved and why she was obliged, Yeter did not say but Nevzat watched her carefully after that conversation. He feared that she might elope with someone he did not know. He made a habit of coming home at unlikely hours in his attempt to keep an eye on her, and to prevent her from making a mistake. But when he discovered that the object of his daughter's affections was Aziz, the boy next door,

Nevzat was furious. He heard rumours that Yeter spent the whole day on the telephone to Aziz.

A good friend of Nevzat's told him not to worry about his daughter's telephone calls to Aziz, but to pay attention to her trips to Istanbul. Nevzat took no notice of his friend's warning because his daughter was always with her mother when she went to Istanbul.

It wasn't until much later that it occurred to Nevzat that he had ignored the most critical part of the conversation with his friend. Rumours had begun to circulate and he thought that the best way to protect his honour and dignity was not to spend time finding out whether there was any truth in the rumours, but to marry Yeter off. Even if he'd managed to prove the rumours false, once a rumour has begun to circulate, Nevzat knew that it was almost impossible to stop it. The only way to escape a rumour was to leave home, but Nevzat was too old for that. So, he thought that if he gave Yeter away in marriage, even though he would not be able to stop the rumours, at least he would have rid himself of the responsibility. Her husband would have to deal with it.

He sat down to talk to his daughter. He said, 'Yeter, sweetheart, people are saying that you talk on the telephone with this thirty-two-year-old grown man. If this is true, child, tell him to come and ask for your hand. I wouldn't be a man if I didn't accept him. But, my dear girl, if he intends to flirt with you and stain your good name and not take you as his bride, then that is a very a different matter.'

Yeter, who had reached puberty earlier than expected, kissed her father's hand in gratitude for his understanding. She rushed to the telephone as soon as her father left the house and joyfully told her lover, Aziz, what her father had said. But Aziz seemed not to hear what Yeter was saying. Her father's unanticipated consent did not excite him; instead he continued to talk about Yeter's body, attempting to arouse her with his words. Yeter, who was only too willing to give in and had found all kinds of reasons to slip into Aziz's bed at other times, was now upset.

'Well, come and ask my father for my hand, then,' she said. 'If you do that, we can do everything you say night and day, without fear, or having to hide from anyone.' Yeter hung up angrily without waiting for Aziz to reply. And then she had a feeling that something was wrong.

Nevzat was still at home. He had hidden in the bedroom closet, wanting to find out what his daughter was up to. The conversation he'd just overheard did not bode well. In fact, it made him shudder. His daughter's deathly silence and her sorrowful face warned him that disaster loomed and because Giresun was a small town and everyone knew everyone else's problems, Nevzat waited at the market crossing for hours until Aziz's mother appeared.

Then he approached her and said, 'The girl is stained. Your son has defiled my daughter; you are obliged to ask for her hand in marriage. Come over to our house on Saturday evening and we shall engage them, and so end the matter.'

Nevzat sighed deeply at this point in his narrative and he remained silent for some time.

He had been avoiding eye contact while he spoke and now he avoided the camera too, and when he began to talk again, it was as if he were speaking into a void.

'I don't know whether things would have turned out differently if that rapist's family had come to our house that night. They sullied my child and they didn't give a damn that she was defiled. But later I found out that my wife had sent them word not to come. She told them I was a nervous type, and that I might get violent. So they did not come.'

Even though the Keşan family did not come to ask for Yeter's hand in marriage, Nevzat's whole family did gather at home early that evening. But when Nevzat saw that his wife had not prepared anything for the guests, he said, 'They will come for Yeter tonight and you haven't made any preparations. That's not going to look good.'

But Fadime, who was unable to meet her husband's eyes, replied, 'The boy's family sent word that they will not come.'

Nevzat was furious. 'How can they not come?' he said. 'This is not up to them. There is an obligation. They defiled the girl.'

This time Fadime looked straight into her husband's eyes. 'Maybe they don't want to come. Maybe they don't want this engagement. Maybe it's because the man of this house has a temper. You can't know what they're thinking.'

Nevzat got up and stood menacingly over his wife. The children took up positions around their mother. They didn't want him to hurt her. But Nevzat had no intention of hurting anyone. His anger had vanished. He only wanted to resolve the matter. He turned to his son and said, 'Go and get the family. Tell them I say they have to come. If they don't, then we will have to go there and that's not good form. People will talk. Tell them that.'

The young man was off before his father had even finished speaking. He knew that something dreadful would happen if his sister's situation wasn't resolved. But he did not return as fast as he had hoped because he wasn't able to persuade Aziz's family to come. Their refusal was final.

This time, Nevzat was unable to control his temper. He had beaten his wife a thousand times since they had married, but never had he felt so upset. He had moulded this frail, small, nervous woman who withstood hardship and feared neither beating nor hard labour, according to his desires. But he had never, never beaten her on account of honour. Now it was altogether a different matter. Now that his wife had sold out his honour, he found he was quite unable to hit her, even lightly. He wanted to stretch her out on the floor and tread all over her, he wanted to do something to make her feel some regret at the fact that she had allowed their daughter to put the family in this disreputable position. But, oddly, he was quite unable to move. He could only scream at her.

And so he yelled at the top of his lungs and his words were cruel. In the family, he shouted, the mother is responsible for the daughter, the father for the son. Yes, the boys had not received an education but they had grown into manhood without getting into trouble. If the boys had taken to gambling or drinking or become burglars, or in some other way gone astray, some friend of his would have warned him before it was too late. 'Nevzat,' somebody would have said to him, 'last night your son was seen doing this or that.' But fathers did not hear of their daughters' foibles; mothers did. Nevzat left at dawn and returned at sunset. How could he know what went on at home all day long? But Fadime surely knew. She knew and she concealed from him what she knew.

Nevzat shouted that he could tell from their whisperings that they all knew what had been going on, and they had hidden it from him. This drove him mad.

The lies his daughter had told whirled through Nevzat's head. Whenever the telephone rang, it was she who jumped up to answer it. If he were to ask her who had called, she always said it was her aunt. How could he know who was at the other end of the damned line? Once, twice, three times; each time he had chosen to believe her, even though he suspected she was lying. He had wanted to believe her.

Determined to elicit every truth that had ever been kept secret from him, Nevzat went to the kitchen. He took the unregistered pistol from the large pot where he had kept it since the trouble with his eldest daughter. Back in the living room, he placed it on the sofa where everyone could see it.

To his wife he said, 'I will kill you if you try to keep anything from me. Don't make me a murderer, woman! You have left my honour in tatters already! Now, answer me: Why does the Keşan family think their seedy son unworthy of my flower? Answer me! Don't you dare conceal it from me. I don't want everyone else to know this information before me. If I hear about it elsewhere, you will have nowhere to run. I have a circle, I have my name. I won't have people saying Nevzat's daughter goes around with so-and-so and does this and that. I will not have people spreading rumours about me. What have we got in life, woman, except our honour? Tell me. I want to be the first to know.'

Fadime hesitated briefly, but Nevzat was by now so angry that she plucked up her courage and blurted out the dreadful secret that would spell her death sentence. 'The girl's with child,' said Fadime. 'Who would take a whore with a bastard inside?'

She begged her husband for mercy. 'I told you, didn't I, to send the girl to Istanbul for good. You never listened to me. But let's send her away now so she can at least deliver the child there. Then we'll see what else we need to do.'

Nevzat told me that he had no recollection of pulling the trigger.

And even later, when he replayed the events endlessly in his mind, he could not remember how he picked up the gun from the sofa, nor when he fired it. There was a black hole in his memory. The last thing he remembered was his wife telling him that Yeter was pregnant. The rest was a blank. The next thing he knew was that his daughter threw herself in the path of the bullet as it was fired. Nevzat found out only during the court hearing that Yeter had died within minutes of being shot.

Nevzat remembered that after his daughter had collapsed, and a pool of blood had covered the floor, his son, in tears, had thrown himself on top of his mother, in an attempt to prevent him from shooting her. He had no recollection of repeatedly firing the pistol, nor of how many shots had hit his wife or how his son had survived.

Then Nevzat had put his head in his hands and fallen to his knees by the bodies of his wife and his daughter. He had wept and howled and wished he hadn't done what he had done. His son had called the police, who had been unable to handcuff Nevzat because his body was rigid with shock. They had had to wait for Nevzat to relax but, as he held out his wrists to be handcuffed, he was still muttering that he 'would not have people say his daughter was all about town with everyone', and that he lived 'for his honour'.

The nut harvest began in Giresun soon afterwards. This was also the season for engagements and weddings, for feasts and celebrations. But in Nevzat's house, the debris from the disaster was being cleared up.

And then the door of that nondescript house at the edge of town was forever closed.

At the court hearings Nevzat discovered that his daughter had been four months pregnant. He felt bitter that he had not realised what had happened. He saw Aziz for the last time in court, when he came to testify against Nevzat. Aziz, said Nevzat, behaved in a lowly, treacherous manner when he testified that, 'the girl who died was like a sister to me; I do not know who got her pregnant. Her father is slandering me. Ask whomever you wish, they will tell you the sort of man I am. I couldn't have had anything to do with such a dishonourable act. They threatened me, to get me to marry a girl who was pregnant out of wedlock. I am an honourable person. I will not have my honour tampered with. Would you sacrifice your honour, just to do a good deed? If I had married the pregnant girl just to do a good turn, it would have ruined my honour. How could I have faced the world afterwards? How could I walk home with my head held high? What have we got in this life but our honour?'

It hurt Nevzat to listen to Aziz and he wished he'd killed him too.

Later, in prison, Nevzat discovered the rumour was that even though Aziz had had sex with Yeter, he had actually sold her to someone in Istanbul. And that even though he had raped her, he had continued to sell her to others and he really did not know who the father of the child was. Even worse, Yeter had not filed a complaint because she had been receiving money from Aziz. She only panicked when she became pregnant and feared that everything would be discovered.

This last rumour dealt the final blow to Nevzat. He realised that even if he had killed himself too, the gossip would never end. The neighbours thought that Nevzat had known about his daughter's dealings all along; they did nothing because they thought he was being paid off by Aziz. They thought that Nevzat had undertaken the honour killing only when Aziz had ceased to pay up.

Nevzat had committed murder to protect his honour, but his honour still lay in shreds. It was obvious to Nevzat that nothing, not even the sacrifice he had made, could halt the rumours. He also realised that the gossip, that had destroyed his life and caused him to kill his wife and his daughter, was in fact something that everyone did, just to pass the time. There were rumours about every family, and every family invented gossip about all the other families. It had done no good to ruin his family for fear of what was really nothing more than a simple, traditional form of entertainment. But if you reacted as Nevzat had done, if you considered your honour to be at stake because of what was being said about you, you risked turning what should have remained a harmless way of passing the time into a devouring monster.

Nevzat had killed two women of his own blood just to stop talk behind his back, but now that talk had reached epidemic proportions. Nevzat, by his own actions, had brought about what he feared most.

Nevzat lost his faith in Divine Justice during the court hearings. He had been taught by his parents that all the evil in the world was ultimately punished, but now, on the threshold of his own private Apocalypse, he found that the principle of Divine Justice was no longer at work. There was no connection between Human Justice and God's Justice and Nevzat could no longer believe in either. God's Justice had left his daughter pregnant, Human Justice had sentenced him to thirty years. But for fear of his doubt of the Divine becoming evident, he tried to conceal it by devoting himself all the more to prayer and worship.

He heard the court sentence with his head bowed. He was a murderer who had killed his wife and daughter. That was irreversible. But with good conduct and with a number of other reductions – the calculation of which was fathomable only to experienced inmates – at the age of fifty-eight he would be able to leave this prison that he had entered at forty-five. Nevzat made only one plea during the hearings. He wanted to be transferred to a prison near Giresun. He did not expect his plea to be granted but the prosecutor, even though he had obviously thought Nevzat a complete monster throughout the hearings, accepted his plea.

The local papers also called Nevzat a monster. His only consolation was the national papers which had understood the problem and written that Nevzat was a helpless man who had felt compelled to kill his pregnant daughter, and his wife because she had consented to the fateful events that led to the pregnancy. The national papers' famous third page – which is devoted to family murders – printed photographs from the hearings that displayed Nevzat's forlorn state, and thereby his innocence. He was grateful for this unexpected understanding and thought that the national papers were not like the Giresun papers which were run by badly-educated journalists, because they were run by highly educated people who grasped the significance of honour.

It is said that the house from where the wife's coffin departs before the husband's is a desperate house. That was certainly the case in

Nevzat's household. After he was arrested, the remaining members of his family disappeared into the vast city that is Istanbul. Nevzat's last unwed child eloped with a girl in Istanbul and married in a hurry. Nevzat was deeply sorry to hear that and wished that he could have asked for the girl's hand for his son and, after the nuts were sold, held as fine a wedding as possible. But, of course, he could no longer do anything of the kind.

From the few visitors who came to see him in prison, Nevzat heard about a grandson fathered by his oldest boy, and that his brothers gathered the nuts which his wife used to gather – the same nuts which had paid for his court fees.

After sentencing, and his removal to the ward for the long-term prisoners, the daughter-in-law he had never known came to see him with an infant in her arms. Nevzat's son had hesitated, sending his wife and child ahead, but the visit did Nevzat good. He thought about Yeter and her never-to-be-born child. Seeing this grandchild, it occurred to him for the first time that he had not killed two, but three people He buried the thought for fear of losing his mind.

By the time I met Nevzat, his hair had greyed, his back pains had increased and he realised that he was aging, but he also realised that, as you aged, you had a greater need of family. He said, not in the tone of voice of one who had been through a terrible tragedy, but more like a person discussing the ordinary troubles of daily life, 'I wake up early. I'm on my feet by five. The ward is unlocked at seven. I pace about all day. Life approaches an end; one gets older. So many people have passed away in my village since my downfall and I'm still alive. All those who died are about my age. I thank God. I'm in prison but I'm alive. I hear the call to prayer here. I never miss the morning prayer, nor the matins.

'I recognise all the voices and sounds beyond these high walls. I know the hour when each street vendor passes, the hour when the dogs bark, the vehicles that come to the prison and when they leave. In prison, one becomes like a clock. A clock that ticks by the sounds of the street.

'It will take a few years for me to pull things together again, but I have the capacity to bounce back fast. I know that my nuts are still growing and if I get out and God grants me a couple of years, I'll pick my nephew's nuts. That will make three or maybe even five tons. Last year the harvest was bad, but in my orchard there was still one or two billions' worth.* My brother told me the other day when he was here. What else can I ask of the Almighty?'

Nevzat had ceased to answer my questions. Instead he complained about his health and the prison conditions. He said that the ward was never warm enough, and that not even three blankets kept him warm when the city's famous winds raged. He told me that, with friends in the ward, he used to buy ingredients and they'd cooked together which helped pass the time and also meant that they ate better. But recently new regulations had forbidden them to put in shopping orders, so now they had to settle for prison food.

'It's no longer like before,' Nevzat said. 'Before, the wards were more spacious; companionship and conversation were good. But now they're bringing in people from Istanbul who are here for things like mugging, not for honour. They've got no money, no honour and they're full of aggression. Being an inmate has become more difficult because inmates no longer respect each other, there's no friendship among them. Everything has changed. Being in prison used to mean you were a man of honour; the new ones haven't got that,' he said.

I said a few polite words of consolation about prison conditions and then brought the subject back to Yeter. I wanted to know what Nevzat thought she might have been thinking. Why, for instance,

---

*   Liras. One or two billion Turlish lira is roughly equal to £700-800 pounds. Now it is a 'thousand' Turkish lira but people still refer to billions rather than thousands.

did he think she'd done what she'd done when she knew she risked her life for it? Surely when Yeter realised she was pregnant, she would have known that her father would kill her?

I prepared myself for the anger that these questions might arouse in Nevzat, but he was not angry. He said, calmly, 'girls don't think about life and death. They plunge headlong into the things they do. If the family's finances are in order, that's enough for them. If they get married, however, even if he's not making a great living, he'll be sure to put some food on the table. But if the man likes wining and dining and goes out on the town each night, an ignorant girl can't manage that kind of fellow. So a man's got to have family ties, so that he can take care of his family. A girl needs that.'

Before I left, I wanted to hear a clear expression of Nevzat's regret. I even hoped for repentance, because something in me said that if I heard that loud and clear, Yeter and Fadime would rest in peace.

'I have,' I began, 'some superstitious beliefs to which I'm deeply attached. I believe that your wife and daughter will rest peacefully in their graves if I hear from you that, from the depths of your heart, you regret what you did. Do you feel any regret?'

But Nevzat said, 'If I thought like that, in here, I would make my friends in the ward uncomfortable. If I thought too much about any regrets for what I have done, life here would become impossible. You get sick in the head in prison if you think like that, and I don't want to get sick because, in prison, doctors don't take a real interest in you.'

I timidly interrupted him. 'Do you ever say to yourself that you wish you hadn't done it, that you wish you had looked for other ways out? When you're alone?'

'We do feel we erred,' he said, as if he was speaking for all those imprisoned for honour killings. 'We do feel this, but you can't feel that day in and day out. Just think: your father dies, your mother dies. Your brother dies in a car crash. And what happens? You eventually forget it. What else can you do? You visit their graves for some days, and then you forget them. If you don't forget your dead, you cannot go on living yourself. You have to forget to be able to live!'

And then Nevzat got up; he didn't want to miss supper. He said, as he left the room, '*Akşam karavanas*ını *kaçirmamak için bize aceleyle veda etti.*' [A daughter is difficult. She's a burden on her father's shoulders.] It was one of the first things he'd said to us.

We gathered up our equipment, but neither my cameraman nor I felt like speaking as we drove towards Trabzon. The fate of a young pregnant girl, which symbolised the fate of so many others, had silenced us. Eventually my cameraman, who had just spoken on his mobile to his wife about their newborn daughter, pulled over to the side of the road and said, 'Probably no one visits the girl's grave. Shall we?'

We rang the prison prosecutor who told us – when we reassured him that we also had good footage of his kiwi production facilities – that the Municipality had buried Yeter with her unborn child still in her womb. She and her mother were side by side in the graveyard for orphans and the homeless. He told us that the grave's registry number was no longer legible, but because the incident was still fresh in public memory, the prosecutor thought that the graveyard warden would show the site to us. He said he would instruct him to do so.

We bought little bunches of flowers and attached the photograph that had been printed in the paper. We found a small stone inscribed, 'Yeter Ayaz 1984–1999'. At the grave of the little mother who died on the eve of the millennium, I prayed for the lives of all the girls who had not yet been killed for honour.

9

ULVIYE

Our driver turned towards Schaerbeek, which is the Turkish district in Brussels. On both sides of the main street, Turkish grocers' shops, halal butchers and Turkish döner kebab restaurants stretched into the distance. This immigrant neighbourhood is equally detested by both the Flemish and the Walloons, who aren't overly enamoured of each other either.

The noise of children's voices rings out in this neighbourhood where the Belgian children of Emirdağli origin, who are unable to express themselves in Afyon Turkish, communicate in their own mixture of Flemish and French, or Flemish and their mother tongues. Heavily pregnant women, who have emigrated illegally from Turkey to marry their cousins, share their troubles in Flemish but shout to their husbands in Turkish. I had heard that the community hadn't managed to carve a new identity for itself from its Albanian, Turkish and Belgian fusion.

When we got out of the car and were fretting about how to ask for directions (as we spoke neither French nor Flemish) a small child shouted, 'It's that house there.'

How did a small child know which house we were looking for? More importantly, how did he know we were Turkish?

We removed our shoes and rang the doorbell. A child answered the door and through the door that opened onto a large living room, we saw men and women of all ages – the women wearing embroidered white headscarves, the mustachioed men clad in dark jackets and smoking pungent cigarettes. They sat together in a cloud of dense smoke while young girls served a vast array of dishes: everyone who came to offer their condolences brought homemade food. Glasses of tea, rich pastry desserts and dried fruit and nuts were passed around on large trays.

The frail, elderly Advil Celili was sitting cross-legged on the large couch. One of his arms was twisted in the opposite direction. He didn't move it at all. His head turned towards the sounds he heard, but he gazed hopelessly, then bowed his head, as though what he heard wasn't what he longed to hear. It crossed my mind that he might be waiting for someone to say, 'Afrim isn't dead'; that he was awaiting a miracle. His son's death seemed to have sent him into a vegetative state.

Everything I had heard about him had led me to expect someone younger, but the light had gone from his eyes and he looked old. He gave us no sign of recognition, though he knew who we were and why we were there. I was afraid of upsetting this weary, grief-stricken, elderly man. I wanted to slip quietly out of the house and allow them all to grieve in peace, but I knew that the family would interpret my desire to leave so soon after my arrival as a lack of respect for the deceased. Moreover, we were a large group and had turned up empty-handed, without so much as a single box of pastries or *börek*. I was ashamed of my own indelicacy. As though he had perceived my intention to leave, Advil Celili patted the couch with his good hand so I sat down beside him. My cameraman too sat down on a chair opposite us.

Eventually he asked, 'Do you still drink *boza** on Wednesdays?' I was taken aback by this unexpected question. I had prepared myself to offer words of condolence. I had never even tasted *boza*, but I couldn't confess that to the elderly Albanian. I babbled something incoherent in reply.

Suddenly he said, 'It was an Arab who killed my son. The brute came up from behind and slit his throat. We've suffered more at the hands of the Arabs than we have from the infidel. The Turkish especially.' When he didn't receive the agreement he was expecting from me, he turned to his relations who were listening intently. 'The Arab gypsies stabbed the Ottomans in the back too. Why does the Belgian government let them into this country? No good will ever come of them. They're all tent-dwelling dogs.' He fell silent.

Some people I didn't know launched into a lengthy diatribe about the cruelty and barbarism of the Arabs. I said, into the old man's ear, 'Can we go somewhere a bit quieter? It might be easier to talk.'

He stood up and said, 'Daughter, Advil Celili's life is a novel. I couldn't tell it to you in a day or even a month. How do you expect me to fit an entire lifetime into an hour?' But his remaining children, understanding that their grieving father had accepted my proposal and was agitated, prepared a small room. Hurriedly, they placed embroidered cushions on the couch and ashtrays and dishes of food on coffee tables.

The interview we thought would be over in two hours lasted five days, during which time we met everyone in the household and lived as part of their family.

We could not know that directly after we left Advil too was to depart from this world and be buried beside his children. It was as

---

*   A warm winter drink made from barley, found only in Istanbul.

though he had quietly taken leave of his refugee existence because once
he had entrusted his tale to us there was nothing left for him to do.

Advil Celili was a Muslim Albanian born in Kosovo, in the Kalista
mountains. He was a robust baby, brimming with health. While his
mother was pregnant his grandmother used to say that if the baby
was a girl they would give her away to be adopted by another family
as their servant, and if it was a boy they would give him away to an
armed gang. They hadn't been able to bring themselves to do either.

According to Celili's grandfather's account, the Kalista mountains
changed hands often, passing from the Ottomans to the Austrians,
from the Italians to the Greeks. Ever since the First World War it
had been difficult to know who the Kalista mountains belonged to:
the Serbs, the Slavs, the Ottomans or the Austrians? It didn't make
a great difference to the Celilis. In their mountains they could speak
Albanian and that was all that mattered. The Serbs' quarrel with
King Alexander's Slavs was a long way away from the Celilis' Muslim
mountains, although Advil spent his childhood counting the dead
described to him by the Serb postman who came to the village once a
week. But the war wasn't between Muslims and infidels. The infidels
harmed one another.

Advil watched over the young Muslim girls on green hillsides and
wondered at the freedom of the Christian girls in the neighbouring
villages. He was a mere boy when he first noticed Kamile. The clothes
his mother dressed him in were too tight for his long-limbed body
and people laughed at him. Until Kamile noticed him and fell in love
with him he had wanted to stop growing so that he could fit into his
undersized clothes.

During his adolescence several different potential owners of the
Kalista mountains began to emerge. In each village a different chief
called the shots. Every village had its own brigand and because Advil's
village had fallen to the Germans, the Serbian militia who supported

them began to enrol the village men as soldiers in their own armed bands. Faced with the choice between the ruthless Slavs and the more innocuous Serbs, the Muslim villagers preferred the armed bands of the latter.

By the time he reached his eighteenth year Advil was aware of his amorous instincts and the desire to be treated like a man. He wanted to be worthy of Kamile's love. He went to the Serbian village on the opposite hillside and had himself measured by the Jewish tailor for a suit. When the time came to collect it, as his grandmother was sleeping, he stole the money she kept hidden in a cloth pouch between her breasts. When he arrived to pick up his suit the Jewish tailor wasn't there. The Serbian villagers told him he had been murdered for being a Jew. Advil's suit had been carefully placed on a hook inside the shop, the door of which had been broken down. He never was able to pay the tailor the stolen money. But neither did he lose sleep over the death of one Jew: to his mind Jews were even greater enemies of Islam than Christians.

For the first time in his life he had a jacket with arms the right length, a pair of trousers with legs that weren't too short, and a brilliant white shirt without patches. Swaggering all the way, he headed for the fields. He lay down, immensely pleased with himself. Every day after lunch Kamile's niece Ulviye passed by on her way back from collecting the lunch bowls she took to the shepherds.

Just as he expected, the small Ulviye arrived as the sun was scorching his head. Her breasts had only recently started to form and protruded through her tight clothes. The scent of the girl's pink cheeks made her seem ready for precocious love. 'It won't be long before she has an admirer,' thought Advil.

'Come and sit beside me for a moment, Ulviye,' he called out. Ulviye hesitated at first, nervously glancing left and right. Then she threw caution to the wind and ran to Advil's side. After all, she wasn't flirting with him. Because her own intentions were blameless she assumed anyone who saw them wouldn't jump to the wrong conclusion. And anyway, who didn't know that Advil was head-over-heels in love with her aunt? She left the food bowls on the grass. She held out a copper bucket of puréed fruit compote to Advil. 'Drink that, it will cool you down,' she said.

Advil pushed the bucket away impatiently, 'Never mind the compote, just tell me whether Kamile has her eye on anyone,' he said. The girl burst out laughing. She too knew her aunt loved Advil but she said, deliberately mysteriously, 'I don't know. But if she saw you in that suit she'd give you her heart even if someone else had it already.'

Advil held out the money he hadn't been able to give the tailor. 'Take this and give it to Kamile,' he said. 'Tell her to buy anything she likes with it.' He was so happy he started to roll around in the grass in his brand new suit at the thought that Kamile loved him too. His high spirits deafened him to all other sounds so he barely heard the explosion of the gunshot. He stood up, brushing off his suit which was now covered in grass stains, and then he saw Ulviye, lying face down.

She was completely still. Her fist was tightly closed but the money she was going to take to Kamile was no longer in her hand. The food bowls were scattered around her and the copper bucket had tipped over. The fruit compote mingled with Ulviye's blood and stained it a yellowish colour.

Three young men stood menacingly before Advil. They were Ulviye's older brothers. One of them was holding a gun. They did not say a word. The thought that their clothes were too tight for them flashed through Advil's mind. They didn't look like grown men, but they had shot their sister like men.

Advil shouted, 'Why did you shoot her? WHY? What did she do to you?'

Ulviye's brother's voice was icy as he said, 'You had no business playing with our honour. You're the cause of this!' He spoke with the indifferent air of a person performing his duty.

'How can you say that?' whimpered Advil. 'She was an innocent young girl.'

Ulviye's brother said to Advil, 'Go away from here. We can't shoot you. You're a Celili. Don't force us to stain our family honour with Celili blood. Don't force a Muslim to sacrifice another Muslim.'

'Wasn't this girl a Muslim too?' wailed Advil. He realised the extent of the tragedy he had caused. He had given the girl what was due to the dead tailor and the twice *haram** money had cost Ulviye her life. For a moment he had forgotten himself and, behaving as though he was in a Croatian village, had rolled around before a Muslim girl as he fantasised about making love to Kamile. The onlookers believed he had seduced the innocent girl. How could these three young boys know that the news he had received had made him wild with joy? They thought he had trespassed on Albanian honour, dared to slander it, and so he had to pay for it.

But Advil knew that everyone would know perfectly well that Ulviye hadn't really committed suicide, even though that is what they would say. Everyone would know perfectly well that Ulviye's brother had killed her, in front of her older brothers and her supposed lover. No one except Advil would care about the truth.

During the ongoing massacre of Croatians, Serbs, Jews, gypsies and anyone opposed to fascism, who would trouble themselves with a fourteen-year-old girl who'd been killed on a hillside by her brothers? Who would give a second thought to a girl who'd been sacrificed for honour when the Communist partisans, led by Josip Broz Tito, and the Serbian nationalists led by Dragoljub Mihailovic, had formed armed bands against the Germans? When Kosovo was under Italian surveillance and they'd duped the Albanian partisan, Enver Hodja,

*   Unlawfully gained.

with dreams of independence? When everyone was killing everyone else and no one was even bothering to collect the corpses?

But Ulviye's dead body lying on the Kalista mountains drove a wedge between Kamile and Advil on that fateful day in 1941. A wedge that was never removed.

Advil would see his lover for the last time on the day he first heard their love declared. He stood outside the back of Kamile's house and she, with the artfulness of a lovesick mistress, escaped from the shame-faced laments that were being said for the girl who had flouted the laws of honour.

'You stole your grandmother's money! She cursed you, and now nothing can save us,' said Kamile hastily to Advil. With her heart pounding, she cut off a lock of her auburn hair and wrapped it in a piece of cloth. She held it out to her lover. 'Don't forget my scent,' she said. She didn't say anything about the clothes Advil was wearing. Advil thrust the lock of her hair inside his shirt. He wanted his lover to notice his suit. He wanted his adolescent good looks to remain imprinted on her memory. Kamile reached over and, with a boldness not to be expected from a Muslim girl, threw her arms around Advil.

'Don't forget my scent,' she said, again.

But they both knew they would never see each other again. Innocent blood had come between them.

Dead men returned to the village, in strange cars. The women buried them silently. Advil's father had gone off to war – which one, he didn't know. Everyone was fighting everyone else in the Kalista mountains.

Advil Celili fled from the murder he had inadvertently caused. He fled even though he knew Ulviye's family wouldn't touch him. As he ran he cursed the carelessness that had made him speak to the girl. He ran away from himself, without knowing where he was heading.

In Drachka Advil's uncle's long-haired dog chased him. The dog never barked, but whimpered; that was his way. Advil sought refuge at his uncle's house.

His uncle said, 'Why run away? So you fell in love with the girl. Is loving a crime? Don't run away, you can hide here!'

Advil believed him. But it *was* a crime. Or at least, it was a crime in his uncle's eyes because his uncle also had designs on Kamile. Advil was about to taste betrayal. He lay down in the barn among the winter provisions. The soles of his feet were swollen and blistered, but he slept deeply all the same. He awoke to the stench of soldiers and realised immediately that his uncle had sent for them.

The soldiers discovered the lock of Kamile's hair inside Advil's shirt and flung it to the ground. Advil was devastated. He didn't dare to wrench himself free and retrieve it. They put his feet in fetters and sent him on a long train journey with other prisoners. He ached with thirst, hunger and the pain of betrayal.

Advil's father was already in prison for opposing the annexing of Kosovo by Yugoslavia, but Advil was completely indifferent to the sovereignty of Kosovo. To him it seemed that dwelling on anything but Kamile was pointless. His father was in prison for being a dissident; Advil now found himself in prison for evading his military service. There was always some pretext for imprisoning a person. But the people in prison were the lucky ones, because they wouldn't be killed in the war.

Advil removed his new clothes, which were now smeared with grass stains, blood and dirt from the barn. He washed and dried them and placed them under his mattress overnight while they were still damp, to press them. He sent his clean, pressed, *haram* clothes to his father's ward. Advil was tall, while his father was short. The suit that fitted Advil perfectly hung off his father and when the soldiers arrived to beat them, they beat father and son together. When they saw that the father was wearing new clothes, they thought he was wealthy and beat him all the more. But they didn't find any money on him.

'Bury me on my own soil and then come and lie beside me afterwards,' said the elder Celili. By 'my own soil' he was referring to Turkey. Shortly afterwards he died before his son's eyes. The soldiers buried him in an unmarked grave.

It seemed that there was no end to the dead tailor's revenge, nor to Advil's grandmother's revenge. Advil hadn't given the money he'd stolen to the Jewish tailor's family. He had added *haram* to *haram*. The curse would never leave him.

He made new friends in prison with Greek, Bosnian, Macedonian and Albanian prisoners. They all tried to comfort Advil. His Bosnian friend told his fortune by scattering beans.

'Tomorrow morning you'll escape, you'll live on dry crusts, and go first to Albania, then to Turkey,' he said. 'You'll have nine children, some of them will die before you. But don't worry, all the ones that are left will be fine.' Then, as if he hadn't said anything upsetting, he gave him a complicit smile, and winked.

The prisoners were made to work on the rail tracks, from daybreak until late at night. Advil was the hardest worker; the youngest and the most robust.

While they were clearing stones his Bosnian friend whispered, 'Now's the time. Run.' Advil flung his shovel as far away as he could and ran after it. Bullets rained down after him. He felt a wet, stinging pain in his left arm. He ran. Running away was what Advil was best at. Months later he would discover, in Greece, that the bullet that hit his left arm had twisted the bone of his elbow around. The bone would knit in that position, rendering his arm useless. That was the reason he became known as One Hand. His past left its mark on his body.

The war ravaged Europe. While he was fleeing Advil heard, on the radios in the Muslim villages where he sought refuge, how Christians were burning Jews, and how Christians were shooting Christians. Nevertheless he didn't have a very clear idea of what was going on in

Germany. In every village he encountered Communists who spoke of freedom, equality and independence. Who would be independent in Advil's village? What difference would it make to Advil if there was independence in the infidel villages of Serbia and Croatia?

Tito became the leader of Yugoslavia. The Communists carved up the provinces and exiled the fascists. Tito promised the Muslims that he would not do as the Germans had done. Muslims would live as Muslims and Serbs as Serbs, in peace and harmony. Kosovo would govern itself. The Italians on the losing side would entrust the Muslims in Kosovo to the Italians on the winning side, for safekeeping. The Serbs would smile upon Kosovo. Advil's family sent word to him:

'Come back,' they said. 'The Celilis have won fame on the Kalista mountains again.'

As Advil made the decision to return, Tito annexed Kosovo. The Prime Minister of Albania, Enver Hodja, abandoned the Kalista mountains to fight, and fled to Albania. But Tito would arrive there not long afterwards. The Russian Communists would also soon be there. Tito and Enver Hodja would make their peace. They would outlaw Islam. They both put their faith in Stalin and believed they would reach a prosperous heaven on earth. Advil was not interested. There was no room for anything in his mind except his yearning for Kamile.

The Greeks were detaining everyone who arrived from Kosovo, without interrogation. Advil, who had lost everything, was sent to a refugee camp in Greece. Independence and Kamile were now nothing but a fantasy. He didn't know how to recite a single prayer. His mother used to say, 'The more the infidels humiliate us the more stubbornly we'll insist we're Muslims.' But because he'd been brought up to be a Muslim out of sheer obstinacy, he never managed to learn any prayers. When he wasn't able to pray he wept in secret.

His grandmother, who had died without forgiving him, used to say, 'Tears are the prayers of repentance.'

In 1950 Advil was still a refugee in Greece. He was still a virgin. He could have found a Muslim girl, but the image of Kamile always stood in the way.

Eventually he received the news he had been waiting for: he would finally be able to escape from Greece to Turkey. As he roved from villages to mountains, the Muslims he met told him they were trying to migrate to Turkey. The news filled him with excitement. With a great deal of trouble he sought out several Albanian addresses and sent word to them, asking for help. Everyone who had gone to Istanbul had become rich. Tales of the great capital city floated in the air like coloured balloons. It took several months for Advil to travel from Korche to Vidina, from Vidina to Drama and from Drama to the River Merich. En route he encountered Greek communists, fascists, immigrants, Muslims. The Greek soldiers were blind drunk and in no fit state to keep vigil on the river. On the opposite bank were Turkish soldiers, who were completely alert, pointing their guns at the tiniest splash. Advil swam across the River Merich at night in pitch darkness, splashing all the way. Soaked to the skin he cried out, '*Um yam Turko ... um yam Musluman ... mos mevrisni!*'*

Miraculously the soldiers decided that the soaking wet cripple with one hand who didn't know any Turkish was a Turk.

They dispatched Advil to Istanbul. He took refuge in a district called Çarşamba where Balkan immigrants lived in cramped, overcrowded conditions in whitewashed, adobe hovels. The old Albanians did not look kindly on the new ones because the immigrants were no longer Albanian, but aspired to be Turks. Advil couldn't speak the language of the Bosnians or the Macedonians. The only language he knew was Albanian, and no one spoke that. And even if he had found someone who spoke it, he had no desire to speak. In the loneliness of his dreams he spoke to Kamile in his native tongue.

But Advil did pick up Turkish. Armed with a *boza* pail he trudged

---

*   'I'm Turkish ... I'm Muslim ... don't shoot me!'

through the streets of the Fatih district from early evening until the night had grown silent, shouting, '*Boza*, anyone for *boza*?'

In Çarşamba he had to get up at the call for dawn prayers, walk up Vefa hill and queue to buy the freshest *boza*. A few times Advil attempted to make his own in his hovel and when he tasted it he thought it had the same astringent flavour, but his customers realised it wasn't the real thing.

'It's not the right consistency,' they said. Advil never mastered the secret of the correct consistency for *boza*. And so, time and time again, lashed by the wind, he joined the *boza* queue at the crack of dawn.

People from Çarşamba drank *boza* on windy days. Advil's hands froze as he sold it in the blustering wind. His nose turned red. He shivered. He yearned for warm summer evenings, but in the summer he couldn't sell *boza*. He needed it to be windy to avoid going hungry, and he longed for it to be summer to avoid getting cold. Not that Advil was complaining, at least he had a job.

During the seasons when he couldn't sell *boza* Advil learned what it was to go hungry. Hunger made him sensitive to the chinking of spoons against soup bowls and he would walk through the streets listening, because where there were clinking spoons there was also soup. When the neighbours spied his shadow in the twilight they would invite the one-armed youth in. Each evening it was a different neighbour's house.

There was a bald, unkempt girl called Gülizar in this overpopulated immigrant community. Her parents and siblings had all perished in a fire; she had managed to escape although her hair had been burnt and it had never grown back. She was one hundred per cent Turkish but she was entirely alone in the world. The Albanian immigrant community married Advil to Gülizar. Their marriage was founded on their desolation: an orphaned girl for the crippled *boza* vendor. Where did love fit in such a match? Love and life, Advil decided, never swam in the same river.

Their first child, Iskender, was born in the immigrants' hovel, their second child, Hüsniye, in a rented hut. Advil had sworn an oath: he was going to ask his bald wife for one child for each member of his family that he had left behind in Kosovo. One child for each person he was separated from ... including his evil uncle. As the children were born the *boza* in Çarşamba seemed more and more insufficient. The summers grew longer and the winters shorter. The only job Advil knew how to do was to sell *boza*, and even if he could do anything else, who would employ a cripple? Cripples were regarded as cursed in Çarşamba.

Even though Istanbul was big enough to accommodate everyone, from the White Russian refugees to the Jews, it wasn't big enough for Advil. The city gave him claustrophobia. News spread from the Belgian Consulate that they were going to take in immigrants from Kosovo. He queued at the door of the consulate for days in order to apply.

They asked him what his occupation was. Though crippled, Advil was a strapping young man. Unaware that no one with a crippled arm could be a welder, he said, 'I'm a welder.' Eventually the Flemish official whose language he could not speak granted Advil a visa, knowing full well he was not a welder. He gave him a modest sum of money to cover travel expenses.

With his visa in his pocket and his wife, screaming with labour pains, on his back, Advil ran to the hospital. But Gülizar couldn't hold out any longer and they rushed into the toilet of the local mosque where Gülizar gave birth to a baby girl.

'Let's call her Ulviye,' said Advil. 'In Kosovo it means "good woman". Let's hope this girl turns into a good woman.'

Advil entered the mosque, at Gülizar's insistence, to give thanks to the Muslim God. Not only did he now have an Ulviye of his own, but his other prayers had also been answered. Europe meant wealth.

They boarded the train at Sirkeci. They would leave the place where Advil had arrived starving and destitute on foot, by train. It may not have been very grand but they were travelling in an unnumbered compartment, with couchettes and meals. Ulviye fell asleep on Gülizar's lap, swaddled in a dirty multicoloured cloth. There was a family sitting opposite them. All of them were neat and prim, as though they had never belched after a meal, as if their noses had never run, as if they had never given birth in toilets.

The woman asked Gülizar, 'Are you gypsies?'

'Yes,' said Gülizar with an offended, wounded obstinacy, 'we are.'

'The war's been over for some time but they still kill gypsies in Europe, did you know that?' said the woman.

Advil remained silent. They weren't gypsies, they were emigrating to Belgium. No one would kill them.

Their last child, Selviye, was born in 1964 in Brussels, in a prestigious Flemish hospital.

'We can stop having children now,' said Advil to his wife. 'We've had a child for every person I've left behind in Kosovo.'

Advil's favourite child was Ulviye. Everyone knew it and the family accepted it. Ulviye spoke in pidgin Turkish, pidgin Albanian and pidgin French. She was French at school, Turkish at home and Albanian in her father's heart. Advil told Ulviye in Albanian, 'You're my bride who flies on a white horse.'

'What does flying on a white horse mean?' asked Ulviye in Albanian.

'It means dying,' said Advil.

'What's dying?' asked Ulviye.

'Flying,' said Advil.

'I want to fly too,' said Ulviye.

'You can't,' said Advil. 'It's not your turn, you're jumping the queue, you've got a long, long time to live yet.'

'No,' said Ulviye, 'I want to fly.'

'You can't,' said Advil. 'Your father's going to fly first.'

Every time Advil looked at Ulviye he remembered the white-skinned, pink-cheeked girl from the Kalista mountains. He had paid his debt to the murder he had caused – he had made Ulviye immortal. No matter what became of his other daughters he would make Ulviye a princess. He would cleanse himself of the guilt that grew in him like a tumour. He would see that the Ulviye he had brought into the world enjoyed life to the full. That was his biggest ambition, and his biggest secret.

The Albanians in Brussels worked out that Advil, father of nine, immigrant in Schaerbeek, was none other than the Celili of the Kalista mountains whom they'd heard about. The community, anxious to shower its heroes with belated idolatry, clamoured round him.

'The invincible Advil who risked death to escape from the Croatian prison, who fought in the mountains for years for Muslim independence ... the Turkish nationalist whom Turkey smuggled to Istanbul to save him from death.' The legend grew and grew, like a snowball rolling downhill, but it protected Advil, although no matter how hard Advil tried to tell them of his suffering, the people thought he was behaving like an ordinary person to avoid revealing a secret mission. Try as he might, he could not persuade his adoring followers that Turkey had no hand in his fate. Eventually he stopped denying it. Myths don't hurt anyone, he thought. They add a little colour to otherwise dull lives. The myth that grew up around Advil endowed his family with a magical, fairytale power.

Never again did Advil go without money, food or a home: his troubles melted away. He opened up a marble workshop and made gravestones for people of every faith. He hired employees of his own. His house overlooked the front garden, while his workshop overlooked the back garden. The gravestones he was most renowned for were the Ottoman tombstones he made mainly for Muslim customers, and which distinguished the rich from the poor in their community. Even some Christians ordered them.

Advil was now a businessman. He had a profession. He was a respected ambassador between the Turks and Albanians in Belgium. They regarded him as their sage. For his community his crippled arm was no longer a sign of God's wrath but of the test God had set him. He had passed God's test. At the age of forty-five Advil Celili was an esteemed immigrant Muslim leader, whom everyone consulted.

Advil turned his attention to Kosovo and followed the events there. Tito died and Yugoslavia resisted. Walls came down. Yugoslavia resisted. War broke out in Bosnia. Yugoslavia resisted. Advil's home became a meeting place for Kosovans. News flew back and forth, half of which was lost and the other half exaggerated out of all proportion en route.

After so many years of silence from home, a letter arrived from Albania via intermediaries from Kosovo. It was a plea to Advil. 'Take me into your home as your second wife.' He didn't know where to hide Kamile's letter.

The Turks in Belgium had two kinds of wives. There were dark-skinned, plump, village girls with securely covered heads who they had brought from Turkey, and there were plump, blonde, village girls with uncovered heads who they had met in Belgium. Far from resenting one another, the wives got on very well. The children had two mothers. The Turkish mothers gave birth to them, and the Belgian mothers raised them. These children, who were outsiders everywhere – Turks at home, Belgians at school and immigrants in the street – grew up within a strange environment. Their Belgian mothers dressed them up, made them look pretty and took them out, while their Turkish mothers fed and watered and washed them. Turkish girls loved their Belgian mothers best, while Turkish boys preferred their Turkish mothers.

Advil envied the emotional wealth of the children with two

mothers. For years, like a caterpillar, he had woven the fantasy of Kamile into a cocoon in which he encased Gülizar's body. But he could not behave like a Turk. He was Albanian. The mere thought of making love to Kamile made him shudder. An innocent death stood between them. As far as he was concerned, a union with Kamile would be a defiance of the God he had come to believe in.

Advil remained imprisoned in his dreams. Kamile held out a lock of auburn hair to him, saying, 'Don't forget my scent,' and he never did forget. Every time he made love to Gülizar he called her Kamile. Advil's heart was as closed towards his wife, who had mothered his nine children, as a sunflower that shuts its petals when the sun goes in. Like a soothsayer, he gazed into the crystal ball of his memory and read his future from his past. He would wait until the next life for Kamile. Gülizar never discovered Kamile's identity. She found it strangely arousing when her husband called her Kamile during their lovemaking. She was not shy in bed, but as brazen as the Belgian second wife at their neighbour's house.

Gülizar said, 'I want you to take a second wife. She can teach the children French and Flemish.' Advil was flustered, suspecting that she might have read Kamile's letter, but then he reminded himself that Gülizar could neither read nor write, and even if she could, he knew she couldn't read Albanian. He barely managed to struggle free from the grip of his guilty conscience. Had Ulviye perhaps read his letter? No, Ulviye wouldn't do that. She was her father's princess, she would never do anything to hurt him.

'I won't smell any other rose but you, Gülizar,' Advil said, 'and besides, the girls can already speak French and Flemish.'

That night Advil dreamt that the roof of his house was on fire. Albanians believe that if the roof of their house burns it is a sign of the imminent death of a family member.

All night long he wept. Would Afrim, his youngest, weakest son, die? Afrim was very frail. When he had told Advil's fortune with scattered beans, his Bosnian fellow prisoner had said, 'Some of your children will die.' It couldn't be Iskender, he was handsome and swarthy and as strong as a lion.

If Afrim died Gülizar would die with him. Gülizar doted on Afrim the same way Advil doted on Ulviye. Ulviye was the only one of the five daughters who had turned out to be a true Albanian. The whole family knew and accepted it. Ulviye couldn't even speak Turkish properly. But her Albanian was flawless. Exactly as if she had been born and bred in the Kalista mountains.

Afrim, even though his name was Albanian, was the only one of their four sons who was a Turk down to the last drop of his blood. Gülizar had brought him up that way. He was Gülizar's secret compatriot. The whole family knew and accepted it. Afrim couldn't even speak Albanian properly. But his Turkish was flawless. Exactly as if he had been born and bred in Çarşamba. Gülizar wouldn't be able to stand it if anything happened to Afrim. Advil and Gülizar had stood by while their other children fell prey to the lax Belgian morals, but they marked out those two children for different treatment.

The following morning Advil was convinced that his dream was an ill omen. Gülizar flew into a panic and summoned the dream interpreter to the house. The woman rushed over knowing that she would receive a generous tip and besides, it was a great honour to be summoned by Advil.

One of the daughters, Hüsniye, served her coffee together with a glass of water on a tray. The woman bided her time. She knew that the neighbourhood worshipped Advil, but his daughters were dragging their father's and older brothers' honour through the dirt. They were attractive, flirtatious girls who were courted by the entire neighbourhood. They pranced around in tiny miniskirts showing their legs; they wore plunging necklines that revealed their cleavages and they got up to God knows what with infidel boys.

It was time someone told their father.

The young boys in the neighbourhood were like rutting beasts. The flighty girls with long black hair and provocative make-up were Albanian, but considered Turkish. They were giving the Turkish nation a bad name. The young boys in the neighbourhood couldn't defy Advil, but the wise woman, the interpreter of dreams, was looking for an opportunity to act as a mediator between the sex-crazed young neighbourhood men and the Albanian girls. Gülizar's request for the dream interpreter to come to their house was perfectly timed.

The woman sipped her coffee and dropped coloured buttons, chickpeas and pebbles into the water. She listened in silence as Advil described his dream. Advil's heart constricted. He was sure that the interpretation would describe bad news from Kosovo. And he had believed unquestioningly in fortune-tellers ever since his fellow prisoner had predicted he would escape and have nine children.

Gülizar sensed what would happen. She wanted to invent some pretext for getting rid of the woman. But it was too late.

The dream interpreter spoke. 'Your daughter slept with this man,' she said. She pointed at the coloured buttons in the water and said, 'Look, that's the man.' Advil leaned over the water but couldn't make out a male form, although he couldn't pretend he hadn't heard. If he did, his life among his people would be ruined that very day. In Schaerbeek prestige is a tenuous and capricious thing. Advil's eyes clouded over. 'Which daughter?' he wondered. 'Hüsniye, Emriye, Filiz, Selviye? Which one?'

He didn't realise that he had left one daughter out. Even if he had realised, he knew that Ulviye wasn't the girl to get mixed up in that kind of thing. She was charmed. The fortune-teller was well aware that she was the most beautiful and the most beloved of all his daughters and Advil wouldn't hear a word said against her.

The woman knew that Muslims have a high regard for silence. She was silent for an eternity. And then she said, 'I can't say for sure,

I can only see the first letter ... it's either a U or a G ... God considers the letter U lucky.'

She stopped speaking for a moment. She passed her hand over the tiny ripples in the water and pointed out the letters U and G in Arabic. She said nothing more, she had said enough.

Advil rose. He put on his boots and slipped a knife inside one of them. Iskender rose to his feet in silence. He removed the knife from his father's boot.

'Father, this is my job, you go and sit on the couch and drink your coffee,' he said.

Advil sat back down without a word. By doing so he had given Iskender his consent. But Iskender wasn't certain which of his sisters had entered the *haram* bed. He looked at his mother, but Gülizar had stuffed the white lace of her head cover inside her mouth and was weeping silently.

Hüsniye froze. She knew what was about to happen. She wanted to warn her sister, but couldn't. It would be impossible for her to reach the restaurant where Emriye worked before Iskender did. How had the dream interpreter known? Hüsniye was unaware of all the gossip; she believed the woman had second sight. She was sure the woman meant Emriye, because Emriye wasn't a virgin.

The woman couldn't have been referring to her, because she was respectably married to a lathe operator from Emirdağ, who later became a supermarket owner. Her womanhood was legitimate. The others may have fooled around, but their virginity was intact. Hüsniye knew because the girls told each other everything.

She knew exactly how Emriye had lost her virginity, because it had been her own husband who had raped her. Emriye was so pretty and so alluring. Her husband thought that girls who were pretty and alluring were whores, just like Belgian girls. And he thought that if they wore make-up and short skirts and revealed their cleavage, they were asking to be raped. The moment a suitor appeared for Emriye she was planning to have her hymen artificially reconstructed by a French doctor, so she would go to her husband's house a virgin. But there had been no suitors so far.

Hüsniye remained rooted to the spot. She could not reach Emriye before Iskender and she was terrified that Iskender would kill her and that, as Emriye died, she would confess everything. When Iskender discovered the truth he would kill Hüsniye's husband too. Because the truth was that Hüsniye had discovered her sister and her husband, Hakan, naked in her own bed. But she had forgiven her husband and she had not cut off ties with her sister either. If she had, she knew her husband would have beaten her as well as Emriye until they were both senseless. Hüsniye neither wanted to be beaten, nor did she want to be a widow. Their lives were safe as long as the secret remained a secret.

If he had had his way Hakan would have liked to bed both sisters at once, but Hüsniye had said, 'Over my dead body. You're free to do what you like, but don't expect me to lie in your defiled bed. Apart from divorcing me you can do whatever you like.'

Emriye's difficulty had been that no one would have believed that she had slept with her brother-in-law unwillingly. People in Schaerbeek and those from Emirdağ believe no one would accost a decent girl. If a girl lost her virginity it was thought that she wanted to lose it. If she had been more forthright in her refusal Hakan would have nonetheless established her as a whore to the whole world. Her sister Hüsniye was in a strong position against her husband, but Emriye's position was weak. To safeguard her sister's marriage and her family's prestige in the community's eyes, and to avoid having the finger pointed at her, Emriye had bowed her head and submitted to the rape. She had tearfully explained this to her sister a thousand times.

Emriye would die, the rapist Hakan would die, Iskender would go to prison and Hüsniye would be condemned to widowhood. In

Brussels it was almost impossible even for young girls from Schaerbeek to find a husband. It was out of the question for widows. Belgians were afraid to marry them because they were Turks and mainland Turks snubbed them as 'Belgian tarts'.

All the Turks with eligible sons put their money together and sent a matchmaker to Turkey. Video camera in hand, the matchmaker would go from village to village. The girls of marriageable age would deck themselves out in their finest clothes, make themselves up and try to look alluring on camera. If the people watching them in Brussels chose them it would be the answer to all their prayers. They would go to Europe as brides. To freedom, money, society ... they had to make sure they looked neither too flighty nor too straight-laced in front of the camera; whoever was watching mustn't think, 'She looks loose,' but neither should they think, 'She looks as though she'd sour the milk.' They had to strike the right balance between flirtatiousness and sensible behaviour.

The matchmaker's return to Schaerbeek unleashed a whirlwind of food preparation and invitations. The senior members of the family would be the first to watch. To spite the infidel girls of Brussels, who had relinquished their virginity on drunken nights, they selected untarnished brides for their sons. The young men would get together in secret and watch the videos amid raucous laughter and crude commentary. But the family, not the young men, had the final say. There was no need to wait around for a visa. They merely had to hand over a month's wages to the network and the girl would be brought over. Before even three months were up they would be serving their guests with lemonade and cake at their wedding, which would take place with *davul* and *zurna** in Schaerbeek's biggest banqueting suite.

Hüsniye never regarded herself as a Turk. The peasants in Schaerbeek didn't consider her a Turk either. Instead of selecting

---

*   Drums and horns, usually played during weddings.

her husband from the matchmaker's supply she chose her own, a Brussels-born young man of Afyon origin. Before their marriage Hakan's family did everything in their power to make Hüsniye's life miserable. They would have married their son to his cousin if this Albanian whore hadn't led him astray. Although they didn't prevent the marriage outright they made the couple rue the day they got married. They cut Hakan off from his share of the money they had saved up and they cut him off from his share of the state benefits they had hoarded. They sold the döner kebab restaurant they had opened for him. Hüsniye was never accepted into the family and she bitterly regretted marrying him, but after a while she stopped caring, and got on with her life.

Yet still she shuddered at the possibility of the end of this marriage that had cost her so much hardship, because of the fortune-teller's allegation. She dreaded living as a widow among these accursed, gossip-mongering peasants.

Late one night Emriye had told her sister about the first time Hakan had raped her. Hakan's supermarket was two blocks away from their house. During the day, after the sons had gone to work, Advil to the mosque and Gülizar to recite the *zikir*, Emriye would give her brother-in-law a hand at the shop. It had started with him occasionally fondling her breasts and stroking her thighs. Emriye had enjoyed it at first. After all, it wasn't likely to go any further. Then Hakan closed the supermarket and locked the doors on the pretext of doing a stock take. Behind locked doors he raped Emriye over and over again.

'Which of your uncircumcised queers has it in him to screw a bird every hour?' he boasted.

Hakan had been born in Brussels but his soul belonged in Emirdağ. For him it was a foregone conclusion that no woman could resist a man. And he was right. Because even though she put up a fight at the beginning, Hakan soon became an inseparable part of Emriye's life. She had stopped working at the supermarket and found a job at a restaurant, but Hakan continued to molest her at every available opportunity. Emriye was incapable of putting a stop to it.

Hakan's threat to tell the inhabitants of Schaerbeek that Emriye had entered his bed of her own free will resigned her to the situation. Hakan did whatever he liked and Emriye accepted anything he imposed on her.

His roughness, the pleasure he took in humiliating her during sex, the way he beat her, the fine line he drew between sex and pain, had taken over her enforced womanhood. When her sister didn't protest, the two of them, bearing the burden of their shared secret, began to live like co-wives.

And yet Hüsniye did not wish death on her husband.

'Dear God,' she prayed. 'I beg you, save Emriye from Iskender. That way you will save my husband too.'

But God had turned a deaf ear to Hüsniye's pleas. Iskender ran into the house, closely followed by his brothers Enver, Afrim and Mithat, marching Emriye before him, a knife at her throat. They had beaten her in the restaurant and were planning to kill her in the house. Her clothes were in tatters and she had two black eyes. The blood that trickled from her nose had dried on her upper lip.

Iskender flung Emriye down before their father. He had always walked with his head bowed in Schaerbeek. He had always had a vague suspicion that his sisters weren't proper Turkish girls, and they had always made him ashamed. He had been prepared for what was about to happen for some time.

Iskender said, 'We're going straight to the doctor's to find out whether she's a virgin. If she's not I'm going to kill her.'

'I am a virgin, Father,' whimpered Emriye. 'Don't believe the fortune-teller. Iskender doesn't believe me, but you at least can believe me.'

Advil felt his heart constrict. If he forgave his daughter his son would revolt, if he didn't he would never recover from the grief. The image of an immortal girl saying 'Drink that, it will cool you down,' flashed before his eyes.

But Advil believed the fortune-teller. Fortune-tellers had been able to predict every last detail of his life. Love and tradition struggled in his heart. He knew that what he was about to do would put an end to all his dreams and slowly kill him at the same time.

Feebly, he said, 'Fortune-tellers don't lie. But Emriye's name doesn't begin with G, let go of my daughter, Iskender.' With a heavy thud Emriye fell onto the rug like a sack.

Emriye's hand went to her throat. For years afterwards, whenever anyone picked up a knife she would shudder. She would never be able to hold a knife again; and to avoid losing her mind she would get rid of all the knives in her house.

'You don't have a daughter whose name begins with G, you have one whose name begins with U, her name's Ulviye!' yelled Iskender. 'Seeing as you believe this slut, you'd better start looking at her!'

'That's right!' wailed Emriye, 'Ulviye's the one to blame!' She was certain Ulviye would turn out to be a virgin and escape from her murderers.

The light left Advil's eyes. The disaster would not be over before it claimed a victim.

'Bring her here,' he said.

Iskender fetched Ulviye.

Hüsniye thought she would faint. Emriye had been saved, her husband had been saved, but who would save Ulviye?

Hüsniye hid in the toilet and rang her husband. She told him in rushed, frightened whispers how he had narrowly escaped death.

'Promise me you'll never touch Emriye again,' she said. 'Look, God saved you, you must have once done something good to deserve it. Everything was just about to come to light.'

Hakan slammed the telephone down. He had ended up with the ugliest of the five daughters. He had resented this for a long time.

Hüsniye had trapped him. But he had the others in his power. He would work his way through all of them, one by one. His mind was set on Ulviye, but he knew he couldn't touch her. He knew she was Advil's sacred child. So Hakan chased all thought of Ulviye from his mind and cast his eye on the youngest daughter, Selviye. He knew he needed to be patient, but because he was the only son-in-law in the house, the girl stood no chance of escaping him. In any case he was sure that sooner or later she was bound to give her virginity to some Frenchman in a bar. These wayward girls knew nothing of fearing their father, or respecting their family's reputation.

After Hüsniye's telephone call Hakan ran out of the supermarket. He knew he must take control of the situation before the girls' tongues were loosened.

While Hakan was on his way home, Advil whispered affectionately to Ulviye, 'Come. Let's go to the doctor. As long as he says you're a virgin we can forget all about this.'

'I am a virgin father,' stammered Ulviye, but her voice was trembling and full of hopelessness.

Gülizar watched what was happening in deadly silence. She felt as though she no longer knew the daughters she had given birth to. She had tried so hard to instil moral values in them but what could she say to Iskender if it turned out to be true that they had squandered their virginity? Gülizar felt as if she had lost her daughters; all she asked now was that the disaster would not affect Afrim.

Advil opened their heavy front door. Ulviye walked out in front of him. While he bent down to look for his shoes among the rows lined up outside, Ulviye too was crouched over the shoes. Then she fell to the ground. She must have stumbled while putting on her shoes, Advil thought. He leaned over her.

He saw a thin trail of blood running between the rows of women's shoes. He realised that it was coming from Ulviye, and that she was lying on the ground. The blood would not stop; it flowed more and more freely, dying the immigrants' battered shoes red.

Advil raised his head. His son-in-law, Hakan, was standing before him, holding a gun. Advil could not say a word. Hakan had shot his daughter. Advil hadn't even heard the gunshot.

Iskender hurriedly pushed his father aside and ushered Hakan inside.

'Hüsniye told me she was soiled,' said Hakan. 'That her virginity was tarnished.'

'Be quiet, don't speak,' said Iskender. 'You've cleansed our honour. If you hadn't done it I would have shot her.'

Lovingly Iskender removed the gun from Hakan's hand. He sat him down on the couch where, in her silent reverie, Gülizar had neither heard the gunshot nor realised that her daughter was dead. She had retreated from the world.

Iskender took responsibility for the murder. He voluntarily turned himself in to the Schaerbeek police. The Turkish journalists took Iskender's photograph. They rushed the news to the Istanbul press under the headline 'Condolences for Your Misfortune'.

Iskender went to prison; the post-mortem showed Ulviye to be a virgin, and the murderer was roaming free in Advil's home. Secrets were held within secrets in Advil's house and Ulviye's sisters knew that Ulviye had fallen victim to a false accusation. Hüsniye knew that Hakan had violated Emriye's virginity. The Turks knew that Hakan had committed the murder. Hakan knew why he had committed it. The Belgian police did not know why Iskender had killed his sister. Gülizar knew that Ulviye hadn't slept with anyone.

The subject of rape was taboo in the family and in the neighbourhood as well. It was as though everyone had taken a vow of silence. They also knew that if they discussed it, it would be Emriye and not Hakan who would be found guilty because the strongly held belief in Advil's family and in the community was that it was impossible for a man to lay a finger on a woman who hadn't encouraged him. They also knew that if they talked about it, another murder would have been inevitable: Advil's sons would have felt forced to kill Emriye too. So, without a word being spoken, they agreed that one victim was enough and that the best thing to do was to act as though they knew nothing about the rape. But they all knew that they all knew.

Emriye and Filiz were hastily married off, as though they had been put up for auction. Emriye didn't even have an opportunity to have her hymen reconstructed. Advil sent word to the Schaerbeek Turks and ordered husbands for his daughters who had Belgian passports. Before nightfall on the day Advil put the word out, his house was packed with contenders. They all had nephews and brothers back home clamouring for the chance to come to Europe. Advil's daughters, with Belgian citizenship, were attractive and provocative, who wouldn't have them? It would be like winning the lottery.

Advil chose a couple of husbands at random. One of his new sons-in-law had been crippled by childhood paralysis and had entered Belgium illegally through the network; he had no residence permit. Emriye was disgusted by his discoloured teeth and wouldn't allow him anywhere near her. Since he had killed Ulviye she hadn't allowed Hakan anywhere near her either. She despised the men around her. She dispatched her husband, who could neither speak French nor find his way around, to work at the Turkish kebab houses in Place de la Reine, while she spent her days shopping at the Grand Place.

Gülizar did not interfere with what was going on but the whole Celili household was plunged into mourning and Advil's prestige rose to legendary heights. In that community, mourning was as effective as silence when it came to raising prestige. Advil was now thought of as something between a sage and a *mehdi*.* His mourning was permanent, but it was through his mourning that he managed to find peace.

---

*   According to Islam, he will be the last prophet to descend to Earth.

Ulviye's body was sent to Kosovo, to be buried in soil she had never set eyes on. Advil oversaw the making of her gravestone himself. On it he had inscribed in Albanian: 'Here lie two Ulviyes in a single body'. Not knowing Albanian, Gülizar didn't understand the words; she mistook them for Albanian prayers.

Advil gave his sons very precise instructions. They were to bury Ulviye in Drachka, on the slope of the Kalista mountains, beside her grandfather whom she had never seen. Enver telephoned from Kosovo. He said that there were no mountains of that name in Albania, no village and no grave.

Advil looked out onto Place de la Reine from his window and sighed. Even if Tito had destroyed his father's grave and the village, how could he have destroyed such huge mountains? Was the mountain range he had kept alive in his memory for the past forty years nothing but a fantasy?

He didn't tell Enver what he was thinking. He simply gave him the address of an elderly woman called Kamile. There was no need to keep Kamile a secret in his life anymore.

Once his sons located Kamile they located Drachka too. The treacherous uncle had gone mad, and kept ranting, 'Advil is going to come and kill me.' When he caught sight of the stocky Enver he mistook him for Advil and died of fright. Enver asked Kamile to recite a prayer against the evil eye, because there were 'black clouds floating above our heads'.

Because she had never married, Kamile was regarded as a saint in Drachka. Her mourning was permanent. Through her mourning she too had managed to find peace. Kamile was also regarded as something between a female saint and a male *mehdi*. She had a prayer to guard against every malediction, a breath to blow away every evil eye.

Enver telephoned his father again. 'My condolences, Father, your uncle's dead.' Ulviye and her uncle were buried in the same grave on the same day. The boys returned to Belgium. Advil made Enver tell him about Drachka and Kamile. As he listened his lame arm hung limply from his shoulder.

Advil had grown very thin. Gülizar knew her husband was exhausted, and she recited prayers for him. Their dream-interpreter neighbour was banned from their home. As was their son-in-law, Hakan. In his turn, Hakan banned Advil and his family from shopping at his supermarket. No one declared these prohibitions; they simply happened. It seemed that destiny was at work.

Only Afrim and Mithat remained at home. Iskender was in prison. Enver had married. Hüsniye had become a mother. Filiz was about to give birth and Emriye had become a slut. Selviye had gone to Lyon and was living in sin with a Frenchman.

Gülizar refused to speak, but Afrim still filled her with pride. He was so handsome, he was the image of Advil Celili's youth. Her daughters had not brought her any joy, but Afrim would. Afrim's existence gave Gülizar the strength that kept her going, after years of living like a Turk who had been forced to become Albanian. Because she had raised him as a Turk, Gülizar felt that all those silent years of her life had not been in vain. Turks call Albanians Turks, but Gülizar knew they were very far from it. Even if hundreds of years passed, Albanians could never be Turks. But Gülizar felt that she had given birth to a pure Turk, even if he had been fathered by an Albanian man.

Afrim had found a job in the Moroccan district. He was making good money. Each day he came home a little later. Gülizar was pleased. He was such a good son, so respectful, deferring to his elders, like a true Turk. He took care of Iskender too. Gülizar had been too poor to be a proper bride with a veil draped with silver thread. She had had to marry off her daughters as if they had been widows. But this time, God willing, she was going to find Afrim a pure, untainted girl from Turkey and give him a spectacular wedding.

As time went by Advil found it more and more difficult to sleep.

Gülizar wished her husband would go back to the dreams he used to have: the ones he'd tried to keep secret from her for so many years. But her pride prevented her from saying so.

Advil heard something and got up. He said, 'May it bode well, inshallah, what's a police car doing at our door?'

Gülizar put her headscarf over her bald head, that not even her sons had ever seen. She ran and opened the door before Advil could reach it. The blond, Flemish policemen looked as though they had escaped from a film set. One of them said something in French. Gülizar didn't speak a single word of French. Mithat came and joined her, sleepily.

'Darling, it's the police, can you see what they want?' said Gülizar.

No one had ever heard her string so many words together at once.

The policeman handed them Afrim's wallet. Before he was even fully awake Mithat translated for his mother. During his bleary-eyed translation he began to weep. A Moroccan thug had slit Afrim's throat in a fight. The Moroccan had caught his sister in Afrim's arms in a bar. According to the police Afrim hadn't even had a chance to stand up.

Advil cried out, 'The Arabs stabbed the Ottomans in the back, and now they've stabbed my son. A century later those tent-dwelling Arab dogs have stabbed another Ottoman. They're never satisfied.'

One by one the neighbours' lights came on. Silent men and lamenting women pushed the police aside and entered the house. The wailing grew louder, but Advil and Gülizar were too stunned to cry.

The window above the forbidden supermarket opened. Hüsniye and her two children cried out and then they ran, Hüsniye in the lead, Hakan behind and the children between them. Enver had already arrived. The police requested that a member of the family accompany them to the scene of the crime.

They lit the stove in the kitchen. 'Prepare soup,' said Advil. 'Distribute soup to the poor.'

'There aren't any poor in Belgium father,' said Filiz. Advil had no idea when she had arrived.

'Distribute soup,' said Advil, his voice icy. They boiled soup on all the rings of the stove. And so, at break of day, instead of *helva*, the sweetmeat of the dead, bowls of hot soup in porcelain bowls were distributed from Advil's house.

The dream-interpreter melted a bullet in a small ladle. She was going to pour it into water in a copper dish to make it sizzle and, according to the forms it took, it would chase away disaster from the house. She brought a large dish to banish the disasters in every corner. She opened the windows, so the disasters the dream-interpreter chased away could fly out.

Advil dreamed of Ulviye and Afrim. Afrim was riding a white horse. Ulviye asked, 'What does riding on a white horse mean?'

'It means dying,' said Afrim.

'What's dying?' asked Ulviye.

'Flying,' said Afrim. 'It's not your turn Ulviye,' Afrim said in his dream. 'Advil Celili's going to fly first.'

10

PAPATYA

Out of all the convicts I had met he was the best-groomed one. He was a light brunette about forty years old. I thought he was southern but his accent was from the east. I thought his family was probably one of the many that migrated to work in the cotton industry. He treated me with exaggerated respect, but did not seem to be timid like the other convicts. His eyes were so full of compassion that if I had met him anywhere else I would find it hard to believe he was a murderer. With some of the other convicts I had to fight the urge to cut the interview short. The man in front of me, however, seemed as though he was not the murderer but the man who had caught the murderer. I soon found out that I was not wrong – I would see that he had managed to catch the murderer inside himself.

Before we met, he sent me a legendary Cukurova breakfast with fresh bread and fresh tea. I would learn much later that he managed to pay for this himself. Only an inmate who carried great weight in the prison could send his guests such gifts.

The prison guard who brought the breakfast also made clear his conditions for allowing us to see him. We would conceal his face and identity and in return we could publish the story. I agreed, and named him Battal with his permission. In a few minutes the signed permission document came.

Ceyhan Agriculture Prison had been built on the abundant Cukurova plains. The prisoners worked as farmers, earning some money and, rather than killing time in their prison cells, they fed their souls with the calming work of the land. I, however, thought they were trying to bury the stories of dead girls and women in the ground.

In the agricultural prison's vast grounds we sat on the wet grass under spring trees that were in bud. I thanked Battal for his gifts. He was embarrassed by our gratitude. We seemed more like friends celebrating the coming of spring than journalists interviewing a prisoner. But as we talked, the spirit of friendship waned and a troubled wind began to blow.

He had killed his sister, who was fifteen years younger than he was, because she fled to a married stranger. If she had gone somewhere where 'there could be a family' he might have forgiven her but she didn't, therefore neither could he absolve her. The scum she fled to failed to protect her honour.

Of course he did not regret it. If he was let out and the same circumstances arose, he would do it again. His only regret was that he left the scum who misled his sister alive.

Every time he remembered his sister he became so angry with himself for not killing this man that he hit his head against the wall and on some occasions he wounded himself. With time he stopped the physical self-abuse but the anger in his heart still burned.

He stopped every once in a while and looked at me to see the effect of what he said. He only continued the story when he was satisfied with my reaction. He was hoping that I would understand, that I might even condone what he had done. If I did, perhaps the dread in his heart would lighten and fate would be the one to blame. Even though he believed what he did was right, he could not find peace.

He was almost begging for someone credible to say, 'You're right, you had to kill her.'

He felt deep anger towards girls who ran away from their homes and families because they thought they were in love.

'The girls don't talk because they are scared. If they don't fear us and talk to us we will find a solution. In fact you need to start when they are children. You need to talk to them not as a son or daughter, not as a sister, but as a friend. You need to be able to talk to them about things like being in love, marriage, creating a home; about honour!

'The girls fall in love and don't talk. They think, "If I tell my brother or my father they won't allow it so I'd better run." Within six months they start to regret what they have done but by then it is too late. How can you forgive them? They stepped on your pride, your honour, your dignity.

'If this girl I killed came to me and said, "I love this man," I would have dissuaded her and would not have had to kill her.' He spoke of his sister as 'this girl I killed'. 'I would have explained to her that she gave her heart to the wrong person, that she could not spend her life with him, that she would be thrown out into the streets in a few months, that our family pride would be hurt; I would have persuaded her. But she didn't tell me. She hid her secret!'

It was as if he was explaining himself to his dead sister, not to me. All of a sudden he stopped. His throat was dry, his voice deeper. He gazed into space. Who knows what point of his life he was remembering. Suddenly he started speaking again.

'You are left with a choice between your honour and your sister. You must choose one. You either destroy your honour or your sister. If you don't choose the latter you can't walk amongst those around you as a man. What do we live for anyway? Why, except to live like a true man?'

Papatya, which means Daisy, was the youngest girl of the house. She had no memories of her father. He died before she was born. Her notion of a father consisted only of a picture above her mother's *çeyiz*** chest. But life had given her a new father, her older brother. Their houses were separate and he had two daughters older than her and two younger sons but she felt more like their friends than their aunt.

Her sister-in-law, who was also her cousin, was the most kind-hearted person she knew. She worked hard all day, and cooked for the family but wouldn't allow Papatya to help her so she could focus completely on her schoolwork. But Papatya did not want to study. School was hard work and boring. Her family, though, was very persistent. They said, 'Study, and have a golden bracelet on your arm.' The golden bracelet meant a profession but the golden bracelet Papatya was dreaming of was the one that she would be given on her wedding day.

She thought about telling her big brother but she was hesitant. Her brother was a respected and much-liked cotton worker. Others showed him so much respect that there was the air of a holy man surrounding him. She was reluctant to ask him questions, let alone tell him what she thought. She couldn't even bring herself to ask him whether she should prepare food or hold his towel or whether to bring hot water for his feet.

Even so he was very understanding. When his oldest daughter told him she did not want to go to school any more he took her out of school without any fuss. They were not giving Papatya the same chance, however. Papatya hated women to be involved in men's affairs and school was a man's affair!

What she hated more than school was her name. It was an embarrassing name. Other girls had familiar names like Ayşe, Fatma, Elif and Zeynep. She thought she was the last girl in the world that

---

*   In Anatolia, girls start preparing for marriage from childhood. The term *çeyiz* refers to the trousseaux girls start putting away to bring to their new house with marriage.

should be named Papatya. She was very dark compared to the snow-white daisies she was named after. The young children of the neighbourhood constantly chased her, mocking her with a rhyme they had invented: 'Papatya, Papatya, are you an insect or a flower?'

According to her mother, the father whose face Papatya had never seen loved the name Papatya, which was also the name of his commander's daughter when he was enlisted in the military. Her mother named all of Papatya's sisters with Muslim names, but in memory of her husband, who had died a few days before her birth, had named her Papatya.

In the school that she hated, she never paid attention in class but instead thought for hours about what she would name her children. She made a promise to herself that she was going to name them the most familiar name of the region – if it was a boy, Mehmet; if it was a girl, Ayşe. She was going to have children as soon as she was married anyway.

She had already found the love of her life and only shared this secret with her best friend Elif. He was the most handsome man in the world. She had already started to meet him in secret, pretending that she was going to school.

The day she met him, her mother had sent her to deliver food to the school for Eid. The unmarried teachers lived in the school dormitories. Her mother had not wanted the teachers to be left wanting during Eid and had sent a large tray of *baklava* and a large piece of sheep rump. The teachers, on the other hand, thought that she made such kind gestures to arouse sympathy, because the old lady sent food and desserts every chance she got.

Her heart's desire was for her daughter to become a teacher. She believed girls who did not study became slaves to their husbands' money. Almost every day, sometimes more than once in a day, like *zikir*, she would repeat to her girls the benefits of becoming a teacher. Papatya could not understand how her mother, who did not even know how to read and write, came to the conclusion that her daughters should work.

After delivering the heavy tray, Papatya was walking out the school gate when she caught a glimpse of a man walking in. He was tall and handsome. Their eyes met and Papatya instantly turned away. She did not want the handsome man to think she was a 'light girl'.* Even so she blushed bright red from shame.

She ran to Elif's house. She had to tell someone. She was struck by the young man whose eyes she had met for an instant. Elif was in love with her auntie's son. But they had it easy. Because they were relatives they could walk into each other's houses and nobody suspected a thing. Even if they were suspected it was always more understandable to be in love with a cousin than to be in love with someone whose identity was dubious, Papatya thought, with a hint of envy.

Just walking in town with another boy or man was enough for rumours to spread. As soon as rumours of this sort began, a young girl's life was over. 'Her death is more welcome than her name being stained,' a member of her family had confessed. But even with this great danger all of her friends had lovers. With a strange talent they managed to keep their lovers hidden in this little town under the watchful gazes of the elders.

Even though they were close friends Elif was very different from Papatya. She had sworn that she would not get married before finishing school. She wanted to become a teacher and leave this town to start a new life in a city with her cousin.

They went to the garden in front of the house. Because it was Eid everyone had worn their best clothes and were about to start a round of visits to neighbours, friends and family members. While Papatya was telling her friend about her 'encounter' with the handsome man in excited whispers, she noticed that he was standing across the street

---

* A Turkish phrase meaning sexually promiscuous.

watching her. Her heart almost stopped. He had followed her. She poked Elif and showed her with great happiness.

Elif was scared. She ran dragging Papatya along with her. If anyone noticed that a stranger was watching girls it could turn into a bloody street war. Last year the most ill-fated girl in the neighbourhood had been killed, along with a young man who had been following her in the middle of the street.

As Papatya drifted home daydreaming, she knew she was being followed. Once home, she saw that the young members of the family had come to kiss the hands of the elders. Her sister-in-law was in the kitchen preparing the sacrificed sheep. Her mother asked, 'Did you give the sacrificed meat to your teachers?' and Papatya had replied, 'Yes,' whilst peeking from behind the net curtain and watching the young man who had followed her walking from one end of the street to the other. The stranger knew that he was being watched and kept gazing at the window. Papatya had been caught by the storm of love.

The man began following Papatya from home to school almost every day. They had not uttered a single word to one another; they didn't even know each other's names. Papatya was scared that they would be caught and wanted to tell him to stop following her. Even if a suspicious person in the street did not catch the attention of her mother, it was bound to be noticed by the gossiping neighbours who liked to add a bit of their own to a story before telling it.

They first had a chance to speak three weeks later. On one of the days she was being followed she had turned around and said, 'Stop following me, if my brother sees he will kill us both.' To this the young man had replied, 'Then tell me of somewhere we can meet.' Papatya hastily suggested the patisserie, the only place she knew.

The two-storey patisserie's owner had allocated the second floor as a 'family lounge' to the hundreds of students who had secrets to keep from their families. Only men with female companions could enter the 'family lounge' and a waiter always stood on watch for teachers who might try to see if any of his or her students were smoking or behaving immorally.

The students who were with their lovers would swap seats at a miraculous pace when they heard the waiter shouting, 'Our family lounge is upstairs, sir, come in.' The boys would sit with boys, the girls with girls. It was the safest location against such danger. Elif had gone there a few times with her lover.

She set a date but regretted it right away. She had agreed to meet with someone whose name she did not even know; it would surely cause him to think less of her. The night descended into a nightmare as she kept thinking about how she had degraded herself.

In the morning her regret was replaced by impatient excitement. She faked a sick note for the school and signed it in her illiterate mother's name. She ran to Elif's house begging her to skive off school. Elif gave in after little protest. She was also wondering what her friend's lover was like.

When the two girls went upstairs in the patisserie, he had not arrived yet. Papatya did not smoke but to avoid looking like a rookie amongst the experienced regulars she lit up a cigarette. By the time her lover arrived her eyes had turned red from the cigarette smoke.

They began talking as if they had known each other for a very long time. His name was Emin. Papatya disliked his name as much as she disliked her own. But he was so handsome Papatya forgave his vulgar name and behaviour. It had been only a few minutes since they met but he was already caressing her under the table. Papatya was shaking with delight; she had found the man of her life.

She left school, replacing it with Emin. Instead of going to class she went to the patisserie, imagining the first time they would make love. Because Emin did not have any money, she paid for their drinks and food with the generous pocket money her brother gave her and slipped the change in his pocket.

When they first held hands and when they first kissed, her body had been taken over by a wild, passionate fire and she yearned constantly for that pleasure. When the patisserie was less full they kissed with a youthful lust.

One day when she was called to school she became very scared, but the school board informed her that due to her poor attendance she was expelled. She was immensely happy. She finally had an excuse against her mother's pressure: she wanted the school but the school didn't want her, she reasoned.

When she got home her mother looked terrible. She had been crying. They had already called her from the school. In tears the old woman said, 'Your brother said, "Let's not force her to study, let's marry her instead," but you will regret leaving school!'

With the privilege accorded the youngest child, Papatya threw a tantrum. She did not want to be married. In truth she did want to marry but not a man of her brother's choosing. Of course she couldn't say that to her mother. But her mother guessed that Papatya was in love. She said, 'Whoever you are meeting with, tell him to come and ask for your hand in marriage. Leave this house with your honour as a bride before your brother learns of it.' In despair she added, 'If you had studied, then you would have been free; girls who finish school can marry whoever they want but you never understood that.' Her voice was barely audible.

But Papatya was too happy to take in what her mother had just said. She gave Emin the good news. It would take a few months at most for her to be a bride and leave her house with her *çeyiz*.

Emin looked frozen. It was obvious he never expected this. He couldn't answer the girl who was so excited that she was mixing up words. Papatya realised something was wrong and begged him, 'I let

it slip to my mother; if you don't ask for my hand I will be ruined.'
Emin replied with a weak tone of voice, 'We can simply run away, and
that will settle it.' Papatya started to get angry, 'Why are you making
this so difficult? Tell your mother to come to our house and ask for
my hand in marriage, they will allow it!' Emin remained silent for
some time. At last he kissed her on the cheek and left.

All of a sudden she realised that she knew nothing about Emin.
Where did he live, who was his father, what did he do? All of these
questions began to run through her head. She was worried. Her lack of
foresight unsettled her soul. But it was too late to begin worrying.

From then on the meetings only took place because Papatya
begged him. Emin was reluctant to meet and did not even consider
sending his mother to ask for Papatya's hand. At their last meeting
Papatya took a few of her belongings with her. The shopkeeper, the
butcher, the greengrocer – everyone in town except her family knew
about her relationship with Emin. She could no longer turn back.
Her brother had been looking for men who held a job to honourably
marry Papatya before rumours began to circulate.

With her few belongings in her hand she begged Emin to abduct
her. He did not reply. He knew if he sent her back he could be in
trouble. But if she came willingly he had a chance to save himself.
He began walking in front of her. Papatya started to follow him, not
knowing the end that awaited her.

Emin did not utter a word to her the whole journey. Papatya
thought he had been uneasy about marriage because he couldn't afford
it. In order to get him back to his old self she told him that she was sure
her brother would forgive her soon and cover the cost of the wedding.
This, however, did not cheer him up. They walked from one end of
town to the other for an hour without a single word. It had been a
while since evening set in and it was completely dark. Papatya was
shocked when the mixed, heavy stench of food and garbage reached
her nose. She always knew Emin was poor but could never in a million

years guess that he lived in such a place. Emin knocked on the door of the most wretched house on the street, which reminded Papatya of a pigsty. A young woman with a tight headscarf and a bare breast, as she was breastfeeding a baby, opened the door.

A heavy smell wafted out. There were three young children, all with dirty clothes and faces covered with mucus. One was nibbling on a piece of bread, another was crawling on the straw floor and the last was in swaddling clothes. Papatya turned pale. She felt like passing out.

She had understood everything but hopelessly she wanted Emin to tell her she was wrong. Emin didn't even look at her. He acted as if Papatya was not there. He picked up one of the children and told his wife to prepare dinner. Papatya stood stock-still. The woman in the headscarf poured tea and prepared food without uttering a word. She laid a cloth on the floor and then put a brass tray on top of it. She brought the tea and the food and sat Papatya down by the tray.

Papatya started to cry every time she caught sight of the woman who was serving the residents of the house with an almost spiritual calmness. She seemed to be devoid of any femininity at all. Papatya had become a *kuma** to a household of three children. She lay with Emin that night despite the pain she felt. Her first sexual experience, which she had been dreaming about for months, was a complete fiasco. Emin hurt her, and fell into a deep sleep after taking her virginity.

She kept staring at the ceiling, thinking of the grave mistake that she knew she had brought upon herself, until she could hear the morning prayer. As the neighbourhood was waking up to the cries of roosters and children, she went to sleep, sobbing.

When she woke up around midday, Emin had come home. The wife was feeding the children. She treated Papatya as one of the household, as if there wasn't anything strange going on.

With great difficulty Papatya uttered a few words whilst still

---

*   Concubine.

sobbing. 'He didn't tell me he was married.' The woman said, 'No need to cry. We will all live together. Allah will provide us with all we need.' With one last hope Papatya asked, 'Are you married?' For the first time since she came into the house the woman spoke with arrogance and replied as if challenging her, 'We have been married by both the imam and the council.' This way she highlighted that she was the real wife, hence the owner of the husband. Papatya had been praying to Allah that they hadn't had a council marriage.

If they had been married only by an imam then she could have fooled her family, hid his wife and children and had a council marriage with Emin. But this hope vanished. She thought of her family whilst fearing her thoughts. Papatya had no choice but to take refuge in this house. She could never return to her old life again.

That night Emin did not come home. Both women waited up for no reason. He didn't show up the following night either. Papatya couldn't muster the courage to ask his wife his whereabouts. She did not seem to be surprised by, or wonder about, anything anyway. Papatya did not know how and where to find Emin if he never returned.

The two women who shared their fate became friends. Papatya helped to look after the children and clean the house. They even visited neighbours together for tea. The woman did not try to hide who Papatya was and none of the neighbours were surprised. The only person who seemed to be constantly surprised was Papatya. Everyone in the neighbourhood seemed to have a *kuma*. According to the neighbours she was different from the other devilish *kuma*s. She was a good person. She took on the heavy loads of work herself.

While the days followed one another with a strange tranquillity, Emin returned home. He had fled to Mersin because he feared Papatya's older brothers would find him. Papatya didn't let on that she was hurt. Emin took both women to the bedroom and took them each in turn. Then, while he had them massage his shoulders and feet, he told them that until the situation was cleared up he would come to the house irregularly. He did not want to be a target in a sudden raid by Papatya's brothers. Neither woman made any objections or even a sound. Papatya was copying her 'co-wife' with a strange intuition. Emin liked the women's peaceful coexistence. To show his happiness he gave them each a small allowance. This was the first time Papatya saw that Emin had taken money out for anything, but even though she was surprised, she didn't dwell on it. There was no longer any significance in small details.

The last night it was extremely calm, as the calm before a storm usually tends to be. Both women had put the children to sleep early and were watching a drama on the television that never had good reception. When there was a knock on the door Emin's wife looked out of the window. Two agitated strangers were outside. With haste she signalled for Papatya to hide.

While Papatya was trying to figure out where to hide in the one-bedroom house, her two brothers entered. One held a rifle. They stood in the middle of the room like statues. They looked impassive, frightening, and stared at Papatya as though she were an enemy.

After a while Battal, with his heavy, mournful voice, asked his young sister, who looked terrified, 'You went into his bed even though you knew he was married, didn't you?' Papatya replied, 'I swear on the *Qur'an* I didn't know,' and started to cry. Her brothers were not listening or even looking at her. They looked around the room and the kitchen for Emin but didn't find him. They became uncomfortable with the three children sleeping in the room. They took Papatya outside.

'You ruined our honour,' said Battal. 'I was like a father to you and you made a mockery of me. Attest before Allah now, before I kill you.' Papatya threw herself at her brother's feet. She did not want to die. She wasn't even sixteen yet. 'I am very young, I was ignorant, I was fooled,' she wailed.

Battal lowered his rifle. He hugged his sister who he loved even more than his own children, his sister who had been born into his hands. Her other brother then hugged Battal who was facing the other way. The three siblings were crying with regret over the disaster that had struck them.

Emin's wife, who until now had been waiting by the door like a silent, dark ghost, ran forward. She pushed Papatya and lay the baby in her arms at Battal's feet. She begged him, 'My husband did not want her, your sister ran away to our house! If a girl doesn't shake her tail, how could a man act upon his desires?' Pointing at Papatya she said, 'My husband didn't even touch her. He told her to return home but she refused.'

Papatya could not believe her betrayal by the woman with whom until a few moments ago she shared a life in peace. Her disbelief gave way to fear.

Her eyes became watery. With astonishment she gazed at the woman who had thrown herself to the ground. She couldn't believe that this woman who had been looking out for her like an angel could betray her so violently.

Battal lifted the baby at his feet and put him on a bundle of straw. Without even looking at the woman he helped his sister to stand.

He turned to the dark ghost who had frozen in her place on the straw floor and said, 'Don't cry, *bacim*.* Just tell your husband never to cross our paths again, never to walk by our door.'

Papatya thought her nightmarish ordeal was at an end. She knew this affectionate voice of her elder brother. She was saved, she was going home.

With gratitude she moved to hug her brother. Then, all of a sudden, she felt a brutal burning sensation somewhere inside. As she fell, curious shadows in unlit windows and slightly opened doors were watching all that was going on like a movie. All she took away

---

*   Elder sister.

from this world was deception. A small pool of blood began to appear where she fell.

Battal and his brother walked into the darkness with proud yet heavy steps. The curtains and the doors opened fully with their departure. The shadows encircled the body of the dead girl. There was no one to mourn for her.

In a desolate place far away two brothers were holding each other, crying. The bullet had restored their honour. 'It is too expensive to regain your honour,' Battal sobbed. 'Crying does not suit an honourable man.'

Battal wanted to kiss the hand of his mother and afterwards he wanted to surrender to the authorities. But the old woman had sworn she would never speak to her sons again and she kept her promise. Her heart couldn't take the pain and during the court proceedings it failed her.

The news was heard in the neighbourhood first, then in the town. Those that heard it embellished the story. The most popular version was that Papatya had been working in a famous brothel in Adana. Her brother Battal had walked in and had killed her on the spot.

Battal surrendered to the *gendarme*. Because the family rejected her, Papatya was buried in the orphan's cemetery. The patisserie where the young student lovers met was shut down on the grounds that it was an immoral influence on young girls. Elif, who was partly blamed for the bad influences Papatya had fallen under, was taken out of school by her family. She was married not to her lover but to a widower twenty years older than her for a much lower dowry than usual. After all, her name was stained now.

The family could not deal with all the rumours that circulated even though they were all very different from the court files. The national newspapers all wrote of the tragic story of Battal, who had no choice but to kill his sister to redeem his honour, without once interviewing or talking to him. Every line written was a lie.

Battal was crushed. In this country the taboo that was family honour was a bear trap. Every family that had a girl in it got caught in this trap.

In the court, Emin's wife testified that Papatya had come to their house of her own free will; that even though her husband had not allowed her in she insisted she could not return to her family; and that once he saw he couldn't turn the girl away he had left the house.

The newspapers wrote of Emin, who had refused the slut that left her home and chased him, as an honourable man.

Battal would always regret not killing him.

He was tried and sentenced to death. His death sentence was later converted to life in prison. Then he benefited from a government pardon. His sentence was greatly reduced; he would serve only a further six years in prison and then be freed.

Battal ended his story with a final note: 'The clueless child had passed into the afterlife, startled. She learned that the mother's milk that men drank turned them evil,* but it was too late.' He was extremely sad.

Throughout each of our meetings he continued to shower us with gifts and treats. With his generous hospitality, he was trying to forget the pain inside. He couldn't see that the more he tried to hide his feelings, the more they became obvious. He was filled with regret.

We left without even being able to say goodbye. Words were unnecessary and inadequate. As we headed towards the large gate of the agricultural prison, we noticed that the garden path was lined on both sides with daisies. Their white petals were spread open towards the sun like delicate umbrellas.

---

* Turkish idiom.

The guard who saw us off said, 'Before, you couldn't grow flowers in the prison. Battal *agha** grew these.'

As we walked out of the gate the daisies began to move with the breeze, or I imagined they did. I would like to believe for a very brief moment that I had some contact with Papatya. Maybe Battal thought the same when he was growing them.

As the iron gates closed behind us with a loud bang, my cameraman whispered, 'I think I figured out who the killer is.'

'Who?' I asked.

'Honour!'

---

*   Elder brother.

AFTERWORD

Fourteen-year-old Mehmet Tamer slit the throat of his sixteen-year-old cousin Sevda Gok in broad daylight in the Urfa public market because she was 'going about in cafés'. When journalists asked if he regretted the murder, Tamer replied, 'Why should I regret anything? I cleansed my dignity, my honour.' An autopsy confirmed that Sevda died a virgin. Her murderer, sentenced to ten years in prison, was pardoned after serving only two years and ten months.

Between 2000 and 2005, 1,806 women were victims of honour killings while a further 5,375 committed suicide in the face of family pressure. Even though women whose deaths are classified as suspicious are not included in these statistics, the figures average one honour killing per day.

The Turkish state was unwilling to defend the rights of what it considered to be a handful of women. The law gave honour killers golden opportunities for years. However, in 2006 the sentences became harsher, but in a society where values were not in line with the law, stricter sentencing did not serve as a deterrent.

Until the day Secretary-General of Amnesty International Irene Khan addressed the issue, honour killings had not interested the national press. Such murders were implicitly approved in the police news sections widely known as 'the third page'. A quote from one such report read:

'The stories of the heroes who killed their sisters who had fallen from the path of righteousness and cleansed their honour.'

According to a 2007 research study, 67 per cent of the Turkish population view crime and sin as synonymous; what is a sin is also a crime. Therefore they live not according to the law, but according to their religion.

In Islamic societies it seems difficult to find a solution to honour killings. There is almost no chance that legislation alone can end the murder of women in the Middle East and surrounding regions.

Religion could help stop honour killing but religious authorities have not used their influence to this end. These authorities have remained silent even when religion is cited as a motivation for such killings. This silence has been interpreted as an endorsement of the murder of 'immoral' women. I realised that religion, in fact, contributed to the murders that were not condemned.

Everyone who remains silent about these atrocities are accessories to crime and I did not want to stay silent. The thought of interviewing prisoners who had killed a daughter, sister or mother sounded so absurd to everyone that gaining access to the prisoners turned into a prolonged ordeal; for a year and a half I awaited an official permit from the Ministry of Justice. I finally obtained the permits with the help of influential friends.

Even the managers of the broadcasting company I worked for did not understand why it was so important to learn what these men had to say. They believed that it would be of no interest to their viewers, so I came up with a news story that would serve as a pretext for my visit to each city in which there was a prisoner whom I intended to interview.

For a year I travelled to ten prisons to interview convicts charged with honour killings. I interviewed sixteen convicts on the record and fourteen convicts off the record. Some did not even have a grasp of simple terminology. They had been told to kill and they had done so without question. I also visited families in Batman, a city infamous for high suicide rates of young girls.

These interviews irrevocably changed the way I thought about honour crimes.

The culture assigned traits such as dignity and virtue to women and gave men the job of supervising women and safeguarding these qualities. When it was decided that a woman could not live up to these ideals then it was unavoidable that she would be killed. A man who chose not to kill had no hopes of continuing normal neighbourhood life; he would be belittled and humiliated. Men killed these women 'to be treated as men by their neighbours, their friends, their families'. Therefore to classify honour killings as domestic violence is misleading. It is an internal, societal violence that goes beyond families.

It is not correct to say that a family or a man gains honour or prestige by killing. But it is certainly true that if a guilty woman is not killed the family's integrity will be ruined.

Nor is it true that prisoners charged with honour killing have great authority and esteem over their fellow inmates. Family and neighbours pressure and harass them until they commit the murder; afterwards they are abandoned to joyless solitude. Honour killings cause a double tragedy for families. The girls lie in the cemetery while the boys or men are thrown into prison. It cannot be said that the fate of Haci, who keeps a photograph of the younger sister he killed in his shirt pocket and cries every time he looks at it, is any less of a tragedy than the fate of the murdered girl herself.

Honour killings are especially widespread in poor families; a rich family can buy their honour. If a girl flees to a rich family, she will live.

But even if a girl survives threats to her life, her life will never be the same. The girls who flee for freedom rather than love realise only afterwards that they have traded one hellish neighbourhood for another. The girl who flees to a man she loves is seen as a sinner by her entire community, including her family, her new family-in-law and even her husband.

My dear friend Mai Ghoussoub encouraged me to write about these powerless young women whose fates were sealed by neighbourhood gossip. 'By writing from the perspectives of these men, who killed to be treated as men, we can help them find alternative ways to be treated as such.' She supported, inspired and guided me. How I wish I could share this book with her.

Ayse Onal